CUBA

ANDREW COE has travelled the world extensively and now works as a freelance writer specializing in Latin America. His books include two previous Odyssey Guides, to *Mexico* and *Mexico City*.

ROLANDO PUJOL has 20 years' experience as a photographer in Cuba. Now independent, he has been a staff photographer for *Bastión* and *Bohemia* and won many awards, including the José Martí National Journalism Prize. His photos have also been exhibited abroad and have appeared in many foreign publications.

CUBA

by Andrew Coe
Photography by Rolando Pujol

© 1999, 1998, 1997, 1995 Odyssey Publications Ltd
Maps © 1999, 1998, 1997, 1995 Odyssey Publications Ltd

Odyssey Publications Ltd, 1004 Kowloon Centre, 29–43 Ashley Road,
Tsim Sha Tsui, Kowloon, Hong Kong
Tel. (852) 2856 3896; Fax. (852) 2565 8004; E-mail: odyssey@asiaonline.net

Distribution in the United Kingdom, Ireland and Europe by
Hi Marketing Ltd, 38 Carver Road, London SE24 9LT, UK

Distribution in the United States of America by
W.W. Norton & Company, Inc., New York

Library of Congress Catalog Card Number has been requested.

ISBN: 962-217-610-0

Although the publisher and author of this book have made every effort to ensure that all information was correct at the time of going to press, the publisher and author do not assume and hereby disclaim any liability to
any party for any loss or damage caused by errors, omissions or misleading information.

Grateful acknowledgment is made to the following authors and publishers:

Scribner's, an imprint of Simon & Schuster New York, and Sterling Lord for *Mob Lawyer* by Frank Ragano and
Selwyn Raab © 1994 Frank Ragano, Nancy Ragano and Selwyn Raab

University of Oklahoma Press for *The Diario of Christopher Columbus's First Voyage to America 1492–3*, translated by Oliver Dunn and James E Kelley, Jr. © 1989

Random House UK & Alfred A Knopf for *The Old Man and the Sea* by Ernest Hemingway

Atheneum Books, New York, for *Trading with the Enemy* by Tom Miller © 1992

Holmes & Meier Publishers for *Major Poems* by José Martí, bilingual edition, translated by Elinor Randall,
edited by Philip S Foner © 1992 Holmes & Meier Publishers, New York

Monthly Review Foundation for *Our America* by José Martí © 1977 by Philip S Foner

Vintage Books, a division of Random House, Inc, New York for *Cuban Counterpoint* by Fernando Ortiz © 1974

The Bodley Head, and Pantheon Books—a division of Random House, Inc, for *The Autobiography of a
Runaway Slave* by Esteban Montejo, edited by Miguel Barnet, translated by J Innes © 1968 by The Bodley
Head Ltd

Editor: Elizabeth Rhudy
Series Co-ordinator: Jane Finden-Crofts
Illustrations Editor: John Oliver
Design: David Hurst
Maps: Tom Le Bas and Bai Yiliang
Cover Concept: Margaret Lee

Production by Twin Age Ltd, Hong Kong
Printed in Hong Kong

We welcome comments, corrections and suggestions
from guidebook users; please write to:
Odyssey Publications Ltd
1004 Kowloon Centre
29–43 Ashley Road
Tsim Sha Tsui
Kowloon
Hong Kong
Fax: (852) 2565 8004
E-mail: odyssey@asiaonline.net

ACKNOWLEDGEMENTS

Any guidebook to Cuba is of necessity a communal effort. I could not have completed this work without the help of Publicitur, Nelio Contreras, Rolando Pujol, Ricardo and McCatty, Fernando, Joli, Yoleni, Luis, Chachi, Aldo, Abraham, Grisell, Diana, Yiyi, Robier, Mirta and my sister Natalie, who got there first. Without the steadfast support of David Tang, this guidebook would not have existed.

This book is dedicated to the memory of my mother,
Sophie Dobzhansky Coe.

Contents

Literary Excerpts

Special Topics

Maps

Tobacco and Barn, Valle de Viñales

Introduction

SOME SAY CUBA LOOKS LIKE A CROCODILE. Or a great fish swimming in a phallus. Whatever shape, Cuba possesses the richest culture and is by far the largest of all the Caribbean islands. The land is made up of lush mountains, rolling hills and flat plains, all covered with a fertile soil from which springs sugar, tobacco and a vast array of tropical fruits and vegetables. Cuba's mountains, swamps and offshore keys conceal a wealth of plant and wildlife that has barely been seen by natives, let alone tourists.

The island's natural riches are equalled by the charms of its people. Cubans are a mulatto race. From the very earliest days of the colony, Spanish blood mixed with that of Indians and of black slaves brought over from Europe. As the island prospered from sugar, thousands of African slaves arrived to work on the plantations and, unconsciously, to Africanize Cuban culture. Other waves of immigrants, such as the French in the late 18th century, also had their influence, and the blend became, like a bottle of aged rum, dusky, flavorful and intoxicating.

Cuba appears to be emerging from one of the most difficult periods in its history. After five years of free-fall, the economy bottomed out in 1994 and is now slowly expanding, fueled largely by the tourism boom. Tourists are enthusiastically welcomed, and not just by the government. Your visit also means a great deal to average Cubans. You bring them news, a glimpse at a different way of life, friendship and, yes, money. Most of all, though, you bring them the hope of a better future—something that is in short supply in today's Cuba.

■ HISTORY

EARLY CUBA

Cuba's earliest inhabitants were the Ciboney, the generic term for preceramic hunter-gatherer groups whose remains date back as early as 5000 BC. The origins of the Ciboney are unknown; archaeologists have proposed South America, Yucatan and the Mississippi River area as possible homelands. The Ciboney survived mainly off the sea, travelling in canoes and living nearby in caves or makeshift villages of no more than 100 inhabitants. When Diego Velásquez encountered them in the early 1500s, he called them 'savages'.

Around the third century AD, the Ciboney began to be dislodged by waves of Taíno, which were Arawak tribes originating in Venezuela's Orinoco River basin. The Taíno island-hopped westward through the Antilles to eastern Cuba, and thus began the tradition of great changes happening to Cuba starting in the east and heading west. The Taíno brought with them agriculture, ceramics and complex religious and burial customs. They settled at fertile, slightly inland locations— Matanzas, Banes, Cienfuegos and Baracoa have the most important sites—and lived in villages of *bohíos,* large thatched huts, with populations of up to 2,000 people.

Around AD 1450 a second wave of Taíno with a higher level of carving and ceramic-making skills arrived and settled in eastern Cuba. These may have had some Mesoamerican influence, because archaeologists have found the remains of a ballcourt at one site near Maisí. By the time of the first European contact, researchers believe that Cuba had a population of about 112,000, 90% of them Taíno. When Columbus met the Taíno, he admired the neatness of their villages and their gentleness and generosity. His men also encountered Indians 'with a half-burnt weed in their hands, being the herbs they are accustomed to smoke'. Thus began the spread of tobacco throughout the world. Despite the fact that they named the country 'Cuba', there are officially no Indians left; there are only 'Cubans,' although many claim to be of Indian descent.

Columbus's first landing on Cuba was on October 29, 1492, somewhere between Gibara and Lucrecia Bay on the northeast coast. His initial impressions were of greenness, perfumed air and hills rich in plant and animal life—a paradise. He spent five weeks sampling the delights of the region and convinced himself of Cuba's vast potential for riches: in his imagination, one precious tree heralded a forest full of them; one gold ornament meant a vast trove up in the hills. A year later Columbus returned to the island, exploring the southern coast in a futile search for gold.

For the next 15 years, the Spanish ignored Cuba while establishing a settlement on nearby Hispaniola (now Santo Domingo in the Dominican Republic) and exploring the rest of the Caribbean. European attention returned in 1508 when Sebastián de Ocampo circumnavigated Cuba, confirming that it was an island, and returned with rumors of gold. In 1511 the conquistador Diego Velásquez and a force of 300 men embarked from Hispaniola with the aim of conquering Cuba.

SPANISH COLONY

Velásquez landed at Cuba's eastern tip, Maisí, and quickly faced fierce Indian resistance. By this time, the Spaniards had established a reputation for cruelty in the Caribbean, and many Indian warriors in Cuba were refugees from battles on other islands. One of these was a semimythic chief named Hatuey, who was captured and sentenced to be burned at the stake. Before they lit the pyre, the Spanish encouraged Hatuey to convert to Christianity so that his soul would go to Heaven. 'Are there Spaniards in Heaven?' he asked. 'Many', he was told. He refused the priest and perished an idolater. He is now revered as Cuba's 'first rebel'.

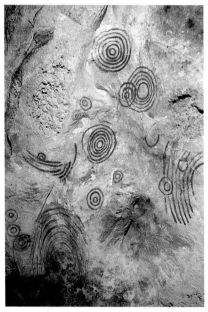

Ancient pictographs on the Island of Youth

After four months of fighting, Oriente (eastern Cuba) was captured and the first permanent Spanish settlement was founded at Baracoa in early 1512. The conquistadors then marched west, leaving a trail of massacred Indians, and all opposition quickly evaporated. Within four years, the length of Cuba was dotted with Spanish settlements. Including Baracoa, the first seven towns were, in order of founding, Bayamo, Trinidad, Sancti Spíritus, Havana, Puerto Príncipe (now Camaguey) and Santiago.

In 1515, Santiago de Cuba, with its excellent natural harbor and proximity to Hispaniola, was named the island's capital. The land was divided among the conquistadors into *encomiendas* and *repartimientos*, and the Indians were forced onto the estates to work as slaves. Maltreat-

Hatuey, 'the first rebel of America', Baracoa

ment and lack of resistance to European diseases tens of thousands of Indians over the next decades. As Indian crops were trampled and eaten by European livestock, many Indians lost the will to live, and whole villages committed mass suicide. By the mid-15th century, there were fewer than 3,000 Indians left on the island. Today Cuba's Indian heritage only lives in the place-names, in some foodstuffs and Cubans' ubiquitous addiction to tobacco.

Cuba's first economic boom was a gold rush, but this soon collapsed as the veins petered out. Thus began the boom-and-bust cycle that has bedeviled the country ever since. Spanish settlers next looked to the sea for economic opportunity. This was the age of New World exploration, and western Cuba, particularly the natural harbor at Havana, was ideally placed to become a base for Spanish expeditions.

In 1519, the conquistador Hernán Cortés fitted out an invasion fleet in Cuba and set sail for Mexico. After the Conquest, Havana became the natural stopping point for fleets returning to Spain, because it lay at the beginning of the Gulf Stream, which heads straight to Europe. For a brief time, Havana reigned as the Western Hemisphere's most important supply and shipping-out port. Then the construction of Veracruz (Mexico) and Portobello (Panama) on the New World mainland undercut that business; Cuba's economy collapsed once again. To make matters worse, Cuba's settlers, seeing on the island only limited possibilities for vast wealth, abandoned their adopted land for greater opportunities in Mexico, Peru and Central America. By 1550, Cuba was nearly depopulated, with only 700 Europeans on the entire island.

By the mid-16th century, Spain was not the only European power in the Caribbean. English, French and Dutch flags entered the region and were soon joined by the pirates' skull and crossbones. They were on the prowl for easy riches, and they saw it in Cuba's unguarded state. In the 16th and 17th centuries, Havana, Santiago and other towns were repeatedly attacked, looted and often burned by foreign fleets or pirates like Peg-Leg LeClerc.

Royal Spanish authorities quickly realized that Cuba, located at the center of the most important sea-lanes, was crucial to the protection of their New World empire and the Treasure Fleet that carried its riches back to the king. They built forts at Havana and Santiago, and enlarged Havana's docks to make it one of the largest New World shipyards. For six weeks every year the enormous Treasure Fleet docked here, and a wide array of services, from sailmakers to prostitutes, sprang up to meet the sailors' every need. As the fleet became the main buyer of everything from cowhides to cigars, the intensely concentrated commerce happening in Havana became the focal point of the island's economy. Havana quickly became the island's largest city; by 1607, when it was named the capital, it held half of Cuba's 20,000 inhabitants. Outside of the Havana area, Cuba was largely deserted, home only to herds of cattle on a few enormous *latifundios* (estates). Santiago and Oriente complained of desertion; no supplies reached them, and they were left open to attack. In revenge, the Orientales (inhabitants of eastern Cuba) turned to contraband, smuggling goods in violation of the strict royal trade laws. They were aided by Cuba's winding coast and thousands of offshore keys —a smuggler's paradise. So widespread was illegal trade in Oriente that whole towns rose up in arms whenever authorities tried to arrest the biggest smugglers, who were usually the town's most prominent citizens.

TOBACCO AND SUGAR

In the 17th century, two crops that would become inextricably identified with Cuba began to make their mark on the island's economy. Sugar started slowly. The early plantations were small and their foreign markets limited. Much larger and more efficient operations on nearby St. Domingue (Haiti) and Jamaica effectively controlled the New World supply. Sugar's main effects on early colonial Cuba were not economic but social. Unlike the French in St. Domingue and the English in Jamaica, the Spanish Crown allowed only small numbers of African slaves to be transported to Cuba. These mainly worked on the sugar plantations and, to a lesser extent, in mines and urban industries. Due to the lack of European women on the island, many white Cuban males took slaves as wives or mistresses. The Spanish had relatively liberal policies about freeing the offspring of these mixed unions, and a significant portion of the population was composed of freed slaves and the freed children of slaves. Thus was born the mulatto, Afro-Cuban nation that we know today.

Tobacco was the most important crop of the 17th and 18th centuries. The first tobacco craze hit Europe in the late 16th century, and within a few years it was Cuba's most profitable—and heavily taxed—export. The search for good tobacco soil led farmers to settle in heretofore empty regions of central and western Cuba, most importantly Pinar del Río, and cigars and snuff became the main cargo of Cuban smugglers. In the early 1700s, when the French Bourbons took over the Spanish throne from the German Hapsburgs, Cuba's new rulers determined to exact the maximum profit from the island. In 1717, they established a royal monopoly on the processing, buying and selling of tobacco, drastically reducing tobacco farmers' income.

Sugar harvesting

The immediate result was the first effective Cuban rebellion against Spanish authority. Armed farmers marched on Havana and forced the resignation of the monopoly's administrators. Before the monopoly resumed operations three years later, Spain reinforced the garrison and a second protest led to battles and the death and execution of many farmers.

The tobacco monopoly was only the beginning; in 1740, the Crown founded the Real Compañía, a joint venture with Spanish merchants that controlled all trade between Cuba and Spain. The Real Compañía bought Cuban products cheaply and sold them flour and other necessities to the Cubans at exorbitant markups. The investors reaped huge profits, while the Cuban people suffered. Food shortages were common, and to survive many moved to Oriente to embark on the booming contraband trade. Through the mid-18th century, Cuba was still a backwater with a repressed economy and little sense of identity as anything but an outpost of empire.

INVASION AND CHANGE

Seventeen sixty-two is the second *annus mirabilus* of Cuban history (after 1492), when another foreign invasion forever changed island society. Spain had become embroiled in Europe's Seven Year's War, and all its colonies were fair game for the English enemy. After a 44-day siege by an English fleet, Havana's authorities surrendered, beginning a ten-month occupation. The surprising result of this invasion was an economic boom. All Spanish regulations were lifted and a horde of foreign merchants descended on a consumption-starved populace. Tobacco, sugar, molasses and hides were traded for imported staples, luxury goods and, most importantly, new sugar-processing machinery. With the disappearance of slave-trading regulations, over 4,000 African slaves were sold in less than ten months, mostly to sugar plantation owners.

In the 1763 treaty that ended the Seven Year's War, Cuba was returned to Spain, while the English took possession of Florida. However, the prosperity did not end there; Spain had a new king, the more 'enlightened' Charles III, who favored freer trade over the monopolistic policies of the past. With over 200 ships docking at Havana per year rather than the six of the pre-1762 years, it was obvious that more trade meant more money. Cuban merchants were allowed to trade directly with Jamaica, St. Domingue and other Caribbean isles, and, after 1776, with England's 13 North American colonies—a market which would eventually dominate the island economy.

The open-door policy meant new opportunities and new instabilities. For the sugar industry, the massive infusion of slave labor and new technology meant larger estates and more efficient production methods. Over the next 30 years, the amount of land devoted to sugar increased 16-fold and production nearly doubled. Although production was still dwarfed by the other Caribbean islands, sugar outstripped tobacco as the most important crop. Cuba was slouching toward the sugar monoculture that has kept the economy in its thrall ever since. From sugar, homegrown fortunes were made, and for the first time Cubans began to see themselves as distinct from the mother country. The first notable works of Cuban literature, painting and sculpture date from this time, and the first newspaper was

started in Havana. Rich planters founded organizations to spread information about new agricultural techniques, and these groups soon became a political force. This new self-awareness led to new resentments among the Cuban-born *criollos* of the Spanish-born *peninsulares* who made up the administrative elite. Bluntly put, the *criollos* felt that they made the money and the *peninsulares* stole it. Cubans heard news of ferment overseas, of revolutions in England's North American colonies and France, and of radical new political ideas. For the first time, Cubans began to contemplate separation from imperial Spain.

WEALTH IN SLAVERY

Foreign turmoil quickly shattered these dreams. In 1791, St. Domingue's half million slaves rebelled against an attempt by white planters to pass new restrictions on slave rights. The revolt turned into a bloody, decade-long civil war that sent 300,000 French fleeing abroad, mostly to Cuba. This immigration was a double bonanza; the main foreign sugar competitor was ruined, and the immigrants brought with them capital and new agricultural techniques. French sugar engineers and their new technologies were soon found in Cuba's mills, greatly boosting production. Many of the immigrants were coffee planters, who set up farms in Cuba's rich eastern interior. For about a generation, coffee was one of Cuba's most important exports, until Brazilian competition and the lure of greater profits in sugar closed many farms. The revolution in St. Domingue, renamed Haiti, also had a chilling effect on Cuban aspirations for independence. For rich and influential Cubans the slave revolt had two lessons: do not give an inch to the African population, and never stir from the embrace of imperial Spain and its all-powerful military.

The first half of the 19th century was an era of turmoil abroad and, by and large, riches at home. From 1796 to 1815, Europe was racked by the Napoleonic Wars; when the sea-lanes were open, Cuba did a booming trade. However, in 1808 Napoleon toppled the Spanish king and installed his brother in his place. Cuba was left without a protector, and for the first time the United States, under Thomas

(previous pages) Morro Castle and the harbour entrance, Santiago

Jefferson, offered to step into that role and purchase the island. Thus began the possibility of annexation that Cubans toyed with for over a century.

In 1809, a freemason named Ramón de la Luz, who had apparently been influenced by too many novels, attempted to overthrow the government, but the fear of another Haiti limited his support. The Spanish Crown was restored in 1814 but in a much-weakened state. Spain's mainland New World colonies saw their chance and under brilliant leaders like Simón Bolivar successfully severed their ties with the empire. Not 'Ever Faithful Cuba'; royalist refugees from Central and South America poured into Havana, while thousands of Spanish soldiers strengthened Cuba's garrisons. Between 1820 and 1868, Cuba became the richest colony in the world.

Cuba's sugar industry was by far the strongest in the Caribbean—Haiti's was ruined and Jamaica's was in fast decline due to the lack of fertilizer. To work their plantations, rich planters imported over 750,000 African slaves between 1763 and 1862. Most of these lived lives of appalling hardship. In the great rural plantations, there were as many as four men for every woman, and twenty-hour days were common during harvest. Planters considered it more economical to work their slaves to death and purchase 'fresh' ones from Africa every few years than give them humane living conditions. There were isolated slave revolts, but, ever fearful of another Haiti, the planters ruthlessly squashed them. Urban slaves had far better living conditions; the male-female ratio was more equitable, and they had the free time to form communal organizations. Called *cabildos*, these groups were instrumental in preserving the dances, music and religious traditions of their homeland and became the main entry points of African culture into Cuba.

Another reason owners worked their slaves so hard is that they knew this cheap source of labor would soon end. England had abolished the trade in 1808 and convinced Spain to follow in 1817. Now English warships patrolled the Atlantic, arresting and hanging slavers; fresh slaves for Cuban plantations had to be smuggled in like contraband. The loss of slaves was a major threat to planters' bank accounts; in 1822, a group of them approached the United States, where slavery was still legal, with the proposal of joining the Union. Spurred by the expansionist 'Manifest Destiny' doctrine, in 1848 President Polk offered Spain $100 million for Cuba. When word of the deal leaked, the ensuing furor caused the Spanish to withdraw.

In the meantime, planters found other ways to increase profits. New technology allowed them to produce the refined, white sugar we know today in Cuban sugar mills, and in 1837 planters built Latin America's first railway. The rail system soon connected all major refineries and the ports, and transportation costs were cut by 90 per cent. These innovations profited most the richest planters, who lived lives of unparalleled luxury. In Trinidad, one planter installed a fountain that spewed gin for the men and, for the women, eau de cologne. However, this idyll was not to last forever. The slave-holders had pinned their hopes on the South in the American Civil War; its defeat in 1865 meant the end of the slave trade (the last slave was sold in 1867). The big planters experimented with stopgap measures, like bringing over 130,000 Chinese laborers—who endured horrendous transport and working conditions—but this was not the permanent answer. It was obvious to most that, in order to protect the island's economy, Spain would have to ease its archaic restrictions on Cuban commerce. That was easier said than done.

THE WARS FOR INDEPENDENCE

Cuba of the 1860s resembled Cuba of the century before. Society was polarized between native-born *criollos* who favored reform and superior, corrupt *peninsulare* bureaucrats who called change tantamount to treason against Spain. This time, however, there was a difference: a wide spectrum of opinion among the *criollo* population. On the moderate end, favoring gradual reform, were the rich planters of western Cuba who had the most to lose. The planters of eastern Cuba had nothing to lose. Their estates were small and far from the rail lines, their slaves few and their methods out of date. Spanish taxes and trade laws fell hardest on them, and many lost their estates to Havana moneylenders. They had no faith in gradualism; many had been educated in the United States or Europe, and they had imbibed the radical political spirit sweeping that world. Immediate, drastic action was their taste, and they saw their chance in 1868, when Spain's tottering monarchy was overthrown in a coup. On October 10, 1868, a sugar planter named Carlos Manuel de Céspedes freed his slaves and declared the start of the rebellion against Spain. His speech, known as the Grito de Yara ('Shout of Yara') was the start of the Ten Years' War, Cuba's first real battle for independence.

The rest of Cuba ignored Céspedes and his little army until they captured Bayamo a week later. The news electrified the anti-Spanish side, and homegrown militias sprang up throughout eastern Cuba. The rebels, called the *mambíses* (from an insulting Spanish term about Cubans), were remarkably successful, adopting the guerrilla tactics of surprise attack and then withdrawal into the countryside they knew far better than the enemy. Cuba was too profitable for the Spanish to lose, however. Despite their own internal problems, they sent over 100,000 troops to the island, including their best officers. Seven years into the struggle, most of the revolt's original, well-born leaders had been killed or exiled, and power fell into the hands of generals from more humble and racially mixed origins, notably Antonio Maceo, the 'Bronze Titan'. In 1875, the tide of battle had turned for the rebels; they were poised to bring the battle to western Cuba. Then a political dispute within their ranks forced the resignation of their brilliant general, Maximo Gómez, and the effort collapsed. In February 1878, the Cubans sued for peace, and the Spanish accepted. The country was tired of war, but not all Cubans were pleased with the terms of peace. In a legendary encounter at Baraguá near Santiago, Antonio Maceo refused to accept any treaty without independence and the abolition of slavery. The Spanish officer was so impressed with his bravado that he called off the plot to assassinate Maceo and let him go into exile.

The legacy of the Ten Years' War was mixed. The Cubans had lost, and the eastern half of the island was in ruins. On the other hand, the Cubans were suddenly a people and proud of it. The war had left a legacy of Cuban heroes, the mambíses, and Cuban patriotic symbols—they now had a national flag to rally behind. Black Cubans had fought at the side of white, melting old fears about a slave rebellion; they were all one people. They were also a poorer people. The old aristocracy had disappeared, and American entrepreneurs descended on the island to purchase sugar plantations at bargain prices, beginning the era of American control over the Cuban economy. Life still revolved around the sugar harvest, but increased competition from Brazil and the European invention of refining sugar from beets cut into profits.

In the early 1890s, higher sugar prices briefly lifted Cuba out of its depression, until 1894 when the Wilson Tariff put a tax of 40 per cent on Cuban sugar imports in the United States, the island's largest market. Once again, Cuba's economy collapsed. The same year saw the increase of tensions with Spain. Cuba's Autonomist Party had failed to win agreement on a plan for gradual independence. It was obvious to all that war was once again imminent.

The flames that swept across Cuba were sparked by an exiled writer and orator named José Martí, today the most revered Cuban patriot. After his deportation at age 17 for criticizing the Spanish military, Martí spent most of his life abroad, writing passionate poems and prose and beating the drum for Cuban independence. Martí was determined to avoid the mistakes of the Ten Years' War. The revolution should be fought by a revolutionary army controlled by civilian leaders, he said, and bring Cuba not only independence but economic and political justice for all citizens. He reserved his deepest scorn for those who wanted to become a territory of the United States: Cuba Libre would never exist under the American flag.

The conspirators' plan was for a mass uprising simultaneously throughout Cuba, and early in 1895 ships filled with rebel armaments were prepared in a Florida port. Unfortunately, they were seized by U.S. authorities and the rebellion was postponed. The uprising formally began on February 24, but the serious fighting did not start until the arrival a few months later of Martí and Generals Antonio Maceo and Maximo Gómez, the Ten Years' War veterans.

Our America

What is this?

Nothing.

Being beaten, trampled, dragged about, insulted on the same street beside the same house and at the same window where, a month before, we were receiving our mother's blessing—what is this?

Nothing.

Spending there, in water up to the waist, with pick in hand, in leg irons, so that the sun bothered our eyes and the heat altered our state of health—spending there the hours that days before we had spent in the bosom of the home: what is this?

Nothing.

To return bruised, wounded, blinded, and lame to the sound of the whip, blasphemy, beatings, and mockery, through the same streets that months before had seen me go by in calm and serenity, arm in arm with my beloved sister and with the peace of happiness in my heart—what is the meaning of this? Also nothing.

A hideous, terrible, heartbreaking nothing!

And you Spaniards were the cause of it.

You sanctioned it.

You applauded it.

And oh, how frightful must be the remorse of the criminal nothing!

The astonished eyes can see; the scandalized reason is amazed; but compassion refuses to believe what you have done, what you are still doing.

Either you are barbarians or you do not know what you are doing.

Let me, oh, let me think that you are still unaware.

Let me think that there is still some honor left in this land, and that this Spain here—so unjust, so indifferent, so similar to the repugnant and ill-tempered Spain across the sea—can still defend it.

continues

Stand up, stand up for your honor; remove those leg irons from the old men, the idiots, the children; take the lash away from the insensitive one who drinks himself senseless in the arm of vengeance and forgets both God and you; erase, uproot all this, and you will enable the man who has not yet learned to hate the lash or the voice of insult or the sound of chains, to forget some of his bitterest days.

—*Our America*, by José Martí

The tomb of José Martí, Santiago

Tragically, Martí was one of the war's earliest victims. Anxious to prove his mettle, he rushed into a skirmish and was slain by a bullet. Power fell into the hands of the military leaders, Maceo and Gómez, who again followed the strategy of fighting their way west from Oriente, destroying everything that could help the Spanish in their wake. The Spanish general Valeriano Weyler retaliated by rounding up the rebels' peasant allies into 'reconcentration' camps that killed tens of thousands through disease and starvation. Early in 1898, with the country in ruins and the Spanish clinging tenuously to the major cities, the United States stepped into the fray.

THE AMERICANS ARRIVE

For the first two years of the war, President McKinley had stayed essentially neutral (although he believed the Spanish were the best protection for U.S. interests in Cuba). In 1898, however, he was goaded into action by pressures from both pro-Spanish businessmen and the rabid anti-Spanish sentiment stirred up by William Randolph Hearst's yellow journalism. The American battleship *Maine* was sent to Havana as a show of force to the island's unruly belligerents. On February 15, the *Maine* mysteriously exploded in Havana Harbor, killing 260 crewmen and leading to conspiracy theories pointing to the Spanish, Cuban rebels and even the Americans themselves. Crying

Wreckage of the U.S.S. Maine, 1898.

'Remember the *Maine!* The hell with Spain!' the American public blamed the Spanish and whipped itself up into a frenzy for war. In April, war was declared.

The American policy in invading Cuba was to oust the Spanish with the help of the rebels wherever needed. However, the rebels were never to be recognized as a legitimate political force. The objective of the American forces was Santiago, where the Spanish fleet was bottled up in the harbor and the army had a large garrison. The only major battle was the bloody fight for San Juan Hill—now a part of American folklore—in which 6,000 American soldiers, including an ambitious officer named Teddy Roosevelt, defeated 700 Spanish defenders. When American troops finally took Santiago, no mention was made of the rebels' assistance; indeed they were forbidden entry into the city. In an insult that still echoes in Cuban memories, no Cubans were allowed at the Spanish surrender in Havana, and the American flag, not the Cuban, was raised at the ceremony.

The American military government that ruled Cuba from 1899 to 1902 had two goals: to rebuild the island and point it toward political independence. It was relatively successful in the first task, less so in the second. One problem was racism—Cubans were seen as lazy illiterates—and the other was a desire to protect American business interests, which were once again buying up the island. In 1900, the American governor, General Leonard Wood, ordered a constitutional convention to build a new political system for Cuba. Work proceeded smoothly until the Americans forced the convention to accept an amendment drafted by U.S. Senator Orville Platt. This much-detested law, known as the Platt Amendment, gave the United States the right to intervene in Cuba at any time and also a lease on the Guantanamo Bay naval base. In 1902, the Americans' candidate, Tomás Estrada Palma, was elected president and the Cuban flag finally flew over Havana.

'INDEPENDENT' CUBA

Estrada's first years in office were relatively successful, marked by governmental honesty and the continued recuperation of the economy. However, cracks soon started to show. Cubans found themselves caught between the Americans, who controlled big business, and new Spanish immigrants who poured into Cuba by the thousands and controlled trade and many urban small businesses. The only openings for ambitious Cubans were found in government, which became a system primarily designed to line the pockets of office holders. For the next six decades, governmental corruption was the rule in Cuba, leading to widespread cynicism in the political system. In 1906, Estrada ran for re-election in a race that saw the murder of his leading opponent. Estrada won, but the opposition began an armed rebellion that forced him to ask for an American intervention. When President Roosevelt declined, Estrada and his entire government resigned, forcing the United States to return. The era of the Second Intervention (1906-09) was greatly humiliating to Cubans, because they felt it showed that they could not govern themselves.

Civilian rule returned under the presidencies of José Miguel Gómez and Mario G. Menocal, whose administrations followed the pattern of electoral unrest, threats of U.S. intervention and more or less—generally more—corruption. A main source of graft was the national lottery, reinstituted by Gómez, which raised money solely to supplement the incomes of top officials. At the other end of society, Cuba's black population was increasingly restless. Afro-Cuban culture was flourishing and a majority of the population were mulattoes, yet blacks had never been acknowledged by mainstream Cuban culture. When they attempted to form a political party, whites passed a law banning parties based on race. In 1912, the black population finally exploded into open revolt in Oriente. U.S. marines landed but only stood by while Cuban soldiers hunted down and killed the rebels. Black political participation was effectively squashed for the next half century.

Despite this turmoil, these were good years for the Cuban economy. World War I destroyed European beet sugar production, and the price of sugar skyrocketed from less than two cents a pound to 23 cents. In the frenzy to make money, huge areas of forest were cut down to make sugarcane fields, and thousands of workers were imported from Haiti and Jamaica to work on the estates. Known as the 'Dance of the

Millions', this boom lasted until 1920, when the price plummeted to below four cents. The Cuban economy, still tied to a single crop, had once again busted.

In the 1920s, the forces that would shape Cuba for the next four decades began to emerge. One of these was radical activism. Students left the universities with no hope of a job and confronted an economy in ruins and their nation in the thrall of the United States (Americans were buying even more of the island's bankrupt sugar plantations). Sons of the new, urban middle class, they began to rediscover the anti-American 'Cuba libre!' writings of José Martí and were also heavily influenced by the Marxist and anarchist philosophies that were sweeping Latin American universities. For the first time, they began to appreciate Afro-Cuban culture and to recognize blacks, factory workers and sugarcane cutters as 'real' Cubans. Many student activists went on to become leading politicians, while many more left their blood in the streets as martyrs to the radical causes that periodically swept across the island.

MACHADO

Another force that has shaped Cuba in this century is *personalismo*, the identification of the Cuban political system with one 'strongman' leader. In 1924, Alfredo Zayas, Menocal's even more corrupt successor, declined to run for re-election and opened the way for the dictatorship of Gerardo Machado. Machado, who began his career as a cattle thief in Las Villas Province, modelled his political philosophy after his idol, Mussolini. His first two years in office were relatively honest; corruption dropped, and he built the Carretera Central, the highway from Havana to Santiago. His thirst for absolute power reared its head in 1928, however, when he named himself the only legal candidate and had himself re-elected to a new, six-year term.

Opposition groups, mainly students and labor-union activists, took to the streets and were brutally beaten by Machado's elegantly uniformed goons. Unrest increased after the effects of the 1929 Wall Street crash hit the Cuban economy. Anti-Machado terrorist cells sprang up, and dozens of young radicals lent their blood to the river of Cuban martyrs. One group tried to start the traditional uprising in the country-side, but military men they were not and the Revolution of 1930 was quickly squelched. By the time of President Franklin Roosevelt's in-auguration in 1933, Machado's thugs were openly murdering people in the streets and strikes par-alyzed the island. Roosevelt's envoy, Sumner Welles, this time sided with the opposition and began to maneuver for Machado's ouster. The dictator held on until August, when a general strike brought Cuba to a halt and the military began to desert him. Machado saw that his time was up and fled into exile.

Sumner Welles anointed Carlos M. Céspedes, the son of the revo-lutionary leader, to succeed Machado. Unfortunately, Céspedes had neither political support nor savvy. Amid a continuing atmosphere of strikes and turmoil, a group of low-level army officers mutinied and, encouraged by left-wing students, occupied the presidential palace. The students were quickly replaced by professional, if liberal, politi-cians, led by Ramón Grau San Martín. This revolutionary government lasted only 100 days but engineered radical changes in Cuban society. The Platt Amendment was nullified (except for the Guantánamo naval base lease), women were given the right to vote and eight hours be-came the maximum workday. Unfortunately, they had no idea how to bring peace to Cuba; senior army officers, unhappy with their subordinate's regime, occupied the Hotel Nacional and were only dislodged with a bloody, full-scale assault. Sumner Welles looked on with disgust and directed his energies at one of the leading junior officers, a sergeant-stenographer named Fulgencio Batista. Known as the *mulato lindo* ('pretty mulatto'), Batista was charming, ambitious and respected by his fellow sergeants. Welles's plan worked; by January 1934, Batista had withdrawn military support for the leftist government and a new, more conservative regime was in place.

BATISTA

For the next 25 years, Batista was the most powerful man in Cuban politics and the second of the nation's strongmen. (In 1934, the third was a mere schoolboy in Oriente Province.) After a brutal repression of the opposition in 1935, Batista ruled through a series of puppet presidents for the remainder of the decade. The military became the most important social force in Cuba, building schools, hospitals and housing and taking a rake-off from every project. They were aided by a steadily improving economy. In the late 1930s, Batista made a surprising alliance with Cuba's communists; he needed support for state control of many industries, including sugar and tobacco, and the communists obliged in return for government jobs.

By 1940, Batista felt secure enough to run for president in a relatively honest election against his old ally, Ramón Grau San Martín. The same year the Cuban Constitution was rewritten following the models of Spain and Weimar Germany; the document was filled with dramatic ideals, such as eight years of education for every child, that were rarely fulfilled. As president, Batista was lucky in his timing; World War II sent sugar prices higher again (although shipping was dangerous and tourism almost nonexistent) and Cuba basked in wartime prosperity. In the 1944 elections, Batista declined to run for re-election and made the mistake of assuming that his candidate would win an honest election. His opponent, once again Ramón Grau San Martín, promised a pot of gold in every Cuban home and won.

Cubans hoping for a return to the idealism of 1933 were quickly disabused by Grau's government. The years between 1944 and 1952, under Grau and his successor Carlos Prío Socarrás, were not the glory years of Cuban society. From the president on down, government officials fell over themselves trying to skim the most money from public coffers, which they then sent abroad, mainly to Miami. Grau soon had a stable of racehorses and estates throughout the island. On campus, leftist opposition groups had been debased into student gangs which stored arsenals in school buildings (the police were banned from the University of Havana campus), shook up professors and had shoot-outs in the surrounding streets. These young gangsters, who cruised Havana in big Buicks filled with machine guns, soon came under the patronage of politicians who used them to intimidate and even kill rivals. In 1946, American tourists began

Cuban dictator Fulgencio Batista

pouring onto the island, looking for sun, sand and sin; Havana was riddled with bordellos. These new riches were reaped by the Americanized citydwellers; in the country, *campesinos* remained poor, uneducated and largely unemployed.

THE MONCADA ATTACK

It was in this atmosphere of widespread corruption that Batista staged a military coup in 1952. In the words of one commentator, the government of President Prío fell like a rotten fruit. For the main political parties, to fight Batista was useless, because either they had lost all moral authority with the people or they were under arrest. It was left to a group of young radicals to mount the first real challenge to the Batista dictatorship. On July 26, 1953—the date is now engraved on Cuban history—a young lawyer named Fidel Castro led a group of

Relics of the Moncada attack can be found inside the Museo de la Revolución in Old Havana.

over 150 men on a daring and utterly foolhardy attack on the Moncada military barracks in Santiago. Within hours, eight of the attackers were dead and over 100 were prisoners. Sixty-eight of the prisoners were shortly tortured and murdered—a crime that appalled Cuba. Those who managed to escape, including Fidel, were captured within the next few days. Amazingly, the military fiasco turned into a public-relations coup, as the details about the Batista soldiers' brutality swept through the press. At his trial, Fidel used the opportunity to deliver a speech, now known as 'History Will Absolve Me', that set forth his demands for a new, free Cuba. Suddenly, he became one of the most famous opposition leaders in Cuba, the bearer of the mantle of José Martí. Fidel revised the speech while in prison in the Isle of Pines (now the Isle of Youth) and, smuggled out, it became the crucial text for Cuba's young revolutionaries.

In May 1955, Batista made his biggest mistake. In celebration of electing himself president, he released all political prisoners, including Fidel, his brother Raúl and the other Moncada conspirators. By this time, Fidel's was only one of many groups fighting the dictator, and a wave of bombings and strikes hit the island. Amid renewed police repression, the Castro brothers decided to go into exile in Mexico. There they made plans for a Cuban revolution that, like so many before, would begin with a landing from the sea. Around them gathered a band of exiled Cuban revolutionaries, as well as a handful of other Latin Americans. Among the latter was a young Argentine doctor named Ernesto 'Che' Guevara, who became the group's political conscience. Their 'secret' training around Mexico City soon drew the attention of the police, and Fidel and the others were arrested, broadcasting their intentions to Batista in large headlines. Nevertheless, they secured their release and resumed preparations. On November 26, 1956, 82 revolutionaries wearing '26 of July' armbands boarded a motor yacht named *Granma* in the port of Tuxpan and embarked for Cuba.

REVOLUTION

Cuba in 1956 was a study in strange contrasts. In the cities, the war against Batista escalated, with bombs and guns fighting the methodical brutality of the Special Police. However, for the Cuban elites and the foreign community, that was just a nasty little sideshow; life was good, with TVs in every home, big American cars on the streets and money pouring in from sugar and tourism. More than 300,000 visitors streamed into Cuba that year, patronizing the American Mafia-run casinos, seeing top entertainers like Nat King Cole in the nightclubs or sneaking into the pornographic movie theatres. In the countryside, life was still poverty-stricken, of course, but if you rolled up the windows and turned on the air conditioners you could ignore the pitiful *campesinos*.

The arrival of the 26 of July Movement fighters in Cuba changed all that. After a miserable boat ride, the landing in a swamp in southwest Oriente Province was a disaster. Batista's troops were watching and later ambushed them in a sugarcane field. Only a little more than a dozen revolutionaries escaped death or capture and made it to

The wheel of chance: a Havana casino

safety in the Sierra Maestra. Somehow, however, that was enough. Their first allies were the Sierra's poverty-stricken peasants, long harassed by the Rural Guard, who gave them food and enlisted in their tiny army. When word filtered back to Havana that Fidel had survived, urban sympathizers began to make the trek to Oriente to join up. In the first months of 1957, the rebels won small but important victories against the Rural Guard, and the Cuban army was forced to send precious troops to the mountains. Just as importantly, a string of foreign reporters climbed the Sierra to interview Fidel— the public-relations battle was half the fight.

The 26 of July Movement was not the only group fighting Batista. The bloodiest battles were led by urban terrorist cells; their campaign of bombings and kidnappings was so widespread that even Cuba's elite could not ignore them. To make matters worse, the military was unhappy, and new plots by disaffected officers were always being uncovered. Sugar prices were dropping, tourists were disappearing and even the United States government had had enough of Batista. By 1958, it was obvious that the dictator's days were numbered.

Teaching reading and revolution: the Alphabetization Campaign, early '60s.

THE TRIUMPH OF THE REVOLUTION

In July of that year, a conference of anti-Batista groups recognized that Fidel Castro and the 26 of July Movement were the vanguard of the opposition. Batista struck back with a full-scale offensive against the Sierra. Within a few weeks, it became obvious that the army's offensive would fail; the inexperienced troops refused to fight, and many, finding the rebels more attractive, defected to the other side. As the government retreated, the rebels advanced westward from the mountains, controlling much of rural Oriente. By December, Batista's army was literally running away, leaving large amounts of armaments in their wake. The rebel army grew by leaps and bounds; in less than two years the ragged handful had turned into an army of almost 3,000 troops. On New Year's Eve, 1958, Fulgencio Batista had reached the end. He and his senior officials boarded a plane and flew into exile in the Dominican Republic. Twenty-four hours later, troops under Che Guevara and another popular rebel leader, Camilo Cienfuegos, took control of Havana's main military posts. That same night, Santiago's main square was the site of a rapturous welcome for a 32-year-old Fidel Castro and his first speech as leader of Cuba. A new era had begun.

The first few months of 1959 were the Revolution's honeymoon. Everything was possible; it remained only to decide what the leaders wanted. One of the first tasks was settling accounts with the Batista regime. Those who had been unable to flee received huge show trials, frequently lacking in due process, that often ended in death sentences. Other anti-Castroites fled to the hills or went underground and began a terrorist campaign to weaken the Revolution. These acts only strengthened Castro's support. From the start, there were problems with the United States, which had never liked Fidel. On the Cuban side, it soon became obvious that anti-Americanism was the basis of the Revolution's philosophy. The Revolution's liberal allies soon detected a drift to the left, and they too began to abandon the island before they were put in jail. Meanwhile, Fidel and the other top revolutionaries solidified their popularity with the masses, receiving near-religious adulation.

Fidel speaks

By the end of 1959, it appeared that the new government had consolidated its power and decided on its goals: all American businesses out of Cuba, greatly improved relations with the Soviet Union and state control of industry and agriculture. These plans sped the flight of the largely white and urban elites from Cuba; from 1960 to 1962 over 200,000 left, settling mainly in Florida and New Jersey. When the Revolution expropriated the last U.S.-owned businesses, the Americans cut off all diplomatic relations and imposed an embargo on all U.S. trade with the island. At the same time, Cuba was signing new trade accords with the Soviet Union, and Prime Minister Krushchev was pledging to fight any U.S. intervention in Cuba.

THE BAY OF PIGS AND THE MISSILE CRISIS

In Washington, the wheels for this intervention were already turning. President Eisenhower had authorized the CIA to begin arming Cuban exiles and training them in Central America. When President Kennedy took office in early 1961, he was told that the operation would be effortless and the political repercussions few. On April 15, a number of Cuban airfields were bombed in order to destroy the Revolution's air force; unfortunately for the mission, they did not complete the job. The bombing also warned Fidel that an invasion was coming. Two days later, 1,300 exile soldiers calling themselves Brigade 2506 landed at Playa Girón on the Bay of Pigs. They were backed by supply ships and, farther offshore, the U.S. Navy. Within 24 hours, Brigade 2506 was surrounded by 20,000 Cuban troops with tanks and heavy weapons personally supervised by Fidel. The invaders' air support was shot down by the Cuban planes that had survived the bombardment. Brigade 2506 radioed desperately for help from the U.S. Navy, but Kennedy was not prepared to step into a direct confrontation. The fleet steamed away, letting the exiles fall captive—they were later ransomed—and giving Fidel a historic defeat of the United States.

The Bay of Pigs Invasion (known as 'Playa Girón' in Cuba) radicalized the Revolution and sent it further into the embrace of the Soviet Union. Over 100,000 opponents of the regime were arrested, and Fidel proclaimed for the first time that the Revolution was 'socialist' and that he was a 'Marxist-Lenin-ist.' The Cuban people were channeled into mass organizations, like the Federation of Cuban Women, the Committees for the Defense of the Revolution (a powerful block-watch organization) and the Union of Pioneers (a Revolutionary version of the Boy and Girl Scouts). If you did not join one, it was assumed that you were against the Revolution. The military, under the control of Raúl Castro, was greatly expanded and armed with the latest Soviet weaponry. Among these were 42 long-range missiles with nuclear warheads capable of hitting most major U.S. cities.

The Bay of Pigs, Fidel alights from a tank

The real reasons for the missile installation remain unclear over 30 years later. According to Fidel, Cuba feared another invasion, although, once bitten, Kennedy had no plans to try again. The Soviets could not resist trying to exponentially expand their first-strike capability on the United States, and they believed Kennedy had been too wounded by the Bay of Pigs to retaliate. What is clear is that the missiles, which arrived on Soviet freighters in September 1962, brought the world to the brink of a nuclear war. In October, American U-2 spy planes confirmed the missiles' presence in Cuba, and Kennedy decided to act. He stated that the missiles were an 'unacceptable . . . aggressive action' and must be returned to the Soviet Union. Until they were withdrawn, the U.S. Navy would quarantine the island to prevent the delivery of any more, which were en route.

After days of tremendous tension, on October 28 Krushchev agreed to dismantle and withdraw the missiles. In turn the U.S. would agree not to invade Cuba.

Fidel and the other Revolutionary leaders, some of whom were ready to risk nuclear war, were furious: the deal had been made over their heads, without even consulting Fidel. A chill settled over Cuban-Soviet relations, and although they thawed out again, it was never the same. Nevertheless, the United States kept its word: no more invasion forces headed to Cuba. The island's leaders turned then to internal affairs and the building of Revolutionary Cuba.

THE NEW MAN

The work took place on two fronts: the economy and social services. The latter was far more successful. Hospitals and clinics were built in hundreds of rural communities that had never seen a doctor, and health care was free to all. Education became a crucial tool of the government, not only for bettering the Cuban people but for transmitting the ideals of the Revolution. Literacy volunteers filled the countryside, where 40 to 50 per cent of *campesinos* could not read or write. Mandatory primary-school education finally became a reality.

The Revolution had a harder time clarifying its goals for the economy. For the first few years, the official policies seemed to be agricultural

One of the sugarmills that was to boost the Cuban economy during the early '60s

Harvesting sugar today

diversity (i.e., no sugar monoculture) and a Soviet-style reliance on heavy industry and mining. These failed to bring in the needed returns, such as enough food, so in 1963 Fidel announced that sugar would once again become a centerpiece of Cuba's economy. The next year he signed a trade accord with the Soviet Union under which sugar would be sold to Moscow at a heavily subsidized price. In return, the Cubans would buy masses of products, from tractors to frozen chickens to gasoline, from the Soviets and Eastern Europe. It became easier to purchase food abroad than grow it at home. All of Cuba's arable land was turned over to sugar production, and this fixation culminated in 1970, in which the plan called for a harvest of 10 million tons of raw sugar. The entire nation was mobilized; the world would watch the Revolution produce another miracle. Unfortunately, when everything was counted up in the end, they only harvested 8.5 million tons of sugar. This shortfall, and the general chaos of the economy, caused a complete reorganization of the Cuban economy on more rational lines.

Although Cuba and the USSR had many trade ties, and Cuba was filled with Soviet advisers, the Revolutionary government pursued a foreign policy that was often at odds with Soviet aims. This was the era of detente, and Moscow did not want to upset the delicate relations between the superpowers. On the other hand, Cuba's leaders were the idols of revolutionary movements around the globe, and saw no reason why they should not spread their ideals. Cuba began subsidizing and training left-wing revolutionary groups from Central America to Africa to Southeast Asia. In early 1965, with support for his policies slipping, Che Guevara decided to resign from the government and rejoin the armed struggle for liberation. He made the mistake of focusing his efforts on Bolivia, a country without the political unrest of Cuba in the 1950s. He spent months in Bolivia's countryside, half-starved and unsuccessfully trying to recruit peasant support. His tiny band of internationalist fighters included at least a few who were traitors or spies. After months of sporadic fighting with no political or military gains, he was captured by the army and executed. In the vast pantheon of Cuban martyrs, Che is now number one, his iconic portrait covering walls and buildings across Cuba.

In the 1970s, Cuba's support for world revolution logged its greatest successes. Two major contingents of Cuban troops were sent to Africa, fighting civil wars on the side of the communists in Angola and Ethiopia. In 1979, the Cuban-trained Sandinista rebels in Nicaragua defeated the Somoza regime and founded their own socialist government with heavy Cuban assistance. There was also a surprising opening to the United States when President Jimmy Carter eased Cuban travel restrictions in place since the Bay of Pigs (this ended with the election of Ronald Reagan). Cubans saw their exiled relatives for the first time in almost two decades and were shocked: the Cuban-Americans had prospered.

THE FIRST CRACKS
In 1980, things were looking up for Cuba. The Soviets had not only agreed to delay payment of the Cuban debt but had increased the subsidies. More goods rolled in; gasoline was nearly free. Then a

small tear in the envelope surrounding Cuba turned into a gaping hole. A group of dissidents broke into the Peruvian embassy in Havana, demanding asylum. When the embassy refused to turn them over to the Cuban authorities, Fidel made the mistake of removing the guards as punishment for the embassy's intransigence—the guards would have prevented the thousands of later asylum-seekers from entering the embassy. Perhaps influenced by their Cuban-American relatives' success, first a few, then thousands streamed into the embassy grounds, hoping for asylum and entry into the United States. More and more publicity appeared in the foreign press, and Fidel decided to allow them to leave, permitting small boats from Florida to pick them up at the port of Mariel. However, Fidel managed to turn the exodus to his advantage; all those who did not wholeheartedly support the Revolution, including dissidents, homosexuals, prostitutes and criminals, were strongly encouraged to join the boatlift. By the time President Jimmy Carter closed the door, nearly 100,000 had left and the Revolution had succeeded in disposing of its most vocal critics.

At home, the mid-1980s were relatively placid. From abroad came faint rumblings that the future was not so certain. In 1983, the socialist regime on the tiny Caribbean island of Grenada self-destructed when its Cuba-supported leader, Maurice Bishop, was killed by radicals in his own party. Seeing his chance, President Reagan sent American soldiers to Grenada ostensibly to protect American medical students but really to topple the regime. The Grenadian and Cuban troops were quickly overcome, and the United States handed Fidel his first defeat.

Two years later, Mikhail Gorbachev became leader of the Soviet Union, and that empire began to totter. When Gorbachev finally arrived for his first state visit in April 1989, everybody knew that change was in the air. The year before, the Soviets had helped prod Angola's warring parties toward peace—a move that Cuba had vehemently disputed—and Cuban troops were on their way out. Gorbachev's reception was distinctly chilly, and he only brought with him vague promises of aid, at reduced levels. By the end of the year, the Berlin Wall had fallen, the East Bloc regimes were on the run and Fidel knew that aid would soon be reduced to zero. In January 1990, Fidel declared that Cuba was in a 'Special Period in Time of Peace.' The subsidies from the communist world had disappeared; the island would have to survive on its own.

AN UNCERTAIN FUTURE

The Special Period has presented the Revolution its greatest challenge yet. The first five years were a time of frightening economic free-fall. Cubans saw their lifestyle erode to poverty level; there were shortages of nearly every essential, including food, electricity, medicine, clean water and transportation. For lack of raw materials and spare parts, factories ground to a halt, and, for most Cubans, the only way to survive was to trade on the black market. The streets of Havana went dark, and the tension was only broken by sporadic riots and a renewed exodus of rafters for Florida.

The turn-around began in mid-1993, when the government legalized the possession of U.S. dollars, which had far more street value than the near-worthless Cuban peso. For the first time in over 30 years, they authorized small private businesses, including restaurants and repair shops. New peso-only agricultural markets brought more money to farmers than selling to the state and provided city-dwellers with previously-scarce meat and fresh produce. Slowly, the economy began to tick upward.

These changes brought a modest form of capitalism to Cuba, but not without stress. Hard-line communists in the government have lobbied strenuously to return the country to a purer socialist state. They see their power being diluted and too many people becoming (relatively) rich, while the rest lag behind. They have allowed private restaurants and other businesses to continue operating but have imposed taxes and other restrictions that make it nearly impossible to stay open. Those that remain are confined to high-tourist areas of Havana, Varadero and other cities frequented by foreigners. For the rest of the population, many of whom lived by their wits during the worst of the Special Period, they are being pressured to return to their government jobs and peso salaries (if they do not, they can be sent to jail for 'potential danger' to the State). The lucky ones work in the tourist industry; the vast majority still struggle to get by, hoping that some relative abroad will send them a remittance of dollars.

Nevertheless, life has gotten appreciably better since the dark days of the early 1990s. In January of 1998, Pope John Paul II toured the island and spoke to enthusiastic crowds. His visit opened the door to a reawakening of the Catholic Church. Priests have been openly critical of the government; mass attendance is up; and churches have become a conduit of all kinds of aid to the public, including the distribution of medicine. At the same time, foreign investment has allowed the rebuilding of Cuba's dilapidated power and telephone networks—the lights are on more often—and funds gained from the tourist trade have allowed work to resume on road repairs and much-needed housing.

The challenge is now to give Cubans hope for the future. The traditional escape valve of a raft to Florida has been closed since the United States and other countries are now returning rafters to Cuba, so the Cuban government must deal with simmering resentments on its own soil. This task still lies in the hands of Fidel. As long as his oratory has the power to cajole his friends and threaten his enemies, the Cuban people will continue to follow him as they have for the past four decades, from crisis to crisis on the heroic island of Cuba.

■ THE NATURAL WORLD

Cuba is an island 1,250 kilometres (780 miles) long and 191 kilometres (120 miles) across at its widest. Its 3,520 kilometres (2,200 miles) of coastline include hundreds of kilometres of beaches, many harbors and over a thousand smaller islands. Millions of years ago, Cuba was formed from three separate islands, none of which had been part of a larger landmass.

Over one-quarter of the landmass is occupied by mountain ranges; these are the Cordillera Guaniguanico in Pinar del Río Province (site of the beautiful Valle de Viñales), the Viñales de Escambray above Trinidad in Sancti Spiritus Province and, in Oriente, the Sierra Maestra and the sierra rising west of Baracoa. At 1,973 metres (6,473 feet), the Sierra Maestra's Pico Turquino is Cuba's highest point. The rest of Cuba's landscape is gentle hills and plains; the percentage of land available for cultivation is extremely high. Cuba has over 200 rivers, of which the largest is the Río Cauto in Oriente.

Cuba's lushness and geographical and biological diversity have made it a paradise for lovers of the outdoors. Micro-habitats like caves, offshore islands, cliffs, swamps and forests shelter a wide variety of unique plants and animals. Like Australia, the island teems with endemic species: more than 6,000 plant types and many thousands of animals species. One of these is the *almiquí*, a ratlike mammal with a long snout and large feet. The forest around Baracoa teems with polymites, a variety of brightly colored land snails. Among the many possibilities for nature tourism, the Sierra Maestra National Park in Granma Province has the richest ecosystem, with one of Cuba's oldest forests filled with a luxuriant plant and animal life. Due south of Havana, the Zapata swamp is the Caribbean's most important stopover for migrating birds and a year-round home to the bee hummingbird, the world's smallest bird. Its lagoons are filled with flamingoes, and Cuban crocodiles and manatees cruise the waterways.

The spectacular, cave-filled hills of the Valle de Viñales abound with the largest number of endemic species, including the pygmy boa which only lives in these cliffs. The hilltops here are the home of the *palma corcho,* a primitive palm tree that is a relic of the dinosaur era. The green peaks of the Sierra de Escambray near Trinidad are covered with a unique rain forest interrupted here and there with splashing cascades. Walks through the woods reveal an abundance of birds and plant species—but bring your rain gear. There is more, like the luxuriant hills around Baracoa and Guantanamo's cactus gardens; it only remains for you to get there. The easiest way is to arrange a trip through one of the big tourism organizations, such as Cubatur, Cubanacan, Gaviota or Havanatur.

Facts For The Traveller

GETTING THERE

ALTHOUGH SOME VISITORS ARRIVE BY BOAT, the vast majority come by air. Havana's Jose Martí International Airport is the most popular entry point. Most international flights arrive at the spanking new, Canadian-built Terminal 3, with glass-walled elevators. There are also international airports at Varadero, Cayo Largo, Ciego de Ávila, Santiago, Camagüey, Cienfuegos, Holguín and Manzanillo. Cubana is the national airline, with a fleet of Russian planes, A300s and Fokkers flying regularly to many destinations in South and Central America, Canada and Europe.

In the Western Hemisphere, the most flights to Cuba come from Mexico, with daily flights from Mexico City and frequent departures from Cancún and Mérida. Cubana also has daily flights from Nassau in the Bahamas to Havana and Varadero. Flights to Cuba also depart once or twice weekly from Curaçao (Netherlands Antilles), Kingston, Montreal, Bogota, Buenos Aires, Caracas, Santiago (Chile), Lima, Managua, Panama City, San José (Costa Rica), Sao Paulo and Toronto. From Europe, Madrid is the only city with daily departures; cities with one or two flights a week include Basel, Berlin, Brussels, Düsseldorf, Grand Canary Island, Moscow, Munich, Paris and Shannon (Ireland). A weekly London–Havana service is planned for spring 1999. Cuba is also the destination of many charter flights, which fly from Guadeloupe, Martinique, Montego Bay, Nassau, Port-au-Prince, Saint Martin, Santo Domingo, Tegucigalpa and Toronto and from Milan and London in Europe.

The U.S. government has recently given permission for charter flights to resume between Miami and Havana. However, only diplomats, employees of international organizations (the U.N., etc.), full-time journalists with accredited news organizations, academics doing professional research and close relatives of Cubans on humanitarian visits (someone dying) are given permission. This can only be given by the U.S. Treasury Department (see Visas). For all others wishing to travel from the United States to Cuba, the only route is through a third country, most commonly Mexico, the Bahamas or Canada.

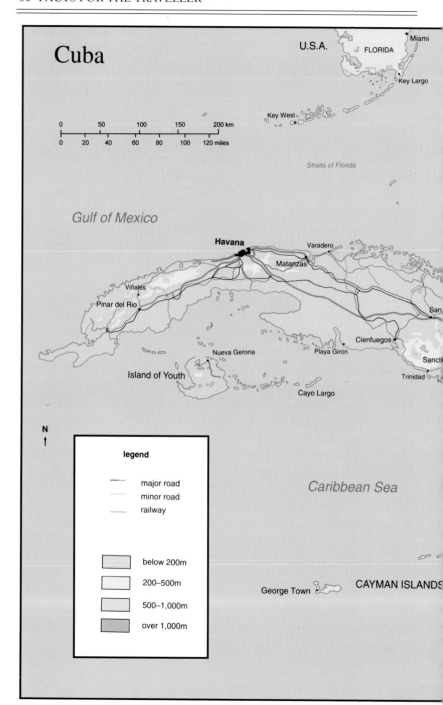

Cuba

U.S.A.

FLORIDA

Miami

Key Largo

Key West

Straits of Florida

Gulf of Mexico

Havana

Varadero

Matanzas

Viñales

Pinar del Rio

San

Cienfuegos

Nueva Gerona

Playa Girón

Sancti

Island of Youth

Trinidad

Cayo Largo

N

Caribbean Sea

legend

— major road

— minor road

— railway

below 200m

200–500m

500–1,000m

over 1,000m

George Town

CAYMAN ISLANDS

0 50 100 150 200 km
0 20 40 60 80 100 120 miles

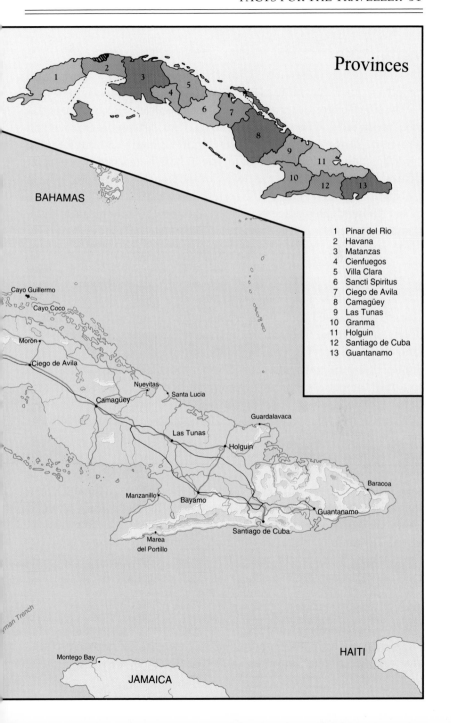

Provinces

1 Pinar del Rio
2 Havana
3 Matanzas
4 Cienfuegos
5 Villa Clara
6 Sancti Spiritus
7 Ciego de Avila
8 Camagüey
9 Las Tunas
10 Granma
11 Holguin
12 Santiago de Cuba
13 Guantanamo

BAHAMAS

Cayo Guillermo
Cayo Coco
Morón
Ciego de Avila
Nuevitas
Camaguey
Santa Lucia
Las Tunas
Guardalavaca
Holguin
Baracoa
Manzanillo
Bayamo
Guantanamo
Santiago de Cuba
Marea
del Portillo

Cayman Trench

Montego Bay

HAITI

JAMAICA

VISAS

Visitors to Cuba must arrive with a valid passport and a tourist card (good for up to six months) issued by the Cuban government or a Cuba tour operator or travel agent. Those countries whose citizens still need a visa include Italy, Japan, Malaysia, Peru, Singapore, Sweden and Thailand. Visitors in transit may stay up to 72 hours without a tourist card. It is now legal for a tourist to stay in both hotels and private residences. In the latter case, the owner of the house is obliged to inform Cuban immigration and pay the corresponding taxes.

For United States citizens, legal Cuba visits are significantly more complicated. Since 1961, the United States has had an embargo on trade with Cuba, and this embargo specifically prohibits travel for purposes of tourism or business (although according to the Cuban government, over 26,000 U.S. citizens visited Cuba in 1992).

Aside from U.S. government officials, three groups of United States citizens are allowed to visit the island: full-time journalists, academics doing 'professional research' in Cuba and relatives of Cubans with 'circumstances of extreme hardship' such as grave illness or a death in the family. Full-time journalists for U.S. news organizations do not need to apply for permission; academics, athletes, religious leaders and those seeking humanitarian permission must apply to the Licensing Division, Office of Foreign Assets Control, U.S. Department of Treasury (tel 202-622-2480). If you want to travel to Cuba as a journalist, you then must apply for a visa at the Cuban Interests Section (2630 16th Street N.W., Washington, D.C. 20009, tel 202-797-8609). This may take months to process. With your permission, you then may purchase a ticket for the Miami-Havana charter flight from Marazul Tours (800/223-5334). Many U.S. citizens circumvent their government's restrictions and visit Cuba without Treasury Department authorization. Once you are in Cuba, there are also limitations on financial transactions involving U.S. credit cards and traveller's checks.

CUSTOMS

Tourists are allowed to bring in duty-free two bottles of alcohol and one carton of cigarettes per adult and any electronic equipment (camera, video recorder, computer, etc.) that is for personal use only. If they believe that you are bringing in goods for sale in Cuba, the Customs fees can be punitive. Pornography, 'morally offensive' material and illegal drugs are forbidden. For most visitors, customs formalities are usually brief—an x-ray and a cursory look through your luggage.

CLIMATE

Cuba is a tropical country. July and August are the warmest months, with average temperatures around 30 degrees C, 86 degrees F; in January, the coldest month, the temperature averages 21 degrees C, 70 degrees F. The driest months are December and August; May through November is the rainy season, and June is the wettest month. June through early November is also hurricane season; most storms hit in September and October. During winter, the weather (particularly on the northwest coast) usually alternates between beautiful sunshine and cold fronts from the north bringing clouds and drizzle. In the cities, July and August can be stifling, with no wind and day after day of oppressive heat. The hottest and coldest regions in Cuba are both in Oriente: the Pico Turquino, Cuba's highest point, occasionally gets frost, and the area around Guantanamo Bay is a cactus-filled desert.

CLOTHING

The Revolution is not formal. In the cities, men wear long pants and T-shirts. Young people wear shorts and flip-flops at the beach as well as in city streets. The *guayabera* (a light cotton shirt with ribs down the front, always worn over the belt and never tucked in) is the uniform of the government functionary. Jackets and ties are only worn by top-level officials when meeting with important foreign dignitaries and businessmen. Some of the fancier restaurants may require men to wear long-sleeved shirts or *guayaberas*. Women have considerably more leeway, appearing in everything from starched, conservative dresses to spandex shorts and tube tops that leave nothing to the imagination. In the oppressive heat of July and August, cotton is a must. At the beach, almost everything comes off, of course, al-

(following pages) Guantánamo Bay from Caimanera

though toplessness is confined to the foreign tourist areas. Always bring a few long-sleeved shirts to survive over-air-conditioning of tourist hotels and restaurants. During the 'Winter', Cubans complain bitterly of the 'cold', but visitors from northern climes rarely need anything heavier than a sweater and a light jacket.

HEALTH

The tropical diseases that once ravaged Cuba have essentially been eradicated. If you are coming from a country with yellow fever, you must show a vaccination certificate. Due to Cuba's current economic problems, the health-care system is undergoing severe strains. Even in Havana, medicine is difficult to find (try the dollar pharmacy in the Camilo Cienfuegos Clinic at Calle L #151 between Linea and 13th, Vedado or the Cira Garcia Clinic at Calle 20 at 41 in Miramar). Outside the capital, it can be nearly impossible. You should bring with you all medications, including antibiotics and antidiarrheal drugs, that you possibly might need. If you need to see a doctor, every tourist hotel has one on call. There are also special tourist clinics in Havana (Ave. Las Terrazas #36, Santa Maria del Mar, Playas del Este), Varadero (Calles 60 and 1), Santiago (Calle 13 and 14, Reparto Vista Alegre) Cayo Coco, Cienfuegos, Trinidad, Santa Lucia, Guardalavaca and Marea del Portillo. However, outside the tourist areas, health-care facilities can be crude and wholly lacking in supplies. Those travelling rough should consider bringing first-aid cream, an Ace bandage, a water filter and a first-aid kit. The two most common health problems encountered by tourists are the *catarro Cubano,* the 'Cuban cold', and the pan-Latin-American stomach and diarrhea problem known as *la turista.* The big resort hotels filter their water; outside them you should only drink bottled or boiled water, generally available in dollar stores.

MONEY

Cuba's official currency is the peso. This comes in coins of 1, 2, 5, 20 and 40 centavos (100 to one peso) and one and three pesos. The paper money circulates in bills of 1, 3, 5, 10, 20 and 50 pesos. Upon leaving Cuba, you may change up to 10 pesos into foreign currency at the official rate, which is one peso to one U.S. dollar.

Cuba's peso has regained slightly more of its buying power compared to the depths of the Special Period. For tourists, however, the U.S. dollar is far more useful: It is the only currency you can use in hotels, restaurants, shops and nightclubs. The only reason to have pesos on hand is to take the bus (not recommended) or buy a movie ticket or some food at the agricultural market.

Although the official dollar-peso rate is one-to-one, the government recently opened money exchange booths named CADECA that trade dollars for pesos at a floating rate that approaches the black market price (20 pesos to one dollar at this writing; 120-to-one a few years ago). For tourists, using these exchanges is far preferable to changing money on the street. It is both legal and safe—you will not be given out-of-circulation notes.

There are not enough dollars in Cuba to meet the demand, so the government has printed "convertible pesos" that are exactly equivalent to the dollar in price. Issued in notes of 1, 5 and 10 dollars and coins of 1, 5, 10, 25 and 50 cents, this currency is accepted throughout Cuba (but is worthless everywhere else).

TRANSPORTATION

The Special Period is still hurting Cuba's transportation sector. It is nearly impossible to purchase tickets for peso transport, like buses and trains, on short notice; the lines for Cubans can be days long. Even with dollars you should buy your tickets well in advance, particularly for internal flights.

AIR

Cubana, the national airline, has daily flights to Santiago and Varadero, and one-to-three-times-a-week flights to Baracoa, Bayámo, Camagüey, Ciego de Avila, Guantanamo, Holguín, Las Tunas, Manzanillo, Moá and Nueva Gerona. The planes are the veteran Russian workhorses, Yaks and Antonovs. Two charter airlines, Aerocaribbean and Aero Gaviota, also fly some of these routes and may have seats if

Cubana is booked—ask your hotel travel agent. Aerocaribbean is the only local airline that flies to Cayo Largo.

All three airlines leave Havana from Jose Martí International Airport in the suburb of Boyeros south of downtown. Most domestic flights (except for Aero Caribbean departing from its separate facility at the west end of the airport) depart from Terminal 2. You must pay in foreign currency for your tickets and they should be bought at least a week in advance. Cuban citizens may only buy tickets 14 days in advance of flying and must line up for days for the privilege.

CAR

Renting a car is by far the most efficient way to see the most of Cuba. Unfortunately, it is not cheap; it is difficult to rent a car for less than $100 a day (including a tank of gas, insurance and unlimited mileage); weekly rates are less. The main car rental agencies are Havanautos (the largest), Cubacar, Transautos and Gaviota. Automatic shift cars are few and expensive.

Vintage taxi jam, Santiago train station

The 'Ship of Gold'

Gasoline is available—for dollars only—at the Servi Cupet and Oro Negro gas station chains that have sprung up across Cuba. At this writing, one litre costs 75 cents. The Cupets also house small convenience stores selling sodas, beer, sandwiches and auto supplies. On long distance trips, it does not hurt to bring an extra can of gasoline.

By Latin American standards, the quality of Cuba's roads runs from very good to poor. The best is the expressway that runs from Pinar del Río, through Havana and ends east of Santa Clara. Country roads away from the main tourist routes can be full of potholes, and you may have to ford some rivers. Outside of Havana, there are rarely many cars and trucks to worry about. During the day, the greatest danger is bicyclists, who swerve across city streets and rural roads without heeding oncoming traffic. In the country, the main nighttime danger is cows, which like to congregate on blind corners.

Due to the lack of public transport, Cuba's roads are lined with hitchhikers, some of whom sleep on the roadside, so care should be taken, particularly at night. At the entrance and exit of most cities and towns there is almost always a motorcycle policeman. Havana's policeman also like to give tickets, usually for making an illegal turn when the prohibiting signs were all but invisible. Fines are marked on your car rental agreement and must be paid, in dollars, when you return the vehicle. Note that Cuba's stop sign is white with a red triangle with the word 'pare' for 'stop'.

TRAIN

Before the Revolution, Cuba's train system was the glory of Latin America. It is no longer; this sorry condition predates the Special Period. The current top-of-the-line service is the overnight train that runs the Havana-Santiago route. For dollars, tickets for this train may be purchased at most hotel travel agents and at the Ladis (ex-Ferrotur) office behind Havana's central station (just south of Old Havana on Calle Egido). For pesos, you have to line up for days or weeks. The #1 train leaves from Havana about 5 pm and, as the #2 train, returns the following night. The trip takes 17 hours, more or less, and features extremely bad food, comfortable assigned seats and air conditioning turned up to a bone-chilling cold. Because most of the journey is at night, there is very little to see from the windows. Ladis will also sell you tickets for multiple destinations, but due to the vagaries of the train schedules, you must allow lots time for the inevitable delays.

The other principal routes are Havana-Bayamo, Havana-Las Tunas, Havana-Cienfuegos and Havana-Pinar del Río. Cuba's only electric train is the Hershey train (named after a sugar mill), which runs from Casablanca on the other side of Havana Harbor to the city of Matanzas. The trip, which takes about three hours, is extremely picturesque, but once again the problem is getting tickets—you should try to buy them two days in advance at the Casablanca station.

BUS

Big, comfortable, air-conditioned tourist buses run from Havana to the major tourist destinations, including Varadero and Santiago. You may purchase tickets from any hotel travel agent. Small, uncomfortable, non-air-conditioned Cuban buses run infrequently between all the major cities. Tickets for these are only purchasable in pesos, and there is a line, of days; dollars will get you a ticket in minutes (although for a bus departing in hours or days). In Havana and Santiago, you might also be tempted to try a local bus (in other cities these are even rarer). They can only be recommended to try once, for the experience. The wait is frequently an hour or two; it is a brawl to get on; you are squeezed together like pigs in a stockyard; it is a brawl to get off (and you might even have to pay for the privilege—10 or 20 centavos). Outside Havana, most 'buses' are actually converted flatbed trucks. In Havana, many buses are the distinctive *camellos* ('camels') hauled by truck cabs.

COMMUNICATIONS

Most of the larger tourist hotels have an office of the Ministry of Communications called *Telecorreo International* which acts as post office and long-distance telephone service. These also often possess telex and fax machines and are the local representatives of the DHL international courier service (sends business documents only). International mail sent through a regular post office box generally takes longer. Many Cubans believe that their mail sent overseas will never arrive, so they ask tourists to mail it abroad.

For shorter communications, both within Cuba and international, the telegraph office is more reliable. Most tourist hotels offer international direct dialing; obviously there is a significant surcharge. ETECSA prepaid **telephone cards** from Cuba's phone company are a less expensive option and can be purchased at *Telecorreos* and hotel front desks. These can be used in a growing number of pay phones that accept only these cards; the phones are strategically situated on key streets and buildings. Local telephone service has gone from bad to poor or even mediocre. Cut-offs and blackouts of whole regions are far less frequent. One drawback of the improvements is that phone numbers for hotels and other tourist destinations constantly are changing. There are a few working pay phones on the streets of Havana; these accept 5-, 10- and 25-centavo coins.

It can be difficult getting news in Cuba. The official newspaper, *Granma,* is much diminished due to the Special Period; no longer a daily, it rarely has more than six or eight pages, and the international coverage is sketchy at best. On Saturdays the government publishes an expanded *Granma International* in English, French, Spanish and Portuguese. Two other national newspapers, *Juventud Rebelde* and Trabajadores, appear once a week with coverage similar to *Granma's.*

Book lover, Havana

Outside of Havana, it is very difficult to find any of these papers; even in the capital, kiosks receive a limited number early in the morning and they usually sell out immediately. The post office at the Habana Libre almost always carries the latest *Granma.* Every province also has a local paper, but these also appear only rarely and in small press runs. Cuba's most famous newsmagazine, *Bohemia,* has recently reappeared. Various tourist-oriented publications are sold at hotels and tourist shops, notably *Opciones* and *Gramma Internacional.* In Havana, the free monthly *Cartelera* describes upcoming cultural events and gives a good listing of restaurants and nightlife. Other Cuban monthlies include *Prisma, Cuba Internacional,* and *TIPS,* which focuses on business and investment opportunities. Newsstands at the larger Havana hotels carry a few European and U.S. newspapers and magazines. The best selection is available at the **Newsprensa** kiosk outside the Cubalse supermarket (Calle 70 and Ave 3ra, Miramar) and at the Meliá Cohiba, Nacional and Habana Libre hotels.

Every city and town in Cuba has at least one bookstore. Unfortunately, the shelves rarely contain new books (dusty copies of Marx and Lenin generally line the walls) because demand far outstrips supply. After years of near collapse, Cuban book publishers are now issuing around 100 titles yearly; most of these are destined for dollar stores and export. The most important dollar bookstores are the **Librería Fernando Ortíz** (Calles L and 27, Vedado—near the Habana Libre), and the **Libería Internacional** (Calle Obispo 528—near El Floridita) and **La Bella Habana**, on the north side of Old Havana's Plaza de Armas. For Cuban and Latin American literatue, try the small bookstores inside the Casa de las Américas (Calle G and Ave 3ra, Vedado) and in the UNEAC building at the corner of Calles 17 and H, Vedado. In Varadero, the bookstore is **Libería Hanoi** at at Calle 44 and Ave Primera. Lively markets for **used books** have sprung up in the Plaza de Armas in Old Havana and along L Street in Vedado across from the Habana Libre.

Cuba has two national television stations, Cubavision and Tele Rebelde, which broadcast between 6 pm and midnight Monday through Friday, Saturday until 2 am and Sunday 10 am to 12 midnight, with children's programming in the morning and family shows and films in the afternoon. Tele Rebelde airs news (12:30 pm, 8 pm), sports and talk shows, while Cubavisión broadcasts the much more popular *telenovelas* ('soap operas', usually Cuban or Brazilian), music programs and movies—a foreign drama on Thursdays, an old film on Fridays, and on Saturday nights, two back-to-back action films, usually Hollywood shoot-em-ups. You can hear their guns blaring and tires screeching from every doorway in Cuba. Outside Havana, there are also provincial TV stations. Most large tourist hotels now have satellite TV, generally offering a selection of U.S., Mexican and European channels. TV Martí, the anti-Castro propaganda station of the U.S. government, is being jammed; the only place you can see it is on videotape in the U.S. Interests Section (see page 129).

There are also a number of radio stations, including **Radio Taíno**, the only one with advertising, oriented toward tourists but listened to by everyone, and the all-news **Radio Relój**, with the unique background of a ticking clock, the exact time every minute and a programming of continuous, 30-minute news segments. Depending what part of Cuba you are in, you may also get overseas stations. Havana receives many south Florida stations (Radio Martí is widely heard), on the south coast you can hear Jamaica and, in Oriente, Haitian stations come in loud and clear.

TIME, MEASUREMENTS, ELECTRICITY

Cuba is in the eastern standard time zone (same as New York) and uses daylight savings time from April to October (EDT starts and ends a couple of weeks before and after it does in the United States).

The metric system is the standard in Cuba, although you may occasionally hear references to American or traditional Spanish weights and measures.

Cuba's electrical system uses 110 volts, with outlets taking same-sized flat-bladed plugs.

HOLIDAYS

The official holidays are January 1 (anniversary of the 'Triumph of the Revolution'), May 1 (May Day), July 26 (anniversary of the Moncada attack) and October 10 (start of the Wars of Independence). All offices, stores and factories are closed on these days, and, in the past, they have been times of mass meetings and marches. No religious holidays are officially celebrated in Revolutionary Cuba.

OPENING HOURS

Hours are flexible in Cuba. Most museums are closed Mondays. Tuesday through Saturday, they generally open sometime between 9 and 11 am and close around 5 pm. On Sundays, museums usually stay open from 9 am to noon. It is impossible to guarantee that a museum will be open—they like to change the hours or close for no discernible reason—but midafternoons from Wednesday to Saturday are your best times for visiting.

Most tourist stores open between 9 and 9:30 am and close around 5 or 6 pm. They are often shut for inventory. Book and record stores usually open around noon and close at 7 pm. Tourist stores generally stay open seven days a week, while the others are closed on Sundays. Government offices are generally open 8-5, with a lunch break between 12 and 2 pm. There is no siesta in Cuba.

CRIME

Cuba is generally a very safe country, with a very low crime rate. However, in some parts of Havana there has been an upsurge in purse snatchings and other petty theft. Calle Obispo in Old Havana seems to be a center of this; one grabs the purse while another drives the getaway bicycle. In the most heavily touristed areas, there is almost always a policeman within calling distance ready and eager to give chase. Another area of possibly more violent crime is the side streets of Central Havana, particularly at night when there are no street lights. Tourists also put themselves at risk when they venture into the netherworld in search of prostitutes or illegal drugs.

Breaking into rental cars—easily identifiable because of their "TUR" license plates—has become disturbingly common. To prevent it, do not leave any belongings visible inside the car or valuables in the trunk. Always park in established parking areas or get one of the ubiquitous watchmen to look after it (cost: $0.25-1.00). This will save you the cost of the insurance deductible and the hassle of a visit to the police station. Nevertheless, if you get into an accident or you are the victim of a crime, either call for a *patrullero*—patrol car—(tel 82-0116) or go to the nearest police station.

TRAVELLER'S AID

Visitors with financial, medical or legal emergencies can go to the Havana offices of Asistur, which specializes in helping travellers in distress. They will help you find lost luggage or replace your tourist card. Asistur also makes reservations for all types of tourist services, including hotels, nightclubs and transportation. Asistur's offices are at Prado #254 (tel 33-8527; fax 33-8087).

TOURIST INFORMATION

In Havana, the main Cubatur office is at Calle 23 #156 in Vedado.

Havanatur's central office is at Calle 2 #17 in Miramar, while Cubanacan's main travel agency is located at Calle 164 at the corner of 17D in Playa (west of Miramar). Nearly every tourist hotel also has its own travel desk; one of the best can be found in the Hotel Habana Libre lobby. Abroad, Cuban tourism offices are located in Frankfurt (Steinweg 2, 6000 Frankfurt/Main 1), Madrid (Paseo de la Habana #28, 28036), Mexico City (Insurgentes Sur #421, Edificio B-310, Col. Hipódromo Condesa, C.P. 06100), Milan (Via General Fara #30, terzo piano, 20124), Montreal (440 Blvd. Rene Levesque Ouest, bureau 1402), Paris (24 Rue du 4 Septembre, 75002) and Toronto (55 Queen St. East, Suite 705, M5C 1R5). Numerous private travel agents also handle Cuban tourism. In the United States, there are many organizations—mainly religious or academic—that arrange fact-finding tours of Cuba. The best known is the Center for Cuban Studies (124 West 23rd St., New York, NY 10011), which runs frequent special topic visits to Cuba for academics and researchers.

EATING AND DRINKING

FOOD

While Cuban food is not one of the great cuisines of the world, what they do, they do well. Some Cuba specialties, like *lechón asado* (roast suckling pig), would be savored by gourmets around the world. The natural abundance of fruits and vegetables also makes eating on the island a delight. Unfortunately, the Revolution has not been kind to Cuban cuisine. As the upper classes left after 1959, so did those fanatic about Cuban food, and the Revolution cared more about the industrial task of feeding the people than about fine dining. Many of the traditions have been lost.

Cuban cuisine received a second blow when Special Period food shortages cut back the supply of every foodstuff. In response, the Ministry of the Food Industry invented less-than-appetizing meat and soybean products such as *jamonada* (also known as 'jamon-nada' or 'ham-not') to stretch scarce commodities. Luckily, food production is now increasing, and Cuban chefs, pressured by thousands of tourists expecting great food, are becoming ever more inventive. Even in the

huevos ~ eggs
huevos fritos ~ fried eggs
revoltillo ~ scrambled eggs
tortilla española ~ omelet with
  potatoes
hotcakes ~ pancakes
jugo de naranja ~ orange juice
pan tostado ~ toast
caldo de pollo ~ chicken soup
potaje de chícharo ~ pea soup
ajiaco ~ stew with a little of
  everything
tamal ~ cornmeal wrapped in
  corn husk and steamed (in
  Oriente it is made out of green
  plantain meal and wrapped in
  banana leaf)
frijoles negros ~ black beans,
  usually in broth
pollo frito ~ fried chicken
pollo asado ~ roast chicken
paella valenciana ~ rice with
  chicken and seafood
picadillo ~ chopped meat
biftec palomilla ~ thin roast steak
albóndigas ~ meatballs
pierna de puerco asada ~ roast leg
  of pork
jamón ~ ham
croquetas de jamón ~ ham
  croquettes
chuletas de puerco ahumadas ~
  smoked pork chops
lechón asado ~ roast suckling pig
cordero ~ lamb
ternera ~ veal
sandwich de jamón y queso ~ ham
and cheese sandwich
bocadito ~ small sandwich
pescado a la plancha ~ broiled fish
filete de pargo ~ snapper filet
camarones ~ shrimp
langosta ~ lobster
arroz blanco ~ white rice
congrí ~ rice with red beans
moros y cristianos ~ rice with
  black beans
plátanos maduros ~ fried sweet
  bananas
tostones ~ fried green bananas
puré de papas ~ mashed
  potatoes
papas fritas ~ french fries
fufú ~ mashed green bananas
boniato ~ root vegetable like a
  sweet potato
malanga ~ another potato-like
  root vegetable
yuca ~ fibrous root vegetable
ensalada ~ salad
col ~ cabbage
lechuga ~ lettuce
aguacate ~ avocado
pepino ~ cucumber
remolacha ~ beet
zanahoria ~ carrot
dulce de toronja ~ candied
  grapefruit
dulce de fruta bomba ~ candied
  papaya
arroz con leche ~ rice pudding
helado ~ ice cream
flan ~ egg custard

top tourist hotels, however, there are occasional scarcities, and it is impossible to guarantee consistent quality. Gourmets have better luck in the *paladares*—the new private restaurants—where the food is more traditional, fresher and far less expensive.

When the Spaniards arrived on the island, they found the native peoples living among an abundance of wild game, sea life, fruits and native vegetables. The colonizers imported the basics of the Spanish diet—bread, oil, wine, cheese, sugar, pork and beef—and adapted the native produce to their tastes. Today Cuban food strongly resembles Spanish cuisine; meat is emphasized (vegetarians may find life difficult), vegetables are boiled or fried and, aside from salt—lots—seasonings are minimal. The use of Tabasco sauce or chile peppers to spice up the meal seems to depend on one's social class; those with Spanish tastes abhor it, while the more Africanized use it freely (restaurants usually have some Tabasco on hand for tourists).

The classic Cuban meal is *cerdo asado* (roast pork) with *congrí* (rice with beans) and *maduros* (fried sweet bananas) on the side. The meal usually begins with soup or salad and definitely ends with a sweet dessert and very sweet and strong Cuban coffee.

If you are invited for lunch or dinner it is in good taste, and highly appreciated, for you to bring a gift, namely beer, wine, rum, chocolate or practically anything sold in the dollar stores. When a visitor comes over to a Cuban household, they are required to eat or, if not, at least drink a cup of coffee. The hosts do not join in but repair to another room while the visitor is dining so as not to disturb him or her (of course, they may just not have enough dishes for all to join in).

DRINK

Rum is Cuba's national drink. The island is filled with distilleries producing dozens of brands (for the best selection, try the Casa del Ron above El Floridita at Obispo and Bernaza in Havana). The main brands are the dry Havana Club and the slightly sweet Caribbean Club, which is preferred by locals. Both of these come in three-, five-

and seven-year-old varieties. Among the best of the other labels are Havana Club Gran Reserva, an extremely aged rum that costs over $60 a bottle, and Ron Matusalen, which is only available in Santiago. Other popular brands are Bucanero, Caney and Varadero.

If factory rum is unavailable, there is an extremely active home-distilling industry; its products are known as *chispa del tren* (train spark) and *wolferina*—after a popular rat poison—and are not recommended unless you want to flirt with temporary blindness.

Most Cubans drink their rum straight; nevertheless there is an abundance of delicious rum cocktails. The most famous is the *mojito* (specialty of the Bodeguita de Medio in Havana), which is made from light rum, ice, sugar, lime juice, mint and a splash of soda water. Following close behind, and entwined with the Hemingway myth (he drank them at El Floridita), is the daiquiri; this is mixed from light rum, ice, sugar and more lime juice and then blended into a frappé. Other popular cocktails are the Cuba Libre (rum, cola, lime and ice), the Cubanito (a rum Bloody Mary) and the Piña Colada.

Beer is also very popular in Cuba; Cristal, Bucanero and Mayabe are the main national brands, and many of the provincial brands also are worth trying (Hatuey was formerly the most popular brand but use of the name was discontinued after the trademark was claimed by Bacardi). The amber Bucanero Negra is a favorite among Cubans. Imported brands, particularly Heineken, Bavaria and Lagarto, made in Holland for Cuba, are universally available.

Imported wine is also available at stores, restaurants and bars at reasonable prices. Cortés is the newest brand, selling table wines and 'champagnes' from the Fantinel estate in San Cristóbal. It joins the other Fantinel labels, Castillo del Morro, Soroa and San Cristóbal.

Cuban bottled water, both natural and gassed, is high-quality and much cheaper than imported. The main brands are Ciego Montero and Levissima.

CRAFTS

Quality crafts can be discovered, but you have to look hard. In Havana, the best selections can be found in one of Old Havana's open-air markets (eventually, they all will be located in the Plaza Vieja), and the **Palacio de Artesania** (Cuba #64, Old Havana) and **Bazar 43** (Calle 22 between Calles 41 and 43, Playa). Both offer a wide variety of well-made straw, wood, leather, textile and metal objects. Che Guevara T-shirts, straw hats and the like are available in the big tourist shops on the ground floor of the Hotel Habana Libre.

In the provinces, craft production has stalled due to the lack of raw materials. It is only beginning to thrive in tourist areas such as Trinidad, where many of the locals are turning their hands to artisanry in order to earn dollars. Some regions are still known for their specialized products. In Nueva Gerona on the Island of Youth, there are factories producing imaginative ceramic tiles; in Camagüey, you can purchase many sizes of simple pottery jars.

FISHING AND HUNTING

Three fish-filled bodies of water surround Cuba: the Caribbean, the Gulf of Mexico and the Atlantic Ocean. Inland there are numerous lakes teeming with trophy-sized largemouth bass. December through May is the best all-around fishing season, although big billfish run in the summer. In 'The Old Man and the Sea,' Ernest Hemingway immortalized the blue marlin fishery off of Cuba's north coast. The Hemingway mystique is revived yearly during the Ernest Hemingway International Marlin Fishing Tournament, based at Havana's Marina Hemingway. Other deep-sea species abundant here are sailfish, wahoo, dolphin, swordfish, kingfish, bonito, shark and tuna. Closer to shore, the coast is lined with reefs filled with grouper, snapper and barracuda. The main north coast fishing fleets leave from Havana, Playas del Este, Varadero and Cayo Guillermo. The shallower waters off the south coast attract schools of tarpon and bonefish; due to the lack of fishing pressure, the latter are almost easy to catch. Cayo Largo and Jardines de la Reina off of Ciego de Avila Province are the centers for the south coast fisheries.

According to Hemingway, largemouth bass was introduced to Cuba in 1929. They have flourished, and some experts think that the next world record will be taken from Cuban waters. The bass-fishing centers are Lago La Redonda in Ciego de Avila, Hanabanilla Lake in Villa Clara, Zaza Lake in Sancti Spiritus and the Laguna del Tesoro on the Zapata Peninsula. For both fresh and saltwater fishing, it is highly recommended that fishermen bring their own rods, reels and terminal tackle.

Cuba has long been a popular destination for hunters, particularly those gunning for birds. Their main targets are white-crowned pigeon, mourning and white-winged doves, snipe, quail, pheasant, guinea fowl, coot and many types of ducks. The pigeon season is July through October; for the rest of the birds, the seasons are either September through February or October through March. Their are 15 hunting preserves throughout Cuba, usually located near lakes, at the mouths of rivers or on offshore keys. Some of the best known are Cayo Saetia in Holguín (until recently reserved for the government elite), Aguachales de Falla in Ciego de Avila, El Taje and Manati in Sancti Spiritus and, in Pinar del Río, Guanahacabibes, Maspoton and La Vibora. Although mammal hunting is less developed, many of these hunting preserves also offer the chance to bag deer, wild pig and many other species. You must pre-arrange for a hunting trip in order to bring in firearms; if you pay for the trip, you get a license.

DIVING

Surrounded by crystal-clear water, coral reefs and 500 years of shipwrecks, Cuba is a natural destination for divers. The south coast has the most extensive coral reefs. The main diving resort here is the Hotel Colony on the Isla de Juventud; offshore there are over 56 dive spots with a wide variety of underwater seascapes. María de la Gorda at the western end of Pinar del Río has the Black Coral Valley and the remains of many shipwrecks. Other south coast dive spots include Cayo Largo, Playa Girón (many underwater caves), Cienfuegos (eight sunken ships), Trinidad and Jardines de la Reina off Ciego de Avila. The main north coast diving resorts are Havana (leaving from the Hotel Copacabana), Playas del Este and Varadero. Cuban diving instructors are recognized by the CMAS (World Confederation of Subaquatic Activities), and only European-made 12- or 15-

liter tanks are used. The only dive resort with its own hyperbaric chamber is the Hotel Colony; other resorts have emergency arrangements with the Cuban air force to fly divers to the nearest chamber.

CULTURE

M U S I C

Cuba's musical heritage is a blend of Spanish and African influences. The Spanish colonizers imported their song forms and melodies and, perhaps more importantly, their instruments, notably the guitar and violin. Dance music became the popular genre for urban and rural whites; the best-known forms were the *guajira*, Cuban *bolero, zapateo, habanera* (used in Bizet's *Carmen)* and the *danzón.*

With the arrival of African slaves, a completely different, but eventually complementary, tradition entered Cuba. The songs were based on African forms, sung in languages like Yoruba, and the principal instrument was the drum, including the hourglass-shaped *bata.* Through religious societies, dances and parades on feast days and Carnival, these African forms began to spread through Cuba. The white population refused to acknowledge African music, of course, but little by little both African and Spanish music began to be infected by each other.

The 'marriage of the guitar and the drum' finally occurred with Independence, when whites discovered that the black half of the population was also Cuban. Suddenly, serious musicians and composers were incorporating African forms and drums in their works; the piano, trumpet and trombone were picked up in Afro-Cuban neighborhoods. In the early 1900s, one of the most popular dances was the rumba, a form of exhibition dance performed to the beat of a percussion band. A less frenetic form that developed at the same time was the *trova*, a type of romantic or patriotic ballad sung to a solo guitar. The 1920s saw the birth of a style that continues to impel dance floors today: *Son* came from sugar workers' dances, but urban musicians adapted the *son* rhythms to orchestras with large percussion sections and violins and horns for the melody.

Rumba drummer

Meanwhile, serious composers like Ernesto Lecuona were blending gentle rhythms with traditional Spanish songs to produce a new type of romantic ballad that filled the serious theatres. Rita Montaner and Bola de Nieve were this form's foremost interpreters. In the 1950s, this genre evolved into *filin* ('feeling') music, and either influenced or copied the style of Nat King Cole.

In the dancehalls the bandleaders were not idle. In 1938, Orestes López saw that dancers were bored during the slow part of a *danzón*, so to speed things up he added a percussion section and called the song 'Mambo'. In the 1940s, a bandleader named Dámaso Pérez Prado adapted the mambo rhythm to a large scale jazz band arrangement with his song 'Qué rico el mambo'. A craze was born. Pérez Prado took his band to Mexico and became a huge hit; mambo spread through the dance-happy world. In 1951, Enrique Jorrín wrote a song called the 'Chachachá' after the noise feet made while dancing to his new rhythms. The sound swept Cuba.

The world, already Cuba-conscious after the mambo, went crazy for the cha-cha-cha. Cuban musicians toured the Western Hemisphere and Europe; top Latin and United States performers appeared in Havana's nightclubs. One of the products of this interchange was Cu-Bop, a fusion of Afro-Cuban rhythms with bebop. Perhaps the most influential musician to appear during this era was Beny Moré, 'the Barbarian of Rhythm', who, as musician, composer and bandleader, performed all the musical genres and put his unmistakable stamp on each. He died at the age of 44 in 1963.

After the Revolution, Cuba's music industry was severely curtailed; far fewer foreign performers visited, and many top Cuban musicians went into exile. The greatest loss was Celia Cruz, the queen of salsa, and the other members of the Sonora Matancera Orchestra. In 1967, Cuba's musical prominence was revived by the appearance of two young singers at a festival of protest songs. Their names were Pablo Milanés and Silvio Rodríguez, and, backed only by their guitars, they sang songs that celebrated Revolutionary Cuba. Their genre, which is known as the *nueva trova,* was the right music for the time; they became stars not only in Cuba but in Latin America and

Europe. That same year the American folksinger Pete Seeger performed Joseíto Fernández's orchestration of 'Guantanamera' (based on a poem by José Martí). It swept the Americas and, returning to Cuba, became the unofficial anthem.

As Cuban musicians came in greater contact with the outside world through increased travel, and Cuba's radio and TV granted greater access to popular music from the rest of the world, the musical genres flourished. Afro-Cuban jazz sprang up, as did groups playing *son,* salsa, merengue and even rock. Today, Silvio and Pablo are still wildly popular. However, it is the dance bands that have the lock on people's ears. Besides Los Van Van, other groups to look out for are Irakere (Afro-Cuban jazz), N.G. La Banda, Adalberto Alvarez, Issac Delgado and the funny, profane (and occasionally banned) Charanga Habanera. In the last few years, Cuban sounds have burst into the U.S. and international music scene with explosive force. In 1998, a collection of classic popular songs performed by traditional musicians, produced by Ry Cooder and titled *Buena Vista Social Club* won the Grammy Award for Best Latin Record. The annual **Cubadisco** is fast becoming an important event for Latin and especially Cuban music, where music executives gather, and new records and artists are launched before huge crowds.

D A N C E
Ballet is the most notable success of Revolutionary culture. The driving force behind dance in Cuba is its 'prima ballerina', Alicia Alonso, who is still dancing well into her 70s. In 1948, she helped found the Ballet de Cuba, which was renamed the Ballet Nacional de Cuba after 1959. Influenced by Soviet ballet, the Ballet Nacional quickly became recognized for the outstanding talents of its dancers and the originality of its choreographers. The company has toured all over the world, receiving accolades and winning prizes. If you are lucky enough to be visiting while the Ballet Nacional is in Cuba, their home is Havana's Gran Teatro (Prado and Calle San Rafael, tel 613078); most hotel tourist desks should be able to get you tickets.

After the Ballet Nacional, the best-known dance company is the Bal-

(following pages) Dancers in Trinidad, Sancti Spíritus province

let de Camagüey, founded by Alicio Alonso's ex-husband, Fernando Alonso. Its dancers are younger and the choreography is considered more innovative. You will be lucky to see them in Havana or even in Camagüey, because they almost always are on the road. Other top dance groups include the Modern Dance Company and the Conjunto Folklórico Nacional. Every other November, Havana hosts an international ballet festival.

THEATRE

After the Revolution, theatre was defined as a medium of mass consciousness and became one of the most heavily politicized art forms. The Teatro Escambray was founded to transmit Revolutionary ideals to the peasants of the Escambray Mountains; they performed in village squares and forest glades to audiences that may never have seen movies or television, let alone a play. Today the revolutionary content has largely disappeared from Cuban theatres. The more thoughtful groups, such as Teatro Estudio, have replaced it with veiled criticism of current policies and dramatization of the hardships of Special Period life.

CINEMA

In 1959, the Revolution founded the Cuban Institute for the Art and Industry of Cinema (ICAIC) to revive Cuba's almost nonexistent film industry and turn it to Revolutionary goals. Its track record has been spotty—not that many feature films have actually been produced—but as a propaganda tool it has been a smashing success, particularly when Gabriel García Márquez was named the head of the film school. The Revolutionary classic is *Memories of Underdevelopment*, the story of a bourgeois man trying to come to grips with post-Revolutionary changes. Other popular films include *The Other Francisco, Lucia, Se Permuta* ('House for Swap')—a comedy about Cuban real estate) and the feature-length cartoon 'Vampires in Havana'. A new Cuban-Mexican coproduction, *Fresa y Chocolate (Strawberry and Chocolate)*, has become a runaway success and a hit at international film festivals.

It is the story of the unlikely friendship between a dedicated young socialist and a homosexual outcast set at Havana's Coppelia ice cream parlor. The script pulls no punches in its criticism of the current regime, and lines in Havana have been blocks long.

Havana is the home of the Escuela Internacional de Cine (International Film School), which was founded in 1985 by Gabriel García Márquez to train Latin American film-makers. Every December, UICAIC sponsors the Festival de Nuevo Cine Latinoamericano; for two weeks, dozens of films from around the world are shown in Havana theatres and compete for the Coral Negro awards. For more information on the festival, contact UICAIC at tel 33-4634, fax 33-3281.

Despite official support for the film industry, you rarely see Cuban films in the movie theatres. Their usual fare is Hollywood action hits from the previous year, Disney cartoons, kung fu movies, Mexican thrillers and the like. Although the tickets are cheap, less than a peso, the moviegoing experience is not always a joy. The power may go out, the projector may break or its bulb may be so weak that the entire film looks as if it was shot at night. In Havana there are two good repertory theatres: **Cine Chaplin** at UICAIC headquarters, Calles 23 and 10, and **Cine La Rampa**, Calle 23 e/ O y P, both in Vedado. Other good movie houses in Vedado are: **Cine Yara**, on L and 23 across from the Habana Libre; **Cine Riviera**, Calles 23 and G, **Cine 23 y 12**, Calle 23 e/12 and 14 and **Cine Acapulco**, Calle 26 and Ave. Kohly, Nuevo Vedado. Probably the best movie theatre in Cuba today is the one located at the **Fundación de Nuevo Cine Latinoamericano**, Calle 212 esq. a 31, La Coronela.

Carmen Miranda at the Cabaret Tropicana

Havana

■ INTRODUCTION

YOU USED TO ARRIVE AT HAVANA BY SEA. Two imposing stone forts guarded the harbor entrance, while to the west a filigree of lights illuminated Havana's seaside drive, the famous Malecón. If you listened carefully as the boat sailed into harbor, you could hear the clack of dice, the clink of ice in cocktail glasses and the whispered enticements of Virtues Street. Under the Revolution, those sinful ways have largely been eradicated, of course, but otherwise the city is little changed (if somewhat more dilapidated). Today the aura of the past is Havana's greatest attraction.

This sense of history is strongest in Old Havana. Its cobblestone streets and tree-filled plazas are flanked by a gallery of architectural styles, from Moorish early colonial to neo-classical to art nouveau. The grand avenue called the Prado just to the west was Havana's most elegant district in the early 1900s. Here you find graceful old hotels, ornate theatres and the Capitolio—a white marble reflection of the U.S. Capitol building. The streets teem with life, from vendors to schoolchildren playing games to baseball fanatics disputing fine points in the park. From here to the hill at the west is Central Havana, a depressed commercial and residential quarter that is not without its fascinations, where those drums coming from a window could be part of a Santería ritual.

Modern Havana begins at Vedado. Atop a hill at its eastern border, the classical columns of the university buildings are shaded by a grove of enormous, ancient trees. From here you descend to Havana's main artery, Calle 23, better known as La Rampa. Many of the towering hotels, from the elegant Nacional to the modern Habana Libre, are relics from when Havana teemed with U.S. tourists and U.S. gangsters. The space-age Coppelia ice cream parlor at Calles 23 and L is a temple to the island's frozen-dessert cult and a center of Havana social life. The tree-shaded side streets are lined with art deco apartment buildings and old mansions in every stage of decay.

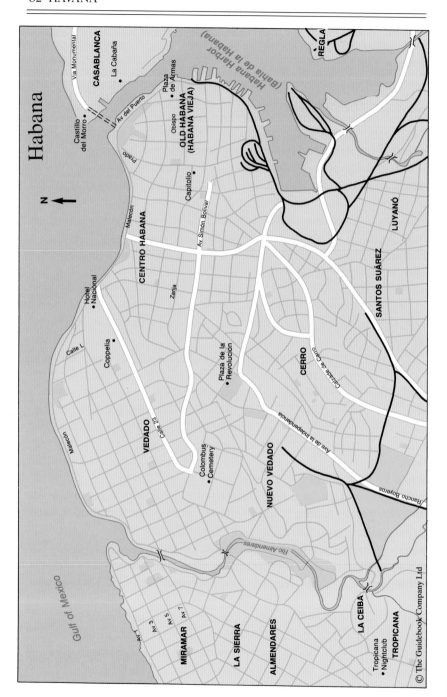

Habana

N

Gulf of Mexico

Via Monumental
CASABLANCA
La Cabaña
Castillo del Morro
Av del Puerto
Plaza de Armas
Habana Harbor
(Bahía de la Habana)
REGLA
Obispo
OLD HABANA
(HABANA VIEJA)
Prado
Malecón
CENTRO HABANA
Capitolio
Av Simón Bolívar
Zanja
LUYANÓ
Hotel Nacional
Calle L
Coppelia
Plaza de la Revolución
CERRO
SANTOS SUÁREZ
Calzada de Cerro
VEDADO
Malecón
Calle 23
Colombus Cemetery
NUEVO VEDADO
Ave de la Independencia
Río Almendares
Rancho Boyeros
MIRAMAR
Av 1
Av 3
Av 5
Av 7
LA SIERRA
ALMENDARES
LA CEIBA
Tropicana Nightclub
TROPICANA

© The Guidebook Company Ltd

West of Vedado spreads Miramar, Havana's ritziest suburb at the Triumph of the Revolution. Its palatial residences have been converted into embassies, government offices and exclusive shops for those with dollars. The beach is lined with resort hotels offering every facility and at the same time easy access to Havana's attractions.

Farther afield, Havana's outskirts are well worth exploring. To the east run the beaches of Playas del Este, where you find many sports facilities and numerous moderate-priced resorts. Just inland lies the traditional town of Guanabacoa, home to the most important museum of Santería. Nearby is Finca La Vigia, Ernest Hemingway's country house, one of the many landmarks from the writer's life found around Havana. To the south extends Lenin Park, a rolling tree-filled expanse where you can find easy escape from the heat and clamor of the downtown streets.

■ HISTORY

The exact place and date of Havana's founding are unclear. A settlement called San Cristóbal de Habana—named after a local Indian chief—was founded by the conquistador Pánfilo de Narváez on Cuba's southwest coast sometime around 1514. The community was moved three times due to mosquito infestation and generally unhealthy conditions. Finally, in 1519 it arrived at the west side of what is now Havana Bay. On December 17 of that year, the first mass was celebrated under a ceiba tree which, according to legend, is an ancestor of the one standing at the east end of the Plaza de Armas. Around it rose the center of the original city—the plaza—and the first government buildings. The port quickly became the embarkation point for Spanish expeditions to the New World mainland, and the settlement thrived. Havana's wealth also attracted enemy fleets and pirates. The first of many invaders were French pirates who, with the help of disgruntled local slaves, in 1538 burned and sacked the city. In response, the Spanish built the first of a number of forts, the Castillo de la Fuerza (just east of the plaza), to protect the city. This, like all subsequent fortifications, was a failure; another group of French pirates plundered the city in 1555.

Despite these occasional depredations, Havana flourished. In 1553, the Spanish governor made the Castillo de la Fuerza his home, and its population had become the largest in Cuba. Once a year, huge Spanish fleets made round trip voyages between Spain and the New World, and Havana was their port of rendezvous. The fleet was the city's main industry, and all types of businesses sprang up to service its needs. The ships were repaired and outfitted by carpenters, sail-makers, provisioners and mechanics; prostitutes, gamblers and other entertainers lightened the heavy purses of the sailors. The citizenry, called 'habaneros', were not just Spaniards but African slaves, a few remaining Indians and riffraff from Europe's seafaring countries. The city had already assumed what the historian Hugh Thomas calls its 'semi-criminal, maritime and cosmopolitan character'.

Continued attacks by pirates, mainly French and English, led to renewed military construction. In 1597, the Castillo del Morro was completed above the eastern entrance to the harbor and opposite rose the Batería de San Salvador de la Punta. Neither was sufficient, because the English raided the city in 1622, 1623 and 1638. Colonial authorities decided to make Havana itself a fort and in 1633 began constructing city walls that eventually ringed what is now Old Havana.

In 1607, Havana was officially named the island's capital, and for the next century and a half it was by far the most important city in Cuba. As the seat of the government, all laws and taxes emanated from here, and all the money squeezed from the hapless citizens was collected in Havana coffers. Corruption was rife in the colonial ad-ministration, and the city's plazas soon glittered with new mansions boasting red tile roofs, courtyards and *mudéjar* ceilings like those in Sevilla. The Spanish elite travelled in fine carriages and dressed in the latest fashions from Madrid. Many of the local rich drew their fortunes from vast estates in the countryside which they rarely vis-ited. The *habaneros'* ostentation, arrogance and lock on political power bred resentment in the provinces (this centuries-long rivalry continued until the 1959 Revolution and encouraged a number of rebellions and wars for independence). Havana's largest buildings were monasteries and nunneries; these sheltered rich young ladies from the uncouth world and educated the Spanish population (blacks, mulattoes and Jews were forbidden the privilege). Beyond the plazas, the streets were unpaved, unlit, fetid and dangerous at night. Diseases were common and periodic outbreaks of yellow fever —transmitted by mosquitoes—decimated the population.

Through the early 18th century, Havana was primarily a mercantile metropolis. Even though it was the third-largest city in the New World (after Mexico City and Lima), culture came slowly. The university was founded by the Dominicans in 1728, and the same decade saw the founding of the first printing presses. Still, Havana and the rest of the nation languished under the repressive colonial rule; aside from a few minor rebellions, the first half of the 18th century was somnolent. The year 1762 dramatically changed all that.

In January, England declared war on Spain, and two months later an invasion force departed for Havana. They had studied detailed plans of the city's three forts and decided that the best way to defeat them was to avoid them. On June 6, English troops landed at Cojímar, 15 miles east of Havana, while the fleet distracted the Spanish by hovering off the city. Despite widespread malaria and dysentery among the troops, the English captured Morro Castle on July 30, and from that moment on Havana was undefendable. Their ammunition almost gone, the Spanish surrendered on August 11. England's six-month rule instantly nullified all the restrictive Spanish regulations and taxes. Hordes of foreign merchants descended on the city, and the economy leaped forward. Havana's merchants and planters were the opening's greatest beneficiaries. The island's brief separation from Spain also encouraged Cubans to think of themselves as a separate people. As part of this new self-consciousness, Havana's intellectual elite began to publish the first newspaper, *El Papel Periodico*, and print the first books on the island's history, flora and fauna.

In the first half of the 19th century, Havana's rich enjoyed the profits of the country's sugar boom. As in many other Spanish colonial cities, the mansions of the rich were built amid the bustle of the

central city and could easily have as neighbors a market on one side and a slum tenement on the other. The ground floors were often used for storing goods, while the family lived in the upper stories.

Outside, the streets were, according to Anthony Trollope, 'narrow, dirty and foul'. Street life was almost oriental in its richness, thought visitors. Aside from the vendors of meat, fish, fruit and sugarcane juice—each with their distinctive cry—Havana's streets teemed with Spanish soldiers, lottery-ticket sellers, prostitutes and all manner of beggars, bandits and hustlers living by their wits. At night, murders were common. Then, as now, Calle Obispo was the center of Old Havana. The city, which had 160,000 inhabitants by 1860, grew at such a rate that it quickly burst the old city walls (these were mostly razed in 1863).

In the 1830s, Cuba's first railway line was built and ended at a terminal just outside the city's southern gate. In order to provide a proper promenade for the city's elite, the captain-general (the governor) ordered the construction of the Paseo del Prado from the San Salvador de la Punta fort to the Parque Central. Farther to the west, the wooded hills known as Vedado were being divided into residential districts. The city glittered like no other in the Caribbean, and the *habaneros* were not going to let a mere civil war undermine their comforts.

During the Ten Years' War, the seat of the colonial government was naturally the center of pro-Spanish feeling. Middle- and upper-class Spanish immigrants banded together to attack rebel sympathizers among the *habaneros* and forced the captain-general to imprison all those against Spain. In 1871, eight Havana medical students were cruelly executed after being accused—wrongly, many believe—of desecrating the grave of a Spanish supporter. The country lay in ruins, but the life of Havana's wealthy was as luxurious as ever. Their time would come in the 1880s, when the bottom dropped out of the sugar market, forcing many planters to sell their estates to North Americans. These changes took a while to affect Havana, where the elite now gathered in cafes surrounding the Teatro Nacional's square for coffee, ice cream and champagne. For foreign visitors, the height of elegance was the neighboring Hotel Inglaterra, the first to offer single rooms

Castillo del Morro

and private baths. Despite this gloss, money was slowly seeping from Havana and following the sugar profits to New York. Meanwhile, red light districts flourished, with over 200 brothels in the city in 1885. By the onset of the 1895-98 war, Havana had become distinctly seedy.

When the Americans arrived in 1898, they found a city that was run-down but far better off than the devastated provinces. Perhaps the greatest success of the American military government was the elimination of yellow fever, a plague that had periodically attacked *habaneros*. Building on the work of Dr. Carlos J. Finlay, a Cuban, an American doctor named Walter Reed confirmed that the disease was carried by mosquitoes; the destruction of their habitats ended the disease.

In the first two decades of the century, American money poured into Cuba, and the country's new overlords built their mansions in Vedado. For the nouveaux riches, the rage was art nouveau, and ornate mansions and hotels sprang up all over the city. The zone between Old Havana and the rich western suburbs, now known as Central Havana, began to fill with cheap apartment buildings, brothels and commercial districts. As wealthy families moved out, Old Havana's colonial palaces were converted to more prosaic uses as factories, schools and hotels. Calle Obispo, the old city's main street, was lined with imposing neo-classical edifices built by foreign banks. For tourists, the area between the Paseo de Martí and the Parque Central was the most important; here were the jewels of the hotel industry, the Biltmore-Sevilla, Plaza and Inglaterra. To play, foreigners travelled out to the new western suburb of Miramar, where the first country clubs were being built. The major public-works project of this era was the Malecón, the seaside drive that began under the guidance of American engineers around 1901.

Money and power gradually moved westward over the next decades. In 1920, the seat of the presidency moved from Old Havana's Palace of the Captains-General to the new Presidential Palace to the northwest. Nine years later the legislature moved into the imposing Capitolio, a copy of the U.S. Congress building. In the struggle against the string of dictators that ruled Cuba from the 1920s to 1959, Havana's streets became the stage for a frequently violent political theatre. In

1933, dissident army officers ensconced in the Hotel Nacional were attacked by soldiers loyal to then-Sergeant Batista. Over 80 were killed and 200 wounded in the battle, and the hotel was severely damaged. Between bombings and shootings, Havana became steadily richer and more Americanized, especially when compared to the provinces. Even the student gangsters of the 1940s wore zoot suits and cruised the streets in big Buicks. (One of them was a future politician named Fidel Castro.)

Havana's wealth peaked in the 1950s. Skyscrapers like the Hilton (now the Habana Libre) and the FOCSA building sprang up in Vedado. The zone south of the university around the Plaza Cívica became the new seat of the Batista government, with modernist towers for each ministry. The country was enthralled by the new; everything that was old, including Old Havana, was allowed to collapse. American tourists and the Cuban rich ignored incidents like the 1956 bombing at the Tropicana nightclub—just intramural squabbles. The following year a left-wing group called the Directorio Revolucionario attacked the Presidential Palace. Unfortunately, Batista had been forewarned, and 35 rebels died in the assault and many more were executed afterward. By 1958, bombings were a daily occurrence, blood flowed in the streets and tourism dropped off. When Fidel's army arrived in early 1959, they were greeted by rapturous throngs numbering in the hundreds of thousands.

One of the Revolution's first orders of business was to clean up the seedy, semicriminal aspects of the capital. Prostitutes and beggars were taken off the streets, and brothels, casinos and nightclubs were closed down. The once glittering nightlife ground to a halt. Following the Soviet model, the government ordered the construction of dozens of utilitarian five- and six-storey apartment buildings on the city outskirts. These were given to 'militants' of the Revolution—those whose labour had furthered Revolutionary goals. The Revolutionary government abandoned the Presidential Palace and the Capitolio—these became museums and libraries—and occupied Batista's new ministries around the Plaza de la Revolucion. The centre of the action remained Calle 23, which cut through the heart of Vedado. Very few new buildings rose in Old and Central Havana, and many of the old continued to deteriorate.

In 1982, Old Havana was named a Patrimony of Humanity by UNESCO, which gave millions of dollars for the restoration of this zone's colonial core. Over the last two decades, most of the new construction has been to the west and east of Havana proper. In the western suburbs rose the convention centre and the Expo-Cuba exhibition grounds, and Playas del Este to the east became the site of the Panamerican Games stadiums in the early 1990s. Since the advent of the Special Period, both old and new Havana have fallen into disrepair due to the lack of fuel and building materials. Tragically, many fine old buildings will have to be torn down, if they have not collapsed already. The only ray of hope is Old Havana, where Eusebio Leal, the city's official historian, is presiding over the renovation of the district, beginning at the Plaza de Armas and working outward. For the rest of the city, however, the job will take years or even decades.

■ GETTING AROUND

For some areas, like the labyrinth that is Old Havana, it is easiest to walk. If you do not have a rental car, the easiest option is to take a taxi. The main taxi services are Turistaxi (tel 335539), Taxis OK (tel 249518), Transgaviota (tel 331730) and, the cheapest, Panataxi (tel 555555). There are taxi stands at every major hotel, and they also operate by radio call. All taxi services offer special hourly and long-distance rates. You also see peso taxis on Havana's streets; these run fixed routes, only accept pesos and generally do not allow tourists.

Havana's buses, called *guaguas*, used to be the easiest and cheapest way to travel. Unfortunately, they run rarely—the wait is often an hour or more—and the fight to get on resembles a rugby match involving both sexes and all ages. The fare is only 10 to 40 centavos, but for tourists any saving is erased by the time and pain involved. Many Cubans now travel by bicycle; if you want to share their experience, be warned that bicycle accidents are one of the leading causes of death in Cuba.

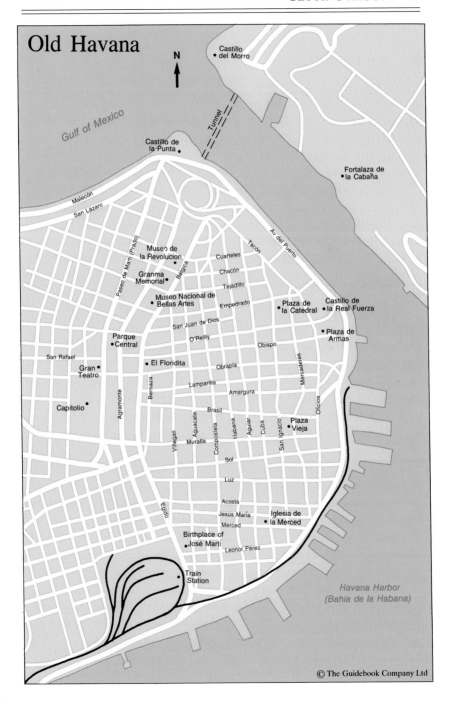

Old Havana

N

Castillo del Morro

Gulf of Mexico

Tunnel

Castillo de la Punta

Fortalaza de la Cabaña

Malecón
San Lázaro

Paseo de Martí (Prado)

Av del Puerto
Tacón

Museo de la Revolución

Cuarteles

Bélgica

Chacón

Granma Memorial

Tejadillo

Museo Nacional de Bellas Artes

Empedrado

Plaza de la Catedral

Castillo de la Real Fuerza

San Juan de Dios

O'Reilly

Plaza de Armas

Parque Central

Obispo

San Rafael

Mercaderes

Gran Teatro

El Floridita

Obrapía

Bernaza

Lamparilla

Agramonte

Amargura

Oficios

Capitolio

Brasil

Aguacate

Habana

Aguiar

Cuba

San Ignacio

Plaza Vieja

Villegas

Compostela

Muralla

Sol

Egido

Luz

Acosta

Jesús María

Iglesia de la Merced

Merced

Birthplace of José Martí

Leonor Pérez

Train Station

Havana Harbor
(Bahía de la Habana)

© The Guidebook Company Ltd

■ OLD HAVANA

PLAZA DE ARMAS

Our tour starts where it all began: at the west side of Havana Bay. At the eastern end of the Malecón, the road turns south along the harbor and becomes Av Carlos M. de Céspedes, better known as Av del Puerto. On the right is a series of grass-covered squares containing monuments and fountains that ends at a four-sided fort called the **Castillo de la Real Fuerza** (1558-77). This site was originally Havana's first plaza, and the present structure is an amplification of the city's first fort, the Castillo de la Fuerza. Although its designers used the most advanced designs of the time, the fort was quickly criticized because it was easily dominated by the hills across the harbor. The critics were proved correct when French pirates successfully raided Havana.

Until 1762, its main use was as the seat of Cuba's colonial governors. The fort now houses rotating exhibitions of modern ceramics that clash with the severe stone setting. However, a tour of the building is worth it; you enter via a drawbridge over a moat and pass through the six-metres-thick (9.5 feet) walls. There is a good view of the port from the battlements. From the center of the fort rises a 17th-century tower topped with a bronze weathervane in the form of an Indian woman. Called La Giraldilla, she is now the symbol of Havana (she is also a replica; the original is in the Museo de la Ciudad de La Habana). A nearby dock is the embarkation point for ferries across the harbor to the town of Casablanca.

We now walk a few steps inland from the fort entrance to the **Plaza de Armas.** In the 16th century, it was originally called the Plaza de la Iglesia because on it stood Havana's main church (demolished in the 18th century); the plaza soon became a parade ground for the Real Fuerza's troops and took on its present name. For its first two centuries, the Plaza de Armas was a rustic, weed-filled square with little charm. After 1750, the government began building a series of elegant administration buildings around the plaza and filling the interior with trees, benches and fountains. For most of the 19th cen-

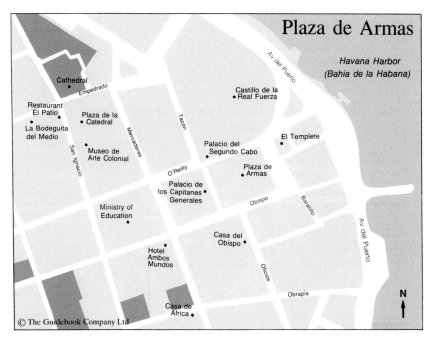

tury, the plaza was Havana's most elegant meeting point, the pride of the city. As money and wealth moved out of Old Havana early in this century, the plaza and its buildings became dilapidated and semi-abandoned. Restoration began in 1935, and today the Plaza de Armas is one of the most beautiful squares in Cuba. In the center is a statue of the rebel leader Carlos Manuel de Céspedes; this monument replaces one of King Ferdinand VII of Spain that, insulting patriotic sensibilities, stood here until 1955.

A ceiba tree at the northeast corner of the plaza is traditionally the site of Havana's founding. In 1754, a memorial column was erected here, and in 1828 it was replaced by a small, Greco-Roman structure known as **El Templete**. You enter El Templete's small courtyard through a gate and inside you find a ceiba that is supposedly fourth in a direct line of descent from the original (the others were blown down by hurricanes). On December 17, the anniversary of Havana's founding, thousands of *habaneros* line up for the custom of making a wish and walking three times around the tree while touching the trunk—the wish will come true. Six columns hold up the facade of El Templete. Inside are three large paintings by Jean-Baptiste Vernay (1784-1833) that illustrate, from the left, Havana's first council meeting, the inauguration of El Templete and the first mass in Havana. El Templete shares the east side of the park with the **Palacio del Conde Santovenia**, an early 19th-century mansion that later became a hotel. It was recently renovated and now is the luxury Santa Isabel Hotel.

Returning to the north side of the plaza, after the fort you come to the dark limestone **Palacio del Segundo Cabo.** Completed in 1772, this sober, baroque building was originally the post office and then housed a number of governmental offices before becoming the seat of the Senate in the first two decades after Independence. It is now the Cuban Institute of Books and houses the Bella Habana bookstore (good selection, dollars only) on the ground floor. The two-storey courtyard is worth a look.

Continuing west, the west side of the plaza is occupied by the **Palacio de los Capitanes Generales** (1776-91). It was home to the

Monument to Céspedes, Plaza de Armas

captain-general, Cuba's colonial governor, and rumor has it that the wooden paving on the street in front was to muffle carriage wheels so as not to interrupt his sleep. From Independence until 1920, this fine baroque limestone edifice acted as the Presidential Palace and then served as Municipal Palace until the Revolution. Today it houses the office of the city historian, important historical archives and the **Museum of the City of Havana**. In the charming courtyard are relics from excavations in the building's basements, including a mysterious metal casket with a sword decorating the lid. A monument to the right commemorates a leading Havana debutante who in 1557 died at this spot as the result of a tragic arquebus accident. In one corner stands a huge pot, called a *tinajón,* which held rainwater, and you may also peek into tunnels in which ran water for the city's baths. A room to one side contains an excellent collection of 18th-century religious art, including silver and many sculptures. A stairway leads up to the apartments, a series of luxurious rooms that hold a number of the most important relics of Cuban history. The first room houses uniforms of colonial and rebel officers and many 19th-century weapons,

Throne room (never used), palacio de los Capitanes Generales

including an ingenious rebel cannon made from leather. Next you enter a long, very well air-conditioned hall whose walls hold portraits of all the most important fighters for independence. Here is the first Cuban flag (1850)—much like today's—whose design symbolizes: 'red of blood, blue of sea, white of sky and star of triumph'. Many other rebel flags are also displayed, as well as the personal articles of Cuban fighters for independence, including Maximo Gómez's death mask and Antonio Maceo's boat. A candle always burns in the memory of the heroes. Another room is devoted to the struggle against imperialism, i.e., the United States and the dictator Batista. Here lies 'The Eagle of Imperialism'; that is, the broken wings of the U.S.S. *Maine* monument that was partially destroyed in the early post-Revolutionary euphoria. Other chambers include a huge dining room filled with ornate ceramics given to the captains-general, a throne room for the king of Spain (he never used it), a ballroom called the Hall of Mirrors, a music room and a chapel.

The south side of the Plaza de Armas is lined with a number of very old businesses. Starting at the corner of Oficios and heading west, these are the Cafe Habanero, the La Mina restaurant and the Casa del Agua 'La Tinaja', where *habaneros* used to buy their drinking water during the early colonial era. They are now moving the **Museum of Natural History** into a building here.

Calle Obispo, the pedestrian-only street which begins along the south side of the square, is Old Havana's main thoroughfare. **Calle Oficios,** which heads south from the middle of the plaza, is worth a quick stroll. A half block south on the right is the 17th-century **Casa del Obispo** (Oficios 8), the original residence of Havana's bishop and now the **Museum of Numismatics.** The next building south, the **Colegio San Ambrosio** (18th century), originally a religious school, houses the **Casa del Arabe**, a museum of Arab art and culture with a second-floor restaurant. It also contains a prayer room which is the only space dedicated to Islamic worship in Cuba. Across the street is the **Auto Museum,** which exhibits a diverse collection of cars, from a 1902 Cadillac to a white Rolls-Royce.

Arco de Belén

Returning to the plaza, we now head west on Calle Obispo. Until the city burst its walls in the late 19th century, Obispo was the center of Havana's business and social life and the site of the most elegant shops and hotels. One of the latter, the newly renovated **Hotel Ambos Mundos**, stands one block west at the corner of Obispo and Mercaderes. Originally the mansion of an 18th-century marquis, the building was expanded in the 19th century and converted into a hotel. Its most famous resident was Ernest Hemingway, who during the 1930s had a number of long stays in Room 511, where he was trying to escape from his wife. It was here in 1939 that he began writing *For Whom the Bell Tolls*, his novel of the Spanish Civil War. Supposedly unchanged since his departure for the Finca Vigía (see 'South of Havana' section), the room is now a Hemingway shrine, preserving his typewriter, a model of his boat, an empty bottle of Chivas Regal and a few other artifacts.

One block south on Mercaderes, there are a number of sights worth a quick detour. A few steps down on the left is the **Torre de Marfil**, a Chinese restaurant that is better known for its decor than its food. Opposite, a stairway climbs up to the **Casa de Puerto Rico**, which houses a small but interesting exhibition of Cuban cigar paraphernalia, like wrappers and humidors. At the northeast corner of Mercaderes and Obrapía stands the **Casa de la Obra Pía**, an early-17th century mansion—then the finest residence in the city—that was renovated in 1780. Inside the fine baroque entry is a museum with a diverse collection. Two rooms are dedicated to Alejo Carpentier, the great 20th-century Cuban writer, and include the Volkswagen Bug in which he negotiated Paris (his home for most of this life). The other exhibits are devoted to the Spanish king Charles III.

Across Obrapía is the **Casa de Africa**, the most important museum and gallery dedicated to Africa and Cuba's African heritage. In addition to possessing a huge collection of artifacts from 26 African nations and many objects used in Afro-Cuban ritual, the museum also houses a study center and library and stages dance and music performances on the most important Santería festival days. This is a must for those interested in Afro-Cuban culture. Diagonally across Mercaderes stands the **Casa de Benito Juárez**, a museum of Mexican art and culture largely donated by the Mexican government.

PLAZA DE LA CATEDRAL

Returning to Obispo, you continue west one block, past the drab **Ministry of Education building**, turn right on Calle San Ignacio and walk two blocks to the Plaza de la Catedral. The crafts vendors and artists who once crowded this square will be moved to the Plaza Vieja once that square's renovation is completed. The north end of the block opens onto the **Plaza de la Catedral**. Originally a swamp (its first name was Plaza of the Swamp), it was later drained and became the terminus for the Chorro aqueduct, the first Spanish aqueduct in the New World. The plaza remained something of a slum until the 18th century, when the cathedral and a number of baroque mansions were built around its circumference. Today this cobblestoned square preserves a charming colonial ambiance and some of the finest architecture in Cuba.

The *Cathedral of Havana* (1748-77) dominates the north end of the plaza. The Jesuits began construction of this edifice, but they were expelled in 1767, and the final stages were completed under orders of the king of Spain. In 1789, Havana's main church was transferred here from the Plaza de Armas, and a decade later it was named a cathedral (Cuba's first cathedral is in Santiago). The elegant facade, constructed in the style of the Italian baroque, was once far more ornate, but weather and political turmoil have washed away much of the detailing. The larger tower on the right is the bell tower, now silent. The plain stone interior has also been stripped of much of its finery but still possesses a stern grandeur. The inside was renovated for the visit of Pope John Paul II, who in early 1998 celebrated mass here. Two rows of four stone columns separate the nave from the aisles. A huge chandelier hangs from the dome, and wood and gold retables line the aisles. The altar is capped with an elaborate marble and onyx dome that shields a statue of the Virgin Mary. The cathedral is open to visitors Monday through Friday 9-11 am and 2:30-6 pm and Sunday mornings 9-11 am; masses are held Saturdays at 6:30 pm, Sundays at 10:30 am and Tuesdays and Thursdays at 8:00 pm.

Returning to the plaza, the first building on the colonnaded east side is the **Casa de Lombillo** (1737) now housing the Education Museum. Next you come to the **Palacio del Marques de Arcos** (1741), an aristocratic residence that later became the post office and then an art school. Today it houses the **Nelson Domínguez Experimental Graphic Arts Gallery**, its walls covered with canvases of this famous Cuban artist. The south side of the square is occupied by one of the oldest mansions in the city, the **Casa de Luis Chacón**, which was begun in the 17th century. The interior patio is particularly attractive. The building is now home to the **Museo de Arte Colonial**, containing a large collection of Cuban-made decorative arts from the earliest days until 1900. Rooms are devoted to architectural elements, carriages, glassware (including stained glass) and lots and lots of furniture. The little alley just to the west of the museum is the **Callejón del Chorro**, the site of the first aqueduct, now marked by a plaque and a small fountain. At the end is the **Taller Experimental de la Gráfica**, where you can watch artists at work and purchase original prints directly from them or at the gallery on the second floor.

The first building on the west side of the plaza is the **Casa de Baños** (House of Baths), a 19th-century mansion that takes its name from the water tank that earlier stood here. The building contains the **Galería Victor Manuel**, an art gallery. Next you come to **Casa del Marqués de Aguas Claras** (1751-77), another mansion that is home to the **El Patio Restaurant**, a good stop to rest for a drink or a meal under the colonnade or in the patio. On the corner of Acosta and Oficios is the **Centro Wifredo Lam**, named for the noted Cuban artist, which displays works by Lam and Third World artists, and sponsors the **Bienal de La Habana** art exposition.

Another dining option is the famous **Bodeguita del Medio Restaurant** (founded 1942), a half block west of the cathedral at #207 Calle Empedrado. This narrow, three-storey restaurant is renowned for its ground-floor bar—a favorite haunt of Hemingway and many other writers, musicians and politicians—and for the Cuban food served above. The Bodeguita also saw the invention of the *mojito*, Cuba's national cocktail, a delicious mixture of rum, soda water, sugar and mint. The restaurant's walls are covered from floor to ceiling with graffiti, while the autographs of the more famous, like Salvador Allende, are preserved in frames. Perhaps the most well known is Ernest Hemingway's advertisement: 'My Mojito in La Bodeguita, My Daiquiri in El Floridita' with his signature below. Unfortunately, this motto was apparently concocted in order to increase the traffic at both restaurants.

A half block west of the Bodeguita, you come to Calle Cuba; three blocks to the right (north) stands the **Palacio Pedroso**, now the **Palacio de Artesania**. When this formidable mansion was built, it verged on the waterfront, which is now on the other side of the park. Its lovely interior patio has been converted into a colonial mall where vendors make and sell crafts—dolls, hats, leather goods, clothing, weavings, etc.—and you can also have coffee and buy rum and cigars. In the plaza in front of this building stands a piece of the old city

Plaza de la Catedral

wall. To the left, the park contains an **amphitheatre** where occasional concerts and political events are staged. The palace faces on Calle Tacón which marked the original border of the waterfront.

CALLE OBISPO AND CALLE CUBA

Beyond the region of the Plaza de Armas and the Plaza de la Catedral, Old Havana's more obscure sights are more widely scattered. An excursion in search of them is definitely worthwhile, because Old Havana's streets have a picturesque, almost medieval quality. Skinny dogs slink down the narrow streets, people call up to friends' windows, music blares out a doorway, water drips from a balcony, planks prop up a deteriorating facade, an underground network of food and alcohol vendors ply their illegal trades, the people hustle to survive. Many of Old Havana's buildings were once one-family mansions; over the last century, they have been converted into decrepit apartment houses for dozens of families. Their roofs are a maze of jury-rigged pipes and water tanks. Inside, colonial-style rooms with 5.5- metre (18-foot) ceilings have been converted into *barbacoas,* two rooms with 2.5-metre (8 foot) ceilings; the name come from the Cuban Indian style house on stilts. The extra weight has threatened many buildings with collapse.

One obligatory excursion is to walk **Calle Obispo** from the Plaza de Armas nine blocks west to its terminus at the Plazuela de Albear near the El Floridita restaurant. Despite hard times, Obispo is the most vital street in Old Havana, nearly always filled with people during the day (watch out for pickpockets) and lined with crafts stores, bookstores, galleries and peso-only fast-food restaurants. Three blocks west of the Plaza de Armas at the corner of Calle Cuba, you come to the old **National Bank of Cuba** building (early 1900s), now the State Committee of Finances offices. The basement of this massive neo-classical edifice houses the **Museum of Finance**, which is dedicated to a Revolutionary history of finance from the colonial days through Che Guevara, the bank's president in the early days of the Revolution. The highpoint of the exhibit is a peek into the massive vault that once held most of Cuba's gold bullion.

Five blocks farther west on Obispo, you come to Calle Villegas, where you can turn left (south) and walk two blocks to the small **Plaza del Cristo**. This area was developed in 1640 and quickly attracted homes of the elite, including the bishop, whose house stands at the west end of the square at the corner of Calles Bernaza and Brasil. In the 19th century, the plaza was home to the Mercado del Cristo; today, the main reason to visit is the small but charming **Iglesia Santo Cristo del Buen Viaje** (1755). Twin towers flank the symmetrical baroque facade, which is topped with a unique woven iron cross. The nave is covered with a decaying but still beautiful *mudéjar* ceiling held up by plain stone columns. The church takes its name ('Holy Christ of the Good Voyage') from the crucifix that is supposed to protect travellers and sailors.

Returning to the intersection of Calles Obispo and Cuba, you will find that **Calle Cuba** is the most fruitful route for a trip through the labyrinth that is southern Old Havana. Three blocks south of Obispo you come to the **Iglesia de San Francisco**, originally the **Iglesia de San Agustín** (1608), at the corner of Calles Cuba and Amargura. The baroque facade is the only remnant of the original decor; the interior was redone in the neo-classical style after the church was taken over by the Franciscans in 1842. The old convent just to the south was renovated in ornate, 19th-century style and converted into the **Antiguo Academia de Ciencias**. The original home of Cuba's Academy of Sciences, this building now houses the **Carlos J. Finlay Historical Museum of Sciences**, with exhibits on Cuban science and medicine, a library and an archive. A large exhibition is dedicated to the life and personal effects of Carlos J. Finlay, the scientist who discovered that yellow fever is transmitted by mosquitoes.

A half block to the south you arrive at Calle Brasil; from here it is worth taking a quick excursion one block to the right (east) to the **Plaza Vieja**. This plaza was built in the late 16th century but remained more or less a swamp until it was finally drained in the late 17th century. Havana's wealthy began constructing their palaces here—seven colonnaded 18th-century mansions remain—and the plaza became the center of city life. In 1835, the Cristina Market was opened in the plaza, reconfirming the area's eminence. The plaza and the surrounding buildings are now being renovated; many of the long-time residents will be moved out and replaced by offices and stores and museums for the tourist trade. Once work is completed, the plaza will become the home to Old Havana's market for crafts and artworks. Lovers of art nouveau will admire the Hotel Palacio (1907) at the plaza's southeast corner, once one of the city's finest and now rapidly deteriorating. The **Casa del los Condes Jaruco** (1733-37) at the southwest corner is now the **Fondo Cubano de Bienes Culturales**, a cultural space that stages concerts and art shows and sells handicrafts. A quick walk one block to the east takes you to the Plaza de San Francisco, now lined with new stores (Benetton) and expensive tourist cafes. Returning to the Plaza Vieja, Calle Muralla heading west will return you to Calle Cuba.

Continuing south one block, you come to the **Antiguo Convento de Santa Clara** (1638-44) a massive building between Calles Sol and Luz. This was the first convent in Cuba, built to protect the flowers of the aristocracy from marauding sailors. The nuns sold the convent in 1919 and moved to the suburbs; unfortunately for visitors, they took most of the religious decorations with them, so all you see are the bare walls. By 1981, the convent was in ruins; that year it became home to the National Center of Conservation, Restoration and Museology, which directs all efforts to restore Cuba's crumbling patrimony. You can tour their studios and labs and see

Altar, Havana Cathedral

the progress of the restoration of their own buildings. The interior
garden is filled with a variety of Cuban medicinal plants and trees.

Walking one block south, you arrive at the **Iglesia del Espíritu
Santo** (1640) at the corner of Cuba and Acosta. The oldest church in
Havana, it was originally built by free blacks and then expanded
about 30 years later. The interior is simple, with a long nave and one
side aisle lined with dark wood and gold retables. To the left there is
a statue of Santa Barbara, the Catholic saint associated in Santería
with the Change, the god of lightning and thunder; both saint and
god celebrate December 4 as their feast day. Continuing south, in
two blocks you come to the **Iglesia de la Merced** at the corner of the
street of the same name. This church was begun in 1755 and only
completed in 1904; much of the money was donated by Afro-Cuban
religious groups. The interior is ornate, with blue and gold *trompe
l'oeil* frescoes, murals on the ceilings and neo-classical retables. On
the left a chapel lined with fake stalactites is dedicated to Nuestra
Señora de Lourdes. The domed main altar holds a statue of the

Virgen de la Merced; stairs circle behind so you can see the statue up close. In Santería this Virgin is a representation of the god Obatalá, who is symbolized by white cloth. Obatalá devotees dressed all in white can often be seen at their prayers here. The Virgin's feast day, September 24, is shared by Obatalá, and that day thousands cram into the church to celebrate. Smaller celebrations are held on the 24th day of the other months. Parishioners state that this church is much more popular than the cathedral.

From here you can walk to the next corner, Calle Leonor Pérez, and head left (west) six blocks to the **Casa Natal de José Martí**, the 19th-century house in which Cuba's national hero was born on January 28, 1853. The exhibits include a personal belongings, a collection of his writings and a history of his life.

It is a few steps west to the Av de Bélgica, which marks the border of Old Havana. To the right and left across the avenue, you can see pieces of the original city wall. Directly in front of you stand the twin towers of the semi-Venetian-style **Central Railway Station** (1912). In the waiting room sits an 1843 locomotive that ran the Matanzas route. North of the station, Cubans without tickets wait days in lines under the colonnades for the chance to buy one.

PASEO DEL PRADO

Our tour continues at the west side of the entrance to Havana Bay. In the early days of the colony, this was a favorite landing spot of pirates. Concerned about Havana's poor defenses, the city fathers in 1589 began the construction of two forts, Morro Castle across the harbor and the fort called **San Salvador de la Punta** at this site. Until recently, the latter quadrangular construction housed a restaurant, but now it is permanently closed for restoration.

San Salvador de la Punta marks the north end of the **Paseo del Martí**, better known as the **Prado**, a broad avenue constructed in 1772 with a tree-lined park running down the center. In the 19th century the Prado was the favorite promenade of the aristocracy. About halfway down the Prado's length, the park is a center for **Se Permuta**, or 'For Swap'; here *habaneros* gather in a kind of informal market to trade their houses or apartments for a different neighborhood or more or less space (as opposed to straight cash sales). We will return to the Prado at its south end.

Just east of the Prado begins the grass-covered **Parque Mártires del 71**, a park dedicated to the Havana medical students executed during the First War of Independence; their monument here is constructed from the remnants of the old military quarter wall against which the students were shot. **Av del los Estudiantes**, which heads diagonally away from the Prado, is the bus pick-up point for pedestrians and bicyclists going to Havana's eastern suburbs through the harbor tunnel. Across this street, another small park marks the site of the old **Havana prison**, which was built in the 1830s and held many fighters for independence in its day. The prison was razed in the early 1900s, and only a small fragment of its wall is left as a memorial. The circle of roads entering the harbor tunnel enclose an impressive 1935 equestrian **statue of Máximo Gómez**, the rebel general who was a hero of both wars for independence. Due south of this circle opens the Plaza 13 de Marzo, at the northwest corner of which stands the ornate 1912 art nouveau palace housing the **Spanish Embassy**. Another early 20th-century mansion on the opposite corner is the home to the **National Museum of Music**, with period instruments and exhibits on the history of Cuban music and occasional concerts. A highlight is the African drum collection of the renowned Africanist Fernando Ortíz.

At the south end of the plaza, just beyond another fragment of the old city walls and an old tank, rises the white, wedding-cake-like structure of the old **Presidential Palace** (1913-20). Originally planned as the seat of the provincial government, in 1917 it was designated as the presidential residence, and Tiffany & Co. completed the interior. Until 1959 the palace was the home to all of Cuba's more or less corrupt presidents and dictators, including Gerardo Machado and Fulgencio Batista. A group of rebels attacked the building in March, 1957 with the intent of assassinating Batista; unfortunately, they did not know that Batista's apartment was only reachable by private elevator. In any event, Batista's forces had been forewarned and slaughtered the rebels.

Since the triumph of the Fidelistas, the palace has been converted into the **Museum of the Revolution**, the most complete exposition of the island's revolutionary history. The exhibits begin on the second floor. You start with the colonial era and its evils: destruction of the Indians, feudalism and slavery. Then you quickly move through the 19th-century struggle for liberation, a room devoted to Jose Martí, the Yankee occupation, the Russian Revolution and its influence on Cuba and finally come to the main plot line of Fidel and his group of rebels. Martyrs are prominent; here you see their blood-spattered clothing and pamphlets they were trying to distribute just before their assassination. After Fidel's early years as a student leader, you come to the 1953 Moncada assault (the rebels were natty—admire Raúl's sport jacket), prison, exile in Mexico and the 1956 *Granma* landing. A diorama shows wax dummies of the hirsute rebels as they fight Batista's army in the Sierra Maestra.

Descending to the first floor, where you can see the interior of the domed cupola and the Hall of Mirrors, the story continues with the final battles, the Triumph of the Revolution and **La Limpia** ('The Cleaning')—the eradication of counterrevolutionary traitors. Here you see exhibits devoted to the Bay of Pigs, the Declaration of the Socialist Character of the Revolution and the founding of the mass organizations that regulate the lives of ordinary Cubans.

On the ground floor you come to the **Rincon de los Cretinos** ('Cretin Corner'), where cartoons depict Cuba telling Batista, 'Thank you, cretin, for helping us to MAKE the Revolution', and telling Reagan, 'Thank you, cretin, for helping STRENGTHEN the Revolution'. Exhibits document the accomplishments of the Revolution in agriculture, industry, education, etc., the crimes against Cuba committed by the CIA and the Cuban armed forces' battles in Angola and Ethiopia. A new permanent exhibit completely devoted the **Ernesto Che Guevara** was opened in 1997, the 20th anniversary of his death in Bolivia. In addition to objects related to the guerrilla leader's life and struggles, you can see a short video on the ceremonies marking the return of his remains to Cuba and burial in Santa Clara. If you need refreshment, a small souvenir shop here sells sodas and coffee.

Museo de la Revolución

The Presidential Palace's rear entrance lets you out into a square containing the **Granma Memorial** (admission only through the museum). Inside a crystal-walled pavilion (1976) sits the original *Granma*, the yacht that in late 1956 carried 82 rebels led by Fidel Castro from Mexico to Cuba to start the Revolution. The pavilion is surrounded by vehicles from Revolutionary history, including jeeps, crude armored cars made by the rebels, fragments of an American B-26 shot down in the Bay of Pigs and a U-2 spy plane destroyed by Russian missiles during the Cuban Missile Crisis.

Immediately to the right (east) of the Presidential Palace entrance rises the white Gothic **Iglesia Santo Angel Custodia**. First constructed in the 17th century, it was destroyed by the 1846 hurricane and rebuilt in its current style over the next few decades. As you can guess from the luxurious marble and mahogany interior, this was the favorite church of Havana's aristocracy. José Martí was baptized here, and the building provided the setting for tragic marriage scene in *Cecilia Valdés*, the great 19th-century Cuban novel of manners.

Directly south of the **Granma** pavilion lies the main entrance to the **Museo Nacional de Bellas Artes**, the most important art museum in Cuba. Luckily, the exterior of this rather ugly 1956 trapezoidal concrete building is largely hidden by the surrounding trees. The building is now undergoing a year-long renovation; at this writing, a reopening date had not been set. The ground floor houses temporary exhibitions, a shop selling art books, prints and cigar labels, and a cafeteria. On the first floor, the permanent exhibitions begin with the collection of the counts of Lagunilla. These are antiquities from Egypt, Rome and Greece and include marble sculptures, vases and mosaics. The following rooms contain European medieval and Renaissance paintings by Italian, Dutch and Spanish artists, the most noteworthy being José de Ribera. The combination of fluorescent lighting and paintings badly in need of cleaning makes the art very hard to see. This floor continues with European painting through Impressionism.

The second floor is dedicated to Cuban art, which began with 18th century painters of religious scenes, such as José de Nicolás Escalera and Juan del Río. (There were earlier painters, but their works have disappeared.) Cuba's Academy was inaugurated in 1818, and for the following century artists copied the fashionable styles of Europe. From this era, the most interesting works on exhibit are those by Vicente Escobar, a room full of early landscapes and a collection of tobacco-label art that may represent the peak of 19th century artistic expression.

In 1925 a group of artists broke with the academy and began to copy European avant-garde methods. Mexican and African art began to have a strong influence, and abstraction steadily increased until the 1950s when it became the prevalent mode. Surprisingly, the art of the Revolutionary era is relatively eclectic (compared to the Soviet Union or communist China); a variety of styles is allowed to bloom, from neo-Diego Rivera to neo-Andy Warhol.

If you turn left on exiting the museum, across Calle Agramonte (also called Calle Zulueta) you see the recently renovated **Hotel Sevilla Accor** (early 1900s). During the first half of this century, this was the Sevilla-Biltmore, one of Havana's finest hotels and a meeting place of the international elite. Beautifully renovated, its arabesque lobby includes a shop that sells a selection of foreign newspapers and magazines. Check out the rooftop restaurant for a grand view of Havana. A block south, under the colonnade at the southwest corner of Agramonte and Animas, a mosaic on the pavement advertises the now-defunct **Sloppy Joe's** bar. A favorite haunt of Hemingway, this watering hole also attracted boisterous crowds of American tourists from the 1920s until the Revolution. Given the current importance of tourism, it is a sure thing that Sloppy Joe's will eventually rise from the dead.

Continuing south, across the street you see the colonial-style **Hotel Plaza**, a late 19th-century residence that was converted into a hotel in 1909. A block to the east on Calle Neptuno rises the magnificent art deco-style **Edificio Bacardí** (1930), once offices for the famous rum manufacturers. The facade is decorated with beautiful ceramic tiles and topped with a row of near-naked nymphs. You can also peek inside at the ornate marble art deco lobby. It is now government offices.

Across the street from the Hotel Plaza stands the **Manzana de Gómez**, a 1910 department store occupying the entire block. Once it must have been marvelous; today it is occupied by a few dollar-only stores selling crafts, records and clothing. The tourism bureau on the west side is open 24 hours. The Manzana de Gómez fronts on the **Parque Central**, which in the late 19th century was the center of Havana's social life. A 1905 statue of José Martí graces the center of the park. A nearby bench is an *esquina caliente* ('hot corner') where Havana's baseball fanatics gather to endlessly discuss the fine points of their favorite sport.

Just south of the Manzana de Gómez rises the rather gloomy **Centro Asturiano**, once a club for natives of this Spanish region and now the Supreme Court of Justice. One block east of the park on Calle San Rafael is the famous **El Floridita** restaurant. Another Hemingway hangout, the Floridita claims to be the home of the daiquiri cocktail. For many years after the Revolution, this space was an abandoned shell; it was recently renovated to its old luxury by following old photographs and the memories of the original employees. Today the daiquiris are still delicious, but the overpriced food could definitely be improved. Above the restaurant is the **Casa del Ron**, a store where you can sample and buy most brands of rum made in Cuba (only some from Oriente are missing). The neighboring **La Zaragozna** restaurant also specializes in seafood but at more reasonable prices. Behind El Floridita, on the corner of Obispo and Bernaza, there is an inexpensive but good Italian restaurant, Gentiluomo.

Returning to the Parque Central, the west side of the square is occupied by the **Hotel Inglaterra**, Havana's first luxury hotel. This originally was the Cafe Louvre, 'the most popular resort of the elité of Havana', which was expanded into a hotel with 'every modern improvement' in the late 19th century. The hotel's roof garden, from which music still blares on weekend evenings, was a favorite of the wealthy aristocracy. Just to the south stands the extremely ornate (a unique mix of art nouveau and neo-classical) facade of the **Gran Teatro de la Habana**, home of the **Ballet Nacional de Cuba Alicia Alonso**, as well as the national opera company. This was originally the site of the Teatro Tacón built in 1837; in the early 1900s it was purchased by the Galician (Spanish) community, which incorporated the theatre into the **Centro Gallego**, the ornate edifice that now occupies the entire block. The theatre is home to Alicia Alonso's Ballet Nacional de Cuba as well as the national opera company, and you can also see a wide variety of theater and classical music performances here.

Just south of the Gran Teatro looms the white marble bulk of the **Capitolio de la Habana** which is a direct copy of the U.S. Capitol building in Washington. It was constructed between 1926 and 1929 at a cost of $17 million by that most undemocratic dictator, Gerardo Machado, as a glittering centerpiece of his regime. Rejected by the Revolutionary government, today it is home to the Academy of Sciences. A tour costs a rather expensive three dollars. Up the marble steps, reliefs on the three bronze doors tell the story of Cuba until 1929; the face of Machado was obliterated when he was ousted in 1933. Statues on either side depict *Work* and *The Virtue of the People*.

Gran Teatro Facade

The dome covers an enormous circular entry hall and soars 91 metres (303 feet) from the floor to its peak. In the center of the floor, a 24-carat blue-white diamond is embedded to mark kilometre zero of Machado's central highway running from Havana to Santiago. The diamond is almost certainly a replica; the original is rumored to be in Fidel's office. Against the rear wall rises a 49-ton bronze statue representing *Cuba* in the form of a massive woman. This side of the building also houses, surprisingly, a wine shop. (There is also a souvenir store to the right of the entrance.) The Capitolio is perfectly symmetrical, and its size generates some weird acoustical effects, such as hallways in which it is difficult to hear others talk. The north wing housed the old Chamber of Representatives, recently restored, while the south was home to the Senate, whose circular chamber is being renovated. In the center is the Salon José Martí meeting room, decorated with murals of the arts and sciences, and the old parliamentary library, a copy of the Vatican's, which is now used by science and technology researchers. On the terraces facing El Prado, there are a cafe

(North side) and a restaurant (South side) offering a fine view and, in the latter, rather good cuisine.

Returning outside, opposite the Capitolio stands the **Sala Polivalente Kid Chocolate**, a gymnasium and boxing ring dedicated to the famous Cuban boxer. Just south of the Capitolio, the Paseo del Prado ends at a traffic island containing the **Fuente de la India** (1837), an allegory of Havana in the form of an indian maiden holding the city's coat of arms. Walking west across the neighboring **Parque de la Fraternidad**, you come to the Tree of American Fraternity, planted in 1928 in soil from all the countries of the Americas. Calle Industria runs along the west side of this park, and a half block to the right (north) behind the Capitolio, you see the **Fábrica de Tabacos Partagás** (late 19th century), the oldest cigar factory in continuous operation. For the price of admission ($5), you can tour the factory and see the cigar-making process from the preparation of the leaves to the packing of the boxes. It is customary for the rollers to tap their knives on the work tables as a greeting for guests. The shop here is one of the most reliable sources of cigars and has an extremely wide selection. This area is a center of cigar manufacture; the parallel block of Calle Amistad just west of Partagás is lined with a number of famous factories, including H. Uppman (but Partagás is the only one that allows visitors).

■ CENTRAL HAVANA

Central Havana, better known as 'Centro', is the neighborhood that stretches between the Paseo del Prado to the east and, opposite, the Calzada de la Infanta, which marks the border with Vedado. The touristic sights are few here; the zone is largely run-down apartment buildings from the early 1900s and a few depressed shopping streets. However, it is worth a stroll; street life is very active, there is lots of local color, and there are a few architectural gems waiting to be discovered. Before the Revolution, this was the center of the red-light district; streets like Virtudes ('Virtues') were lined with hundreds of prostitutes (today they wait outside tourist hotels). Centro's northern boundary is the famous **Malecón**, the seaside drive that runs from the San Salvador de la Punta fort to the entrance to Miramar. (Caution: While driving west on the Malecón, it is very hard to make a legal left turn into the city; until you reach Calle 23. A number of outdoor cafes are located in this area, between the base of Hotel Nacional and La Piragua.) During winter storms, huge waves break over the seawall and flood the nearby streets, halting traffic. The Malecón is Havana's most popular free amusement; here *habaneros* sunbathe, flirt, drink rum, fish or go swimming off the rocks. Every evening fishermen in inner tubes set out from here for the reefs or to the mythical land to the north. Occasionally, the government closes down a stretch, constructs a stage and invites the restless youth to a seaside dance party.

In Centro, the seaside buildings are colorful—you can see hints of art nouveau and elaborate mosaics—but much decayed by wind, wave and salt. Some have recently collapsed. The line of old buildings ends at the plaza in front of the skyscraping **Hermanos Ameijeiras Hospital**, one of Cuba's best, named for two brothers martyred by the Batista regime. This building was originally constructed by Batista to house the Banco Nacional de Cuba; there are rumors that Cuba's gold reserves are now held in vaults in the basement. Just to the west is the small 17th-century watchtower called the **Torreón de San Lázaro.**

Centro's main shopping street is **Calle San Rafael**, which begins at the Parque Central between the Hotel Inglaterra and the Gran Teatro. For five blocks west of here, San Rafael is pedestrian-only and lined with 1950s department stores still sporting the original neon signs. Inside there are more shopgirls than customers. You need ration books to buy most of the items; those which are *venta libre* (free sale) are generally junky trinkets and toys you do not want to buy. There is far more action in the dollar-only stores and the expensive *casas comisionistas*, a kind of pawnshop where people leave articles to be sold and the store takes a commission. The street is also filled with people offering things for sale, from homemade peanut bars and

(following pages) the Malecón at dusk

sandwiches to little plaques that avert the evil eye. Other important shopping streets are Av de Italia and Calzada de Infanta, both of which run north-south.

Under a grove of trees at the corner of San Rafael and Infanta is the headquarters of the **Canary Cultivators of Havana**; huge cages hold hundreds of blue, green, yellow and white birds making a tremendous racket. Calle Neptuno, two blocks north of San Rafael, is home to the friendly **Casa del Tango** (Neptuno #303), which serves as a museum of the dance form, a club of aficionados and a school where you can take lessons.

Calle Cuchillo, a block-long street that runs between Calle Zanja

Eating Stones

Havana is for walking, no matter what neighborhood you're in. The sidewalks are seldom wide enough for people to freely pass each other, but common promenading etiquette allows spilling out into the street. The country wears its history in the streets, from plaques commemorating sixteenth-century structures to busts of Martí to today's unimaginable architecture.

No cardboard encampments ringed the city. Crowded neighborhoods such as Centro Habana, in serious need of replastering, replumbing, repainting, rewiring, and rebuilding, stood out for their ills, yet the utter absence of people so destitute they had to sleep on sidewalks was continuously impressive. The few scavengers know to dig in dumpsters near buildings like mine, where foreigners lived.

One night at two o'clock I saw a couple of middle-aged women sitting half asleep against a store window on Galiano Street. Could they, I wondered, have been the first indicators of the economy bottoming out? It turned out they lived around the corner. They wanted to be first in line for goods at a women's apparel shop that they hoped would stock skirts their size when it opened eight hours later. Both women had ration books that corresponded to the and Calle San Nicolás, is all that is left of Havana's once-thriving **China-town**. In the 19th century over 130,000 Chinese, the vast majority men from Guangdong Province, were imported to Cuba as essentially slave labor for the plantations. Those who survived—with almost no Chinese women, their birthrate was close to zero—eventually moved to the cities, where they became traders and relatively prosperous market gardeners. Before the Revolution, 15,000 Chinese remained in Cuba, and Havana's Chinatown was a thriving tourist attraction and the center for the community. During the 1950s, this area's movie theatres specialized in pornographic films. Today only 700 Chinese—mainly the older generation—are left in all of Cuba. For various rea-

category this store would sell to that day. Nothing guaranteed that the skirts would be in, or that there'd be a selection of size or color or style—nonetheless, they'd be the first to know.

The complex ration procedure and the declining availability of merchandise reflected poorly on the system. People had little, but everyone had access to about the same amount of little. This system, unlike those of any neighboring countries, had found a roof to cover everyone at night, but still couldn't assure city folk that county food would arrive on time—or at all. Fidel, said a joke making the rounds, goes to Santiago de Cuba on the southeast end of the island to make a speech. "I've got some good news and some bad news," he tells the throng. "Which do you want first?"

"*¡La buena!*" they yell back. The good news!

"All right, *compañeros*. The good news is that for the next six months you'll have to eat stones."

A hubbub rises through the crowd. "That's good news?" "Has he finally flipped" "Stones?" *El lider máximo* held his arms out for silence.

"The bad news is that there aren't enough stones to go around, so you'll all have to share."

—*Trading With The Enemy*, by Tom Miller

Nails al fresco (top); 'Havana, faithful to its history'—and the barbers work outdoors

sons (including the experiences of relatives in communist China), they have been unhappy with the Revolutionary regime and have emigrated en masse, largely to the United States and to other Latin American countries. Havana's Chinatown is a shell of its old shelf, but you still can see a few stores, the ornate **Restaurant Pacifico**, the **Casino Chino** and the **Chang Weng Chung Tong**—the Chang family association. (The Pavo Real in Vedado is rumored to be the best Chinese restaurant.)

■ VEDADO

Since the late 19th century, the city's centre has moved west from Old Havana and now can be located on La Rampa in the heart of Vedado. The Vedado neighborhood takes its name from the woods that once covered this hill. In the early 1900s, wealthy Cubans and Americans built palatial homes here, far from the smells of Old Havana. The late 1950s were Vedado's apogee, when skyscrapers rose right and left and the future seemed limitless. Outside of the hotel, nightclub and movie theatre zone around La Rampa, Vedado is largely residential, with hundreds of small apartment houses and old mansions converted into multiple dwellings.

AROUND THE UNIVERSITY

Vedado's eastern border is the shopping avenue Calzada de Infanta. Two blocks to the west, at the corner of Calles San Miguel and Ronda, stands the **Museo Napoleonico**, originally property of Julio Lobo, a wealthy industrialist and collector of Napoleonica. When Lobo fled Cuba after the Revolution the government turned, his luxurious house and collection into a museum. The strongest connection between Cuba and Napoleon is that his personal doctor died in Cienfuegos, and Lobo was able to acquire some of his souvenirs of the Corsican. On the ground floor you see the ballroom and the entry into the small formal garden. The Napoleon collection begins on the first floor with furniture, commemorative vases and an amusing painting of Napoleon planning his coronation with rows of dolls.

Objects from St. Helena are exhibited on the second floor; here are his toothbrush, molar, famous hat, death mask and a lock of his hair. The third floor houses a magnificent dark wood library of Napoleonic lore. From the balcony, you have an excellent view of Centro, with Old Havana in the distance. The massive antenna next door is used to block the signals of TV Martí from the United States.

One block north and west of the museum, at the end of Calle Neptuno, rises the magnificent grand staircase of the **University of Havana**, scene of many political demonstrations up until 1959 and great open-air concerts in recent times. At the top sits a statue of *Alma Mater* in front of the four Corinthian columns and the main entrance. The university was originally founded in 1728 in Old Havana; in 1902 it was moved to these yellow stone, classical-style buildings. The campus is pleasant, with lots of trees and a cool breeze running through the colonnades, but you wonder where all the students are. It is also home to two museums, both found in the Felipe Poey building.

On the ground floor is the **Felipe Poey Museo de Historia Natural**, an old-style museum with many stuffed and pickled animals in glass cases. It is not without its charm, and its cases house an extremely wide array of dead Cuban wildlife, including many rare and weird endemic species. Felipe Poey was the preeminent 19th-century Cuban naturalist and many of his papers and personal effects are also preserved here. On the first floor you find the **Montané Museo Antropologico**, the most important collection of Cuban pre-Columbian artifacts. If you speak Spanish, it helps to request a tour, because the labelling is not very good. The three main eras up until the conquest —hunter-gatherer, proto-agricultural and agricultural—are illustrated with artifacts and reconstructed burials. Carved turtle shells were often used in ceremonies and as ornamentation; today many Cubans keep turtles as pets in order to bring health and good luck. The most important artifacts here are two idols. The first, the **Tobacco Idol** (around AD 1500), is a carved wood figure with shell eyes found near Baracoa. Its precise ritual use has not been deduced. The stone **Bayamo Idol**, a seated man with a grimacing, masklike face, may represent a person experiencing the effects of a hallucinatory drug.

PLAZA DE LA REVOLUCION

Avenida Universidad runs south down the hill from the University to the district called **Plaza de la Revolucion**, the heart of the Revolutionary government. A car comes in handy here, because the sights are spread out and generally not open to the public. At the bottom of the hill, Universidad reaches an intersection; continue south on the right (east) side of all the greenery along Av Rancho Boyeros. Two blocks farther, on the right you see the modern **Sala Polivalente**, a large gymnasium with a blue space frame roof. On the north side is a Museum of Sport, now closed, and a **bowling alley**, which will open for dollars. Opposite this gym stands the **Terminal de Omnibus In-**

Vedado

Gulf of Mexico

N

Casa de las Americas

Calzada

9

U.S. Interests Section

U.S.S. Maine Monument

Linea

Malecón

Edificio FOCSA

Hotel Capri

Hotel Nacional

11

13

Av de los Presidentes (G)

15

Museo de Artes Decorativas

17

Coppelia

Hotel Habana Libre

Calzada de Infanta

19

21

(La Rampa)

San Lázaro

23

University

Museo Napoleonico

25

© The Guidebook Company Ltd   27

Av Universidad

terprovinciales, Havana's long-distance bus station. A rare news kiosk decorates the sidewalk in front.

Continuing south one block, you come to the Ministry of Communications, which houses the **Museo Postal Cubano** on the first floor. Immediately south of the ministry opens a wide, paved square called the **Plaza de la Revolucion**. This is used for mass demonstrations —rare during the Special Period—on holidays such as May 1 and July 26. During Pope John Paul II's visit in early 1998, this was the site of a massive outdoor mass. A huge banner diplaying the Sacred Heart of Jesus even decorated one of the government buildings flanking the plaza. It faced the metal portrait of Che Guevara that adorns the Ministry of the Interior. The modern **Teatro Nacional**, presenting mainly symphonic music and operas, stands across from the northwest side of the square. On the opposite side rises the **Biblioteca Nacional**, Cuba's largest library.

On the south, the plaza is dominated by the looming white marble **Monumento á José Martí**. A white sculpture of the hero of independence sits in front of a tall, four-sided obelisk (pre-1959) of dubious architectural value. The reviewing stand in front of this assemblage is used by Fidel and the other leaders to address the gathered multitudes. In the base is a newly-renovated museum to Martí containing excellent exhibits and holograms of some of his possessions. For an added fee, you can take the elevator to the top of the obelisk, where you have one of the finest views of Havana.

Discreetly nestled among the trees to the south of the monument is the most important government building in Cuba: the Palace of the Revolution, the site, they say, of Fidel's office. Nearby are the headquarters of the Central Committee of the Communist Party of Cuba, the Councils of State and of Ministers and the Ministries of FAR (Revolutionary Armed Forces), Interior, Sugar, etc. Av Rancho Boyeros continues all the way south to the airport.

LA RAMPA

Our tour now returns to the university. North of the campus Calle L runs down to the Malecón. The north-south streets in this part of

Vedado are letters or, farther west, even numbers, while the east-west streets are odd numbers. On first glance, street signs are nonexistent; after some searching you discover that they are placed on nearly invisible low concrete markers at every corner.

Two blocks north of the university on Calle L soars the **Hotel Habana Libre**. Originally built as the Havana Hilton in the 1950s, the hotel was converted into a meeting and study center by the Revolution; Fidel, Che and other Revolutionary leaders were frequently sighted here. In the 1980s it was returned to its more profitable function. After years of renovation, the hotel has now been returned to something like its original splendor, with a grandiose lobby, valet parking, three restaurants, a bank, travel agencies and a variety of well-stocked stores. The **Tienda Artex** across Calle L sells English paperbacks and foreign newspapers and magazines.

The corner of Calle L and Calle 23 here is one of the busiest—and most dangerous—intersections in Havana. Calle 23 is better known as **La Rampa**, 'The Ramp', as it runs down to the Malecón. In a park

Street vendor

Mob lawyer

On my first night in Havana, Santo took me on the rounds of several of his casinos. His favorite was the Sans Souci because it had a nightclub and floor show that was one of the most popular draws for Cubans and tourists.

We visited the nightclub shortly before the first show was to start and Santo gave me a backstage tour. He strolled into the chorus girls' dressing room where many of the dancers and singers were half nude and barebreasted. While I was uncertain about what to do with my eyes, Santo casually chatted with the girls in Spanish, which he spoke fluently. When he introduced me to some of his favorite performers, none exhibited any embarrassment.

In the men's dressing room, all the dancers and singers in the state of undress immediately covered their genitals.

Outside, I asked Santo, "Why are these guys running for cover? The girls didn't."

"You don't know? They're queers," he said, grinning at my naiveté. The men, who never performed in the nude, did not want to expose themselves to heterosexual men.

The next stop was the casino's counting room. A uniformed guard stood outside as Santo pulled out a key and unlocked the door to a small room, about twelve feet square, containing a wide table and a huge safe. The casino was air-conditioned but the room was stuffy, a floor fan providing only a warm breeze.

Two men, one wearing a green head visor and the other making entries in a ledger, were at a table covered with stacks of U.S. money.

"This is Henry," Santo said, introducing me to the man working on the ledger with an adding machine. "This is the most important room in any casino. We deal in cash and either you make it or lose it by what goes on in this room. Henry here is from Tampa and he watches that the count is right and that nothing gets lost. These

people will steal you blind," he added, referring to the Cuban employees. "So I bring people from Tampa to watch the counting
room."

On that first trip, I also accompanied Santo as he made his late
rounds of the casinos. One night, close to dawn, he pointed out a
visitor as the bagman for Batista's wife. She got 10 percent of the
profits from the slot machines in all of Santos' places. "You pay for
everything in Havana," he said without rancor.

Impressed by his holdings in Havana, I asked him why, since he
was so successful legitimately in Cuba, he did not turn an honest
dollar at home.

"Frank, a man who is blind in one eye has a great deal of vision
among the blind," he said with a wide smile. In other words, corruption and loose standards made it easy for him to prosper in
Cuba.

—*Mob Lawyer* by Frank Ragano and Selwyn Raab

at the northwest corner of L and 23 sits the enormous flying-saucer-
shaped **Heladeria Coppelia**, the cathedral of Cuba's frozen dessert
cult (the hours vary depending on supply, but generally it is open
from early afternoon until about nine at night). Cubans acquired
their taste for ice cream in the 19th century; today their expertise in
its manufacture is a matter of national pride—indeed, it is by far the
best in Latin America. Habaneros line up for hours for a chance to
savor this delicay. Before his doctors reigned him in, it is said that
Fidel could devour a dozen or more scoops at a sitting. Recently renovated, the main building is restricted to selling ice cream for pesos.
Cubans line up for hours to savor their favorite treat, usually only
available in two or three flavors. Kiosks in the surrounding gardens
occasionally sell ice cream for dollars, but they are rarely open. If
you do not want to stand in line for two to three hours, you can sample Coppelia's product in most hotels and dollar restaurants.

Heading east down La Rampa, the sidewalks are inlaid with mosaics designed by some of Cuba's best-known modern artists, includ-

ing Wifredo Lam. The five blocks to the Malecón are lined with restaurants, shops (Photoservice at the corner of Calle P sells film and photo equipment and develops in an hour, but watch out for *multas*, or overcharging on your purchases), and airline offices. Turning left on Calle O, in one block you come to the grand entrance to the Italianate edifice of the **Hotel Nacional** (1930), Cuba's most elegant hotel. In 1955, a portion of this hotel was converted into a gambling complex managed by the American gangster Meyer Lansky; for four years it attracted the cream of American gamblers and Mafiosi, who used to play penny-ante poker around the pool. Today the high rollers are gone, but it is still worth a stroll through the lobby to see the tile decor. The Nacional has a number of shops and restaurants, a good pharmacy and the Cabaret Parisien, one of Havana's best nightclubs (reservations required).

A block west of the Nacional on Calle 21 stands another ex-gambling mecca, the **Hotel Capri**, which was built by the U.S. Mafioso Santo Traficante Jr. In the late 1950s the casino's host was the Ameri-

Hotel Nacional

can tough guy movie star George Raft. On January 1, 1959, when a mob sought to destroy the gambling tables in the hotel's Salón Rojo, Raft appeared on the steps and snarled, 'Yer not comin' in my casino'. The mob departed, but all casinos were quickly closed by the Revolutionary government.

Looming just northwest of the Capri is the massive concrete **Edificio FOCSA**, Cuba's largest building, a 1950s apartment building with two restaurants, the rooftop **La Torre** and **El Emperador** on Calle 17. The shopping gallery on the ground floor includes a supermarket, photo shop, cafeteria and the **Teatro Guiñol** children's theatre.

The remainder of our tour should be done by car or bicycle, because the distances are too far to walk. Returning to the Malecón just west of the Nacional, you see the **U.S.S. _Maine_ Monument,** originally erected in memory of the 260 sailors who died when the warship exploded in Havana Bay in 1898. Strangely, this monument does not appear on any Cuban maps. Shortly after the Triumph of the Revolution, an angry, anti-American crowd toppled the eagle from the top of the monument; its broken wings now rest in the Museum of the City of Havana. A 1961 plaque declares: 'To the victims of the _Maine_, who were sacrificed by imperialist voracity in its eagerness to seize the island of Cuba'.

Heading west on the Malecón, in a few blocks you come to the **U.S. Interests Section**, a five-storey box with mirrored blue windows (the entrance is on Calzada between Calles L and M). Until relations between the U.S. and Cuba were broken, this was the U.S. Embassy; now it operates under the protection of the Swiss Embassy.

The Malecón curves around Vedado until it comes to the **Monument to Calixto Garcia**, a hero of both Wars of Independence. Just to the south stands the art deco **Casa de las Americas**, a cultural center founded in 1959 to promote 'sociocultural relations' between Cuba and other Latin American and Caribbean nations. The Casa de las Americas' literature prize and eponymous magazine have long been influential in the region. For visitors, the Casa has four galleries exhibiting art from throughout the Americas, and you can also hear concerts and attend literary events here. The ornate white mansion southeast across the avenue houses the offices of **MINREX**, the Ministry of Foreign Relations.

Nine blocks south of the Casa, on Calle 17 between E and D, stands the **Museo de Artes Decorativos**, housed in a luxurious 1824 mansion once owned by the Countess of Revilla de Camarga. Attended by a team of women guards, your tour begins on the ground floor with the marble-lined dining room and its collection of French ceramics. Up the grand staircase, you come to an exhibit of ivory carvings on the landing, from where you enter the bedroom with its Oriental ceramics and bronze. The tour continues through the pink marble bathroom and concludes in the boudoir with a display of furniture inlaid with mother-of-pearl.

Returning to the Malecón at the Calixto García monument, seven blocks to the west you come to two symbols of the Cuban tourism industry, past and present. First is the enormous, dark glass **Hotel Cohiba**, one of the newest and best-equipped hotels in Cuba; it is a favorite of foreign businessmen. Just to the west stands the blue, Miami-Beach-moderne-style **Hotel Riviera**, Meyer Lansky's pride and joy. The American gangster opened the 21-storey hotel-casino, the largest outside Las Vegas, in late 1957. He crapped out, because in a little more than a year the entire gambling industry would be closed by the Revolution. The interior still preserves the original, joyously tacky decor—concrete fish gamboling in the lobby—and you can peek into the oval, domed nightclub to see where Lansky fleeced the suckers.

Vedado ends about eight blocks farther to the west, when the Malecón dips down into the tunnel heading to Miramar. Just before the tunnel, on the right you see the **Castillo de Santa Dorotea de Luna de la Chorrera**, a 1643 fort meant to protect Havana's west flank from pirate attack. Today it's a cafe specialising in Spanish food and an outdoor night club. A few feet further west stands the elegant **1830 Restaurant**, known for its international cuisine. Next door, at the mouth of the Almendares river, there is another outdoor cafe and bar open until the late hours.

Crowds cheer Fidel's "Declaration of the Socialist Nature of the Revolution", April 16, 1961.

Our tour ends in southwest Vedado near the intersection of Calles 23 and 12. A bronze plaque on the northwest corner commemorates the April 16, 1961, speech in which Fidel declared the 'Socialist Nature of the Revolution' to the machine-gun-wielding masses mobilized to repel the Bay of Pigs Invasion. This corner is also a center of the movie industry; here are two important movie houses, the **Charles Chaplin** and the **23 y 12**, and the **Cuban Institute of Cinematography**, the organization in charge of all film production.

A block to the south stands the Romanesque grand entrance to the **Cementerio de Colón** (1871), Havana's principal cemetery and a trove of architectural and historical riches. The most important tombs line the main cemetery avenue heading south. Here lie the Céspedes family, Martí's parents and Havana's firemen under a tragic sculpture. Just before the chapel on the parallel street to the left (east), sits the **tomb of Amelia Goyre del la Hoz**, better known as La Milagrosa, who died during childbirth in 1901. A sculpture depicts her with one arm around a cross and the other holding a baby. After her death, her grieving husband visited the tomb daily, first knocking to let her know of his arrival and then holding a long conversation with her spirit. When he departed he never turned his back on her, but respectfully backed away. Passersby saw his faith—and how his business was prospering—and word spread that a prayer to her spirit, now called 'La Milagrosa' (the Miracle Woman), could intercede for the faithful. Today her tomb is a pilgrimage destination and covered with flowers and offerings brought by people praying for her help. Little marble plaques give thanks for the miracles.

At the south end of this avenue stands the mausoleum of FAR, the Revolutionary Armed Forces. Interestingly, unlike cemeteries in the old Soviet Union, there are no tombs in the cemetery decorated with the symbols of communism, like the star or the hammer and sickle —they either have Christian symbols or they have none. The mausoleums of the pre-Revolution rich are occasionally astonishing, built in a wide variety of architectural styles, including Egyptian, Babylonian, Gothic, Venetian, art deco and moderne. The more humble must be content with flat, knee-level tombs topped with thickets of marble angels, virgins, Christs and crosses. The office at the main entrance will help you locate any grave. Just across Av 26 from the cemetery's southwest corner lies the cemetery of Havana's Chinese community.

Cementerio de Colón

■ Miramar And West

Miramar was the country club district before the Revolution, and it retains its air of exclusivity. The wide, tree-shaded avenues are lined with mansions from the 1940s and 1950s now largely occupied by embassies, schools, ritzy shops and offices. The eastern border is the Río Almendares, under which plunges the Malecón from Vedado and then emerges as **Quinta Avenida** (Fifth Avenue), Miramar's main street.

At the corner of Quinta and Calle 14 stands the **Museo del Ministerio del Interior**, a must for anyone interested in the spy vs. spy exercises of Cuba and the United States. The exhibition begins with the founding of Cuba's security organization in 1959 to fight the counter-Revolutionaries. Displays show the bloodied shirts of the martyrs to the cause of counterespionage and the insidious weapons used by the opposition, like a deodorant can used as a silencer and a soap dish full of plastic explosive. After an explication of the various plots to assassinate Fidel, you come to a collection of the tools of the trade: codebooks, counterfeit money and plastic rocks hiding radios. A series of candid photos supposedly shows U.S. State Department personnel making a 'secret' drop. The main part of the exhibit ends with the Ministry of the Interior today, fighting criminals and waves of 'pirates' invading from abroad. A separate galley behind the house celebrates the work of Cuba's police, firemen and prison guards.

The **Casa del Tabaco** two blocks west on Quinta at the corner of Calle 16 is one of the best cigar stores in Cuba. One block south at the corner of 16 and Septima Avenida (Seventh Avenue) stands **La Maison**, an old mansion where you can buy the latest ready-to-wear Cuban fashions, as well as jewelry, crafts and cosmetics. The premises also house a restaurant. Back on 5ta. heading west, on Seventh you come to a mini-mall called **Quinta y 42** ('Fifth Avenue and 42nd Street') which is a trove of hard-to-find consumer goods. Originally only open to diplomats, these shops include a toy store, bakery, sporting-goods store, video rental, supermarket and discount store, in addition to an Italian restaurant.

continues on page 140

MOBSTERS IN PARADISE

The U.S. Mafia's Cuban adventure was a unique episode in the history of that criminal brotherhood. It was their experiment in nation building, in constructing a state so crooked that they had no need to break the laws. Their partners were a Cuban political elite whose greed and venality made the gangsters look like pillars of probity in comparison. Castro's revolutionaries hurried the end of this debauched regime, but the truth is that it collapsed of its own corruption.

This saga begins in 1933, the year that saw the end of two eras, of Prohibition in the U.S. and of the Machado dictatorship in Cuba. In order to cash in on legal booze, New York bootleggers built huge rum factories and contracted with refineries in Cuba to guarantee a steady supply of molasses, the main ingredient. Their representative was Meyer Lansky, the brilliant Jewish mobster who formed a lifelong partnership with the Italian Mafia and became the brains behind its national organization. He met with Cuba's new strongman, army sergeant Fulgencio Batista; recognizing kindred spirits, the two began a friendship and business relationship that lasted three decades.

With the vast profits of Prohibition over, Lansky knew it was time to rebuild the mob's business around a new core. Gambling was the safest bet, and he saw Cuba—close to the U.S. and with an amenable leader in Batista—as the perfect place to promote it. In the late 1930s, he took control of the casino at Havana's Oriental Park (the racetrack) and the Casino Nacional in nearby Marianao. Lansky's procedure was to bring in his own men as croupiers and pit bosses to ensure that the games were legitimate. He knew that success depended on attracting high rollers, and they would not come if they heard the casinos were crooked.

World War II and the collapse of tourism from the U.S. brought this experiment to an end, and Lansky returned to his gambling operations in Florida. Nevertheless, the Cuban casinos had been a success and provided the basis for future plans. During the war, Lansky and many other New York mobsters, including Mafia boss Lucky Luciano, worked for the government in a highly successful effort to keep Nazi infiltrators out of New York docks. According to one story, in 1944 President Roosevelt also used Lansky to send a message to then-President Batista: resign and allow honest elections. When Batista's candidate lost to Dr. Ramón Grau San Martín, the dictator retired to Daytona Beach, conveniently near Lansky's Florida headquarters.

After the war, Cuba heated up. In 1946, Lucky Luciano was deported to Italy, where he acquired a false passport and took the next boat to Cuba. He thought he would use the island as a base to rebuild his status as boss of the national crime syndicate until he could gain entry into the U.S. again. Cuba was a perfect center for his gambling and narcotics transshipment operations; he planned to make the Island of Pines (now the Island of Youth) the new Monte Carlo. In 1946, Luciano called a summit in Havana to confirm his authority over the U.S. mob.

The setting was the Hotel Nacional, the elegant pile on the Vedado waterfront; the ostensible excuse was Frank Sinatra's singing debut in Havana (photos of Sinatra and Luciano in Havana recently resurfaced to haunt the singer). In attendance were the top Italian and Jewish mobsters, including Lansky, Luciano, Frank Costello, Tommy Lucchese, Vito Genovese, Joe Bonanno, Santo Trafficante Jr. and Moe Dalitz. Among the topics discussed were problems with the U.S. Federal Narcotics Bureau and Bugsy Siegel, who had been skimming off construction money for the Flamingo, Las Vegas's first big-time casino. Siegel was a childhood pal of Lansky and Luciano, but the mob could not tolerate a thief. Lansky gave the word, and a few months later Siegel was dead.

Luciano's reign was short. A snappy dresser who liked a luxurious lifestyle, he was not exactly inconspicuous; Federal Narcotics agents followed him to the racetrack and to dinners with beautiful women. Within weeks of the Havana convention, the U.S. government delivered an ultimatum: Luciano had to go. In early 1947, the mob boss was back in Italy; before he left he anointed Meyer Lansky as his stand-in, both in the United States and Cuba.

The late 1940s and early '50s were slow for the mob in Cuba. Their stateside investments in Florida and other areas were booming, and

continues

Las Vegas, Bugsy Siegel's turkey, was turning into the golden goose. Nevertheless, Lansky kept in touch with Batista; he knew that the situation could change, and they might again need a safe haven. Meanwhile, Santo Trafficante Jr., the Tampa, Florida, Mafia boss, began to make modest investments in Havana's Hotel Commodoro and in some small casinos. For bettors, however, Cuba had developed a nasty reputation: Many of the games were rigged, and U.S. magazines screamed headlines such as 'Suckers in Paradise', printing horror stories of innocent tourists who lost everything in crooked casinos.

As Lansky had foreseen, things changed. Florida voters declined to legalize gambling, and the police closed down Lansky's huge Miami-area gambling parlors. Then the Kefauver Crime Commission embarked on a campaign against the national crime syndicate that forced many top mobsters, including Lansky, into the public eye. Lansky returned to Batista's Daytona Beach house, and they began to make plans. They were joined by many top Cuban politicians and military men. It was decided: Batista would not only open the way for large-scale gambling, but he would reorganize the Cuban state so that he and his pals could harvest the nation's riches like ripe fruit.

The first step of this plan was to convince President Prío to step aside. Threats and $250,000 personally delivered by Meyer Lansky did the trick; Batista's March 10, 1952, coup succeeded unopposed. Next laws would have to be passed to encourage investment in hotels and casinos. The new government would contribute dollar-for-dollar in every new tourist facility; any hotel investment over $1 million could apply for a casino license; and there would be no import duties on construction materials. At the same time, new private and government banks were founded to facilitate the flow of money between tourists' wallets and the pockets of mobsters and politicos. It took a year to put the new institutions in place; meanwhile Lansky met with his fellow mobsters to divide up the spoils.

Lansky was the center of the entire Cuban gambling operation; all projects had to go through him. His first action was to get rid of the army of sharpies and cheats in Cuba's casinos who scared off tourists and, more importantly, the high rollers. The 1954-55 winter season had the cleanest games ever. Lansky began with the Montmartre Club, three blocks from the Hotel Nacional, where high rollers could play in an atmosphere of quiet elegance, eschewing frivolity that distracted from the serious business at hand. A year later, singer Eartha Kitt headlined the gala opening of the Internacional Club casino in the ground floor of the Hotel Nacional. Lansky's brother Jake was the pit boss and he quickly shocked Cuba's elite by refusing credit to important military officers; business was business. Lansky's partners in the hotel were the Cleveland Syndicate, a group of Jewish mobsters headed by Moe Dalitz, who relaxed by playing penny-ante poker around the Nacional's pool (they knew the casino was for suckers).

Santo Trafficante Jr. controlled the Sans Souci, an indoor/outdoor nightclub and casino along the lines of the Tropicana, as well as casinos in the hotels Sevilla-Biltmore, Commodoro, Deauville and Capri. Movie tough guy George Raft was the emcee at the Capri, providing the *frisson* of gangsterism that electrified the tourists. When someone asked Trafficante about the secret of his success in Cuba, he somewhat enigmatically replied:

'A man who is blind in one eye has a great deal of vision among the blind.' In other words, someone who is half corrupt can be a great success among the totally corrupt, i.e., the elite who ruled Cuba.

Trafficante also revelled in the secondary businesses that kept the gamblers happy. Prostitution was ubiquitous—it seemed that everybody was for sale—and the casinos kept stores of cocaine for players who needed an extra boost to play through the night. In 1957, Trafficante claimed to have provided three prostitutes for a visiting dignitary, Senator John F. Kennedy, and then watched the proceedings through a one-way mirror in the Hotel Commodoro. His only regret was that he did not tape the show—President Kennedy came down hard on the Mafia.

The Mafia was not the only U.S. organization making money in Cuba. For a price, Batista gave contracts to dozens of U.S. corporations for massive construction projects, including the Havana-Varadero highway, the Rancho Boyeros airport, train lines, the power company and a phantom plan to dig a canal across Cuba. The money

continues

was huge, and everybody—in the elite—was taking a piece. Batista started with just a flat fee from the casinos, but when he saw the profits he demanded, and got, 50 per cent of Lansky's slot-machine net. Lansky did not mind, because he had already doctored his books. The bagman for Batista's wife collected nightly 10 per cent of the profits at Trafficante's casinos. In order to process all this money, Lansky founded two banks in Florida solely for Cuban business. Unknown millions were also sent to secret Swiss bank accounts.

To crown his success, Lansky had a dream: the construction of the fanciest hotel and casino yet seen on the island. In January 1957, work began on the 21-storey, 383-room Hotel Riviera, costing $14 million (mostly from the Cuban government) and designed as an amalgam of Miami and Las Vegas on the Vedado waterfront. The hotel opened on December 10 of that year, with a floor show in the Copa Room headlined by Ginger Rogers. Nearby was the egg-shaped Gold Leaf Casino, where tuxedoed men and bejeweled women gambled away their money in an atmosphere of utmost refinement. Lansky's official title was the kitchen director, but he controlled every aspect of the hotel, even complaining that Rogers could 'wiggle her ass, but she [couldn't] sing a goddam note'.

The 1957-58 season was the most glittering yet; a few more like these and the Riviera would pay back its investment. However, there was trouble on the horizon: Castro's rebels in the Sierra Maestra and a never-ending round of bombings and assassinations in the streets. Batista insisted that these were minor problems; in any case, Lansky and Trafficante had too much at stake to pull out now (the lucky Cleveland Syndicate had cashed out to concentrate on Las Vegas). That summer, Batista's army began a major offensive against Castro's Sierra Maestra hideouts; his soldiers, aware of the moral bankruptcy of the army brass, chose to surrender rather than fight. When the 1958-59 season opened in December, Lansky did not know that Batista had secretly requested U.S. visas for himself and his family. On New Year's Eve of 1958, the sold-out floor show at the Copa Room suddenly had 200 cancellations. The word had passed: Batista was already heading toward the airport.

January 1 dawned with joyous crowds in the streets celebrating Day One of the Revolution. The mob quickly turned against the 'thieving machines' that were symbols of the hated dictatorship: parking meters, jukeboxes (controlled by the U.S. Mafia), slot machines and roulette wheels. After destroying the casinos at the Deauville and the Sevilla-Biltmore, they turned on the Hotel Capri. They were met on the steps by George Raft, who snarled, 'Yer not comin' in my casino'. Abashed, they looked for other targets.

One of the first actions of the Revolutionary government was to close down all casinos, lotteries and other games of chance. Nevertheless, Lansky and Trafficante held on, hoping for a counterrevolution or at least a change of heart by Fidel. In February, the government ordered all casinos to reopen so they could pay their employees, but whenever a potential customer tried to enter he was arrested by the police. This farce lasted only a few months, and in June all 'undesirable aliens', including Trafficante and Jake Lansky, were arrested and eventually deported. In October 1960, the new government struck the final blow, nationalizing all foreign-owned businesses, including the Riviera. Lansky, who had staked millions on the hotel, later said: 'I crapped out'.

The Cuba debacle left Santo Trafficante Jr. and other mobsters poorer and angry. They directed their rage at two men, Fidel Castro and President Kennedy, the latter because he was too soft on the former. Some conspiracy theorists claim that Kennedy was assassinated on Mafia orders in revenge for his lukewarm response to the Castro threat. In mid-1960, the CIA began recruiting Mafiosi, including Trafficante, and embittered Cuban exiles for one of their many plots against Castro's life. They were supposed to plant poisoned pills in one of Castro's dishes at his favorite Havana restaurant. Instead Trafficante flushed the pills down the toilet and pocketed the CIA's money. He may have been a criminal, but he was not crazy.

The only mobster who apparently did not hold a grudge was Meyer Lansky. Perhaps he realized that in the reason for the mob's success, the corruption of the Cuban system, lay the seeds of their downfall.

If you leave the shopping behind for a moment and head north to the seaside Primera Avenida (First Avenue), at the corner of Calle 44 stands the **Hotel Copacabana**, a pleasant smaller hotel known for its free poolside nightclub show (call for times). To the west, Primera Avenida ends at the **Acuario Nacional**, an aquarium that has become slighly run-down during the Special Period. The highlight is the dolphin show.

Calle 60 by the aquarium heads south to Miramar's border with the neighboring district of Marianao. Just across the border, hidden in a grove of trees is the world-famous **Tropicana Nightclub**. The nightclub began as Villa Mina, the residence of a wealthy devotee of exotic plants. Named after a song by Alfredo Brito, it opened as a nightclub on December 31, 1939, and has stayed open more or less continuously ever since. Tickets cost $40 and more, before transport, and can be purchased at any hotel travel desk. At the entry, your senses are dazzled by the neon lights, the deferential doorman, a hall of mirrors, and then are returned to earth by seeing the gift shop. On the right is

Old pharmacy

a large disco with a stage. The Tropicana is outdoors; if it rains, the show is held in here.

The nightclub itself is an exotic tangle of huge trees, multiple stages and neon lights—it is impossible to watch all the action at once. Seats are placed in three different zones, priced depending on your proximity to the stage. The choice areas are reserved for tourists while the seats in the last section are offered in pesos through the trade unions to 'vanguard workers'. There are actually four companies of Tropicana entertainers: one here, one in Santiago and two travelling constantly abroad. At 9:30 the lights dim, and here come the showgirls, all enormous *mulatas* on high heels and wearing huge headdresses. There they go—that is most of the show, the entry and exit of the Amazons, each time in a new costume. In between you see dance numbers—some that would cause an Africanist to shudder— and tributes to great Cuban and Latin American songwriters and musicians, such as Beny Moré, Bola de Nieve and Agustin Lara. The high point is the stately Dance of the Chandeliers, in which a train of

Schoolgirls

showgirls appears attached to each other by electrical cords. The electricity illuminates the lamps on their heads; apparently the Tropicana's power supply is guaranteed. The show ends at 11:15, and the audience are encouraged to do their own dancing on stage. A second, shorter show runs from midnight to 1 am.

Returning to Quinta Avenida and continuing west, you cannot miss the spectacular **Confederation of Independent States Embassy**, a relic of an obsolete foreign policy. This enormous complex between Calles 62 and 66, with its soaring, rocketlike tower, was completed shortly before the collapse of the Soviet Union.

Just to the west stands the **Supermercado 70** (at 3rd Avenue and 70th), Cuba's best-stocked supermarket, which is now open to anyone with dollars (it was originally called the 'Diplo', because its aisles were reserved for diplomats). In the parking lot, **Newsprensa** offers the largest variety of foreign newspapers and magazines on sale in Cuba.

After another kilometre or so, Quinta Avenida leaves Miramar and enters Cubanacán, another exclusive, embassy-filled neighborhood. A few blocks to the south stands the **Palacio de las Convenciones** (1979), a white, space-frame structure with numerous meeting rooms and a large restaurant. Larger conventions may also use the **PAB-EXPO** pavilion a few blocks west. The newly opened **Hotel Palco** is one of the best options in Havana today for business or convention travellers. It has a fine array of shops in the covered walkway leading to the Convention Palace. Four blocks south and east is Chef Erasmo's **Restaurant Rancho Palco**, with a reputation for being the best in Havana.

Quinta Avenida continues west as Havana thins out. Just after the Río Jaimanitas, on the right you see the entry to the **Marina Hemingway**, whose only connection to Hemingway the man is the name. Four canals make up an artificial harbor used to shelter seagoing luxury yachts; a neighboring coast guard base and container-storage depot add a slightly industrial air. Between the canals, fingers of land hold a number of tourist facilities, including tourist villas, tennis courts, a disco, shops, three restaurants—**Papa's** (seafood), **Fiesta** (steak) and **Pizza Nuova** (Italian)—and the Hotel El Viejo y El Mar ('Old Man and the Sea Hotel'). The marina is best known as the base for the annual Ernest Hemingway Blue Marlin Tournament. To the west, Quinta Avenida becomes the highway to Mariel in Havana Province. After Santa Fé, the road passes the Granma Naval Academy, the Baracoa industrial zone and a good beach called Playa Salado, before arriving in Mariel. This industrial port was the embarkation point for the 1980 boatlift.

■ SOUTH OF HAVANA

From the Plaza de la Revolucion, Av de la Independencia runs south to Rancho Boyeros and José Martí International Airport. About five kilometres south of the plaza, Av San Francisco heads east to **Parque Lenin**, a rolling 647-hectare (1,600-acre) park that teemed with *habaneros* in times of good transportation. The park's namesake is remembered by a massive white marble bust of Lenin carved in high socialist realist style. A quote from Fidel on Lenin provides the motto, and, when there is power, loudspeakers blare internationalist music. The park is built around two lakes, the larger of which is named Lake Rebel Army (boats for hire). On the western shores of this you find the **Las Ruinas Restaurant**, a modern building erected around the picturesque remains of a ruined mansion. The interior is decorated with a stained-glass mural, and the specialty of the house is Cuban food. There are also cafeterias, art galleries, a small aquarium, a riding center and a theatre in the park, but they're usually closed these days. The one centre of activity is the **Che Guevara Pioneer Palace**, which is decorated with stainless-steel sculptures cut with the hero's silhouette.

One kilometre west of the park entrance is the **National Zoo**, a park where the animals roam free and the humans observe them from well-protected buses. Due south of the park is the **National Botanical Garden**, with a huge variety of Cuban and foreign species, and **Expocuba**, a permanent exhibit on Cuba's economic accomplish-

Moving van, Havana

ments (science, mining, tourism, health, etc.) in a large space-frame structure. There are also restaurants and cafeterias on the premises, as well as a small amusement park with a unique, foot-powered monorail. This is the site of Havana's yearly International Trade Fair. Across from Expocuba is the **Jardín Botánico** with exhibits of native flora, a pleasant Japanese Garden and the **Ecorestaurant**, serving Cuban-vegetarian (something of an oxymoron) inventions. Returning to Av de la Independencia, one kilometre south of the airport you come to **Santiago de las Vegas**, a small, traditional town that marks the border of Havana Province and the beginning of the rest of Cuba.

■ EAST OF HAVANA

From the eastern end of the Malecón, a tunnel runs under the entrance to the harbor and emerges just beyond the **Castillo de los Tres Santos Reyes Magos del Morro**, also known as the Morro Castle, one of the symbols of Havana. An immediate exit takes you to the parking area just east of the fort, which is perched on a rocky outcropping. During the winter huge waves crash spectacularly against the rocks, splashing water dozens of metres. From the ramparts there is an excellent view of the Malecón and Havana's shining edifices.

The Morro Castle was built as a companion to the San Salvador de la Punta Castle across the harbor in order to protect its entrance. Also, it was crucial for Havana's defenders to control this high ground, from which it was easy to lob shells into Old Havana. Construction on this roughly pentagonal structure began in 1589 and ended in 1630. The Morro Castle was the main objective of the English forces when they attacked in 1762; after its capture, Havana's defeat was ensured. The lighthouse was erected in 1845. Today the castle houses a museum with exhibitions devoted to pirates (both classic and modern, CIA-funded), navigation and a history of the castle. Along the rocks on either side of the castle are batteries of cannons, some old and picturesque, others new and apparently in working order. Immediately south of the castle, the **Bateria del Sol** is now the **Restaurant Los 12 Apostoles**, serving Spanish food with an excellent view of Old Havana.

The English capture of Havana proved that the city's defences were inadequate. Immediately after Spain regained Cuba in 1763, construction began on a fourth bulwark, the **Fortaleza de San Carlos de la Cabaña**, overlooking the harbor about half a kilometre south of the Morro Castle. La Cabaña's design was markedly different from the earlier castles; instead of being a compact, roughly equilateral structure, this was a long rectangle, with guns facing not only the harbor but east in the direction of the earlier English invasion. The military quarter inside the fort was capable of housing 5,000 soldiers in case of attack. For many years La Cabaña also doubled as a jail for political prisoners; many are buried in a tomb at the south end of the fort. The fort's museum has exhibitions on military history and weapons.

These days La Cabaña is best known for the ceremonial firing of a cannon at 9 pm nightly in a rite with much pomp and men dressed in

18th-century costume. Package tours often include the cannonade and then a meal at the **La Divina Pastora Restaurant** (seafood is the specialty) in a battery at the north end of the fort. The dock here is also the embarkation point for the **El Galeón**, a faux pirate ship that cruises up and down the coast for daytime excursions to the beach, evening dinner and cannon cruises and a late-night disco (reservations at any hotel travel desk or at the Hotel Habana Libre's travel agency).

The four-lane road east of the Morro Castle is called the **Vía Monumental**. It passes a hospital complex and then, on the left, the **Panamerican Stadium**, built by thousands of 'voluntary laborers' for the 1991 Panamerican Games. Considering the economic straits of Cuba during the beginning of the Special Period, the completion of the stadium and the success of the games was a miracle. Across the highway is a sports complex also built for the games. The housing built for the athletes became the Villa Panamericana residential complex and the resort-like **Hotel Panamericano**. Immediately after the stadium, an exit to the left takes you to the famous fishing village of **Cojímar**. Hemingway docked his boat, *Pilar*, here and immortalized the local fishermen in his Nobel prize-winning novel, *The Old Man and the Sea.* Your first stop should be the 1915 **La Terraza Restaurant** right at the side of Cojímar's little harbor. This charming, reasonably priced restaurant is known for its seafood. The dining room is decorated with photos of the great writer and of the fisherman on whom he modelled the main character in *The Old Man and the Sea.* Hemingway's assistant, Gregorio Fuentes, over 100 years old, still lives nearby.

Just north of the restaurant stands a bust of Hemingway cast from scrap metal donated by the town's fishermen. They look back on the Hemingway era with nostalgia, because over the last decades the fish have all but disappeared offshore, probably due to pollution. Next to this sculpture rises a small, towerlike fort officially called **Santo Dorotea de Luna de la Chorrera y Cojímar** (1643), better known as La Chorrera. When Spain's military experts examined Havana's feeble defenses, they saw that invaders could use Cojímar's harbor to land forces to attack Havana from behind. They were right; Cojímar's defenders (Cubans, not Spanish, say locals) put up a fierce resistance to the English navy, but the fort was not enough to stop them.

East of Cojímar, the Vía Monumental becomes the **Vía Blanca,** the four-lane highway that runs all the way to Matanzas. Immediately

La Chorrera, Cojímar

after Cojímar rise the Soviet-style apartment towers of **Alamar**, a bedroom suburb of Havana, and, a few kilometres farther east, **Celimar**, another fishing village with a smaller fortified tower. The region east of Celimar is known as **Playas del Este**, which is a bedroom suburb inland and a resort area along the beaches. The beachfront avenues of **Mégano, Santa Maria del Mar, Boca Ciega** and **Guanabo** are lined with relatively inexpensive tourist resorts, villas that you can rent by the day or week, cafeterias, pioneer palaces and discos. *Habaneros* flock to these blue waters and wide beaches during the hot months of July and August; on weekends, they are jammed. Tourists will have no problems making friends.

Marina Tarará, inside the Tarará complex, offers boat rentals for fishing, diving and cruising, and has a restaurant. If you prefer to beat the crowds, a private beach is situated on the ocean side of the marina, at the mouth of the Tarará River. Across from the entrance to Tarará there is a restaurant complex called **Taramar** that includes seafood and Chinese restaurants, a cafeteria and a discotheque. At Mégano Beach there is a carting track where young and old can rent and race go-carts.

Returning now to the east side of Havana Bay, immediately south of La Cabaña you come to the towns of **Casablanca** and **Regla**. If you do not have a car, the easiest way to reach them is by ferry from Old Havana; the ferries (20 centavos one way) leave regularly from docks just east of the Castillo de la Real Fuerza and at the east end of Calle Santa Clara just south of the Customs piers. Casablanca's main attractions are colorfully painted houses and, on top of the hill, a huge concrete Christ and an observatory. The train station here is the beginning of the electric train, a glorified trolley, that runs all the way to Matanzas. Tickets for this extremely picturesque three-hour ride with dozens of stops must be bought a day or two in advance.

Regla, at the southeast end of the harbor amid industrial zones, is a gritty working-class town with one-storey colonial-style houses. Two attractions make a visit worthwhile for visitors. Just opposite the ferry terminal stands the **Iglesia de Nuestra Señora de Regla**. This simple, single-vaulted 1810 church houses the Virgin of Regla, the only black Virgin in Cuba. This image, dressed in a blue-and-white robe, came from Spain, and is adored not only as a Catholic icon but as Yemaya, the Santeria goddess of the seas and the patroness of sailors. September 7 is her day, when she is paraded through the town; big masses are also held on the Seventh of each month. The church also has a good small museum, which you can enter with the permission of the priest. Two blocks inland on Calle Martí between Calles Facciolo and La Piedra stands Regla's **Municipal Museum**, with exhibits on the town's history and, more interestingly, the cult of the Virgin of Regla.

From Regla, you can take buses a few kilometres east to the more picturesque town of **Guanabacoa**. The tourist attraction here is the **Museo Historico de Guanabacoa**, housed in a colonial mansion, with good archaeological and decorative arts collections and the best exhibit in Cuba on Afro-Cuban religions. On display are holy objects from the three main Afro-Cuban belief systems, Santeria, Regla de Palo and Abakua. The high-point is the **Munanso room**, which houses the ritual tools of one of Cuba's most famous *babalawos* (Afro-Cuban priests). Performances of Afro-Cuban dances and rituals are frequently held in the museum and in the nearby Casa de Cultura.

Due south of Guanabacoa, on a hilltop in the town of San Francisco de Paula (part of the San Miguel del Padrén district), stands the **Museo Hemingway**, also known as the **Finca La Vigía**. This was Hemingway's Cuba home from the early 1940s until he was forced to give it up after the triumph of the Revolution. Since then this luxurious white country house, with a swimming pool, tower and guest house, has been kept as a time capsule, preserving all of his books, papers, personal effects and furniture. His famous boat, *Pilar,* sits outside. You can only tour the grounds and peek in the windows.

The Old Man And The Sea

He could not see the green of the shore now but only the tops of the blue hills that showed white as though they were snow-capped and the clouds that looked like high snow mountains above them. The sea was very dark and the light made prisms in the water. The myriad flecks of the plankton were annulled now by the high sun and it was only the great deep prisms in the blue water that the old man saw now with his lines going straight down into the water that was a mile deep.

The tuna, the fishermen called all the fish of that species tuna and only distinguished among them by their proper names when they came to sell them or to trade them for baits, were down again. The sun was hot now and the old man felt it on the back of his neck and felt the sweat trickle down his back as he rowed.

I could just drift, he thought, and sleep and put a bight of line around my toe to wake me. But today is eighty-five days and I should fish the day well.

Just then, watching his lines, he saw one of the projecting green sticks dip sharply.

'Yes,' he said. 'Yes,' and shipped his oars without bumping the boat. He reached out for the line and held it softly between the thumb and forefinger of his right hand. He felt no strain nor weight and he held the line lightly. Then it came again. This time it was a tentative pull, not solid nor heavy, and he knew exactly what it was. One hundred fathoms down a marlin was eating the sardines that covered the point and the shank of the hook where the hand-forged hook projected from the head of the small tuna.

The old man held the line delicately, and softly, with his left hand, unleashed it from the stick. Now he could let it run through his fingers without the fish feeling any tension.

This far out, he must be huge in this month, he thought. Eat them, fish. Eat them. Please eat them. How fresh they are and you down there six hundred feet in that cold water in the dark. Make another turn in the dark and come back and eat them.

He waited with the line between his thumb and his finger, watching it and the other lines at the same time for the fish might have swum up or down. Then came the same delicate pulling touch again.

'He'll take it,' the old man said aloud. 'God help him to take it.'

He did not take it though. He was gone and the old man felt nothing.

'He can't have gone,' he said. 'Christ knows he can't have gone. He's making a turn. Maybe he has been hooked before and he remembers something of it.'

Then he felt the gentle touch on the line and he was happy.

'It was only his turn,' he said. 'He'll take it.'

He was happy feeling the gentle pulling and then he felt something hard and unbelievably heavy. It was the weight of the fish and he let the line slip down, down, down, untrolling off the first of the two reserve coils. As it went down, slipping lightly through

continues

Hemingway monument and La Chorrera fort, Cojímar

the old man's fingers, he still could feel the great weight, though the pressure of his thumb and finger were almost imperceptible.

'What a fish,' he said. 'He has it sideways in his mouth now and he is moving off with it.'

Then he will turn and swallow it, he thought. He did not say that because he knew that if you said a good thing it might not happen. He knew what a huge fish this was and he thought of him moving away in the darkness with the tuna held crosswise in his mouth. At that moment he felt him stop moving but the weight was still there. Then the weight increased and he gave more line. He tightened the pressure of his thumb and finger for the moment and the weight increased and was going straight down.

'He's taken it,' he said. 'Now I'll let him eat it well.'

He let the line slip through his fingers while he reached down with his left hand and made fast the free end of the two reserve coils to the loop of the two reserve coils of the next line. Now he was ready. He had three fort-fathom coils of line in reserve now, as well as the coil he was using.

'Eating it a little more,' he said. 'Eat it well.'

Eat it so that the point of the hook goes into your heart and kills you, he thought. Come up easy and let me put the harpoon into you. All right. Are you ready? have you been long enough at table?

'Now!' he said aloud and struck hard with both hands, gained a yard of line and then struck again and again, swinging with each arm alternately on the cord with all the strength of his arms and the pivoted weight of his body.

Nothing happened. The fish just moved away slowly and the old man could not raise him an inch. His line was strong and made for heavy fish and he held it against his back until it was so taut that beads of water were jumping from it. Then it began to make a slow hissing sound in the water and he still held it, bracing himself against the thwart and leaning back against the pull. The boat began to move slowly off towards the north-west.

—*The Old Man And The Sea*,
by Ernest Hemingway

The West

■ INTRODUCTION

FROM THE BREATHTAKING BEAUTY OF THE VALLE DE VIÑALES to Varadero's white sands, western Cuba offers a broad variety of attractions, many offering a fine day-trip from Havana. In Pinar del Río Province at the western tip of Cuba, you find a living Chinese brush painting: jungle-covered summits dropping down limestone cliffs to verdant valleys. This is the Valle de Viñales, Cuba's most famous landscape, featuring an array of unique flora and fauna, tobacco farms and charming colonial towns. A few kilometres south, Pinar del Río City is a typical provincial capital, with a number of low-key sights and a pleasant atmosphere.

Varadero has been Cuba's principal resort for more than a century. Located in Matanzas Province two hours from Havana by car, this assemblage of glittering hotels and graceful villas is built on a narrow peninsula lined with 20 kilometres (12.5 miles) of fine white sand. Cuba is at a distance here; the atmosphere is international, with glitzy nightclubs, restaurants and a growing number of foreign retailers, including Benetton. Due south on the opposite coast of Matanzas Province, you come to Playa Girón, Varadero's polar opposite and the scene of the 1961 Bay of Pigs invasion. Here you can relive history at the small museum or enjoy a quiet beach resort on the brilliant blue bay (excellent diving). The surrounding ecosystem is the Zapata Swamp, Cuba's most important bird refuge.

Fifty kilometres (30 miles) offshore, you find two islands with their own unique attractions. Although long isolated, the Island of Youth has a fascinating history: it was almost a colony of the United States in the first part of the century and, in the 1950s, Fidel Castro was incarcerated in the awe-inspiring Model Prison, now a museum. Today the great attraction is diving. From the Hotel Colony, Cuba's best-equipped dive resort, there are dive excursions to a number of stunning reefs off the south coast. About 100 kilometres (63 miles) to the east, Cayo Largo is a narrow island, little more than a few trees and lots and lots of sand, totally devoted to tourism. Over the last dozen years, six small but comfortable resort hotels have been built here. Cayo Largo's Playa Sirena, a broad expanse of white sand, is probably Cuba's best beach.

■ PINAR DEL RÍO PROVINCE

The province of Pinar del Río, which possesses Cuba's most dramatic landscapes, was long a forgotten backwater. Occupying the western-most end of the island, it was the last refuge of the Ciboney, the hunter-gatherers who were pushed here by the more advanced Taíno. The province's mountainous landscape is riddled with caves, some running for many kilometres, in which Ciboney burial and cave paintings have been found.

After the Conquest, Spanish colonists were slow in settling here. It was only with the development of the European tobacco market and, in the early 19th century, the perfection of the Havana cigar that Cubans realized that Pinar del Río guarded a treasure: soil and climate which produced the world's best tobacco. Today, farmers in Vuelta Abajo, the region south of Pinar del Río city, cultivate tobacco leaves that become filler and wrapper for cigars that cost a ransom in London and Paris. The province's tranquility was interrupted in 1896, when the rebel army of General Antonio Maceo fought Spanish forces in the bloody battle of Ceja del Negro here.

Pinar del Río is still largely agricultural; the main industry is the Matahambre copper mine. This is also the region of the classic *guajiro*, or Cuban peasant, a mustachioed man on horseback with a straw hat and a cigar between his teeth. For some reason, the province's tourist resorts feature some of the best food found in Cuba.

SOROA

The main road into Pinar del Río is the Autopista Nacional ('National Highway') that ends in the provincial capital. A few kilometres after the highway enters the province, take the exit marked 'Soroa' and follow the road six kilometres up into the mountains to the famous

Soroa Valley

Tobacco vs. Sugar

Tobacco is born, sugar is made. Tobacco is born pure, is processed pure and smoked pure. To secure saccharose, which is pure sugar, a long series of complicated physio-chemical operations are required merely to elimate impurities—bagasse, scum, sediment, and obstacles in the way of crystallization.

Tobacco is dark, ranging from black to mulatto; sugar is light, ranging from mulatto to white. Tobaco does not change its color; it is born dark and dies the color; it is born dark and dies the color of its race. Sugar changes its coloring; it is born brown and whitens itself; at first it is a syrupy mulatto and in this state pleases the common state; then it is bleached and refined until it can pass for white, travel all over the world, reach all mouths, and bring a better price, climbing to the top of social ladder.

"In the same box there are no two cigars alike; each on has a different taste," is a phrase frequent among discerning smokers, whereas all refined sugar tastes the same.

Sugar has no odor; the merit of tobacco lies in its smell and it offers a gamut of perfumes, from the exquisite aroma of the pure Havana cigar, which is intoxicating to the smell, to the reeking stogies of European manufacture, which prove to what levels human taste can stink.

One might even say that tobacco affords satisfaction to the touch and the sight. What smoker has not passed his hand caressingly over the rich *brevas* or *regalías* of a freshly opened box of Havanas? Do not cigar and cigarette act as a catharsis for nervous tension to the smoker who handles them and holds them delicately between lips and fingers? And what about chewing tobacco or snuff? Do they not titillate their users' tactile sense? And, for the sight, is not a cigar in the hands of a youth a symbol, a foretaste of manhood? And is not tobacco at times a mark of class in the ostentation of brand and shape? At times nothing less then a *corona corona*, a crowned crown. Poets who have been smokers have sung of the rapt ecstasy that comes over them as they follow with eyes and imagination that bluish smoke rising upward, as though from the ashes of the cigar, dying in the fire like a victim of the Inquisition, its spirit, purified and free, were ascending to heaven, leaving in the air hieroglyphic signs like ineffable promises of redemption.

Whereas sugar appeals to only one of the senses, that of taste, tobacco appeals not only to the palate, but to the smell, touch, and sight. Except for hearing, there is not one of the five senses that tobacco does stimulate or please.

Sugar is assimilated in its entirety; much of tobacco is lost in smoke. Sugar goes gluttonously down the gullet into the intestines, where is converted into muscle-strengthening vigor. Tobacco, like the rascal it is, goes from the mouth up the turnings and twistings of the cranium, following the trail of thought. *Ex fumo dare lucem.* Not for nothing was tobacco condemned as a snare of the devil, sinful, dangerous.

—*Cuban Counterpoint*, by Fernando Ortiz

Orchidarium. Just before the gardens, you come to a parking area for the **El Salto Cascades.** The waterfall is about half a kilometre down a concrete walkway with many steps. Morning is the best time to see the cascades, when the sunlight shines directly on the water falling 30 to 40 metres (100-130 feet) into a basin. Swimming is possible. The Soroa Orchidarium ($2) was founded in 1943 by a wealthy native of the Canary Islands; today it is maintained by the University of Pinar del Río. The hilly grounds contain over 800 species of plants, including 200 endemic to Cuba, all thriving in the humid climate. Orchids in flower are placed along the path, and you can also see a wide variety of other plants, including begonias, bromeliads and a number of tropical trees, such as the weird cannonball tree. The **Castillo de los Nubes** ('Castle in the Clouds') restaurant just above the orchidarium specializes in chicken. A short drive away stands the **Villa Soroa** resort hotel, a pleasant place to get away from it all boasting an excellent view of the Soroa Valley. A campsite near Soroa possesses an enormous Olympic swimming pool.   *continues on page 166*

Tobacco farmer and his fields

Guajiras (*Cuban peasant farmers*), *Valle de Viñales*

Cuban Cigars

Nothing surpasses the Havana cigar. It is one of the finest products of human civilization, a feast for taste, smell, touch and sight. The Cuban art of making the world's best cigars was developed in the early 18th century. Miraculously, it has not only survived wars, revolutions and natural disasters but been improved to near perfection.

The Indians of the New World long ago discovered the uses of the tobacco plant. Some smoked it for pleasure, but it was mainly used as medicine and as a religious sacrament. Indians rolled the first cigars, crude bunches of leaves twisted into a cylinder. It was more common to inhale the smoke through a forked cylinder or simply snort the powdered leaf.

The early European reaction to tobacco was decidedly ambivalent. When explorers returned home with the habit, many onlookers thought that the smoke was demons being conjured up in satanic rites. The Church banned the weed. On the other hand, European doctors, whose cure rate was abysmal, saw tobacco as a panacea, using it to treat everything from cancer to burns. It was only when the state realized that tobacco could be taxed that the plant gained widespread acceptance. In the first centuries after 1492, cigars were rare; smoking in pipes or inhaling as snuff was much more common.

In Cuba, tobacco was also controversial, but more for the economics of its production than for its use. From sowing to harvest, tobacco plants require constant care; it is far more productive to grow it on small farms with knowledgeable personnel than on large estates with slave labor. Consequently, Cuban peasants found that tobacco could make them a comfortable living, a feat that challenged the hegemony of the estate-owning aristocracy. In 1717, the state sought to control tobacco farmers by imposing restrictive taxes and trade regulations on their crop. The farmers fought back by beginning the first Cuban rebellion against Spanish authority and by moving to obscure corners of the island far from the Havana-based army.

This diaspora spread the cultivation of tobacco to four other regions in addition to Havana Province: Oriente, Las Villas and two zones in Pinar del Río Province, Semivuelta and Vuelta Abajo. In the last, they discovered sandy soils and a climate which produced the finest tobacco in the world. When the rich, finely flavored cigars from Vuelta Abajo began to enter the European trade routes, the Havana cigar began to make its worldwide reputation. By the early 19th century, European poets were penning odes in praise of the cigar, and Czar Nicholas I and Napoleon Bonaparte were devoted fans.

The basic steps of the cigar-making process have not changed much since the early 1800s, because the delicacy of the tobacco plant does not allow for much adaptability. The 80- to 90-day growing season begins in October or November when the tiny tobacco seeds are sown in seedbeds. After a few weeks, the seedlings are transferred to the fields and planted by hand—'as if they were a delicate maiden'— beginning the loving daily care which will bring the plant to its perfect state for harvest. Like wine grapes, tobacco is exceedingly sensitive to the climate; the perfect weather is warm days and cool nights with absolutely no rain. Nineteen ninety-two was a great year; 1993 was poor.

The farmers spend all day and many nights in the fields, clearing away weeds and removing by hand the many pests that feed on tobacco plants. Fields of tobacco destined to become cigar wrapper are covered with cheesecloth netting, called *tapado,* to protect them from too much sunlight. When the plant nears maturity, buds begin to appear; these must be plucked off by hand so that the plant will spend all its energy producing perfect leaves.

In February and March, the lower leaves begin to turn a light green, signalling that the harvest should begin. The farmers begin at the bottom of the plant and gradually work their way up in six stages as the upper leaves become ripe. The higher the leaves, the stronger the flavor. The leaves are then sorted as to color and degree of perfection and taken to the barn, called the *casa de tabaco.* There their stems are threaded together, and they are hung upside down for a drying process lasting 40-45 days.

After this stage, the tobacco leaves the farm for good. They are taken to grading shops to be sorted once again according to up to 50

continues

Cigar rolling

Rollers may smoke as many as they want

Montecristo no. 2's waiting to be packed

gradations of texture and color and then packed for fermentation and storage. The fermentation process is crucial to the quality of the final cigar. The bundled leaves are placed in piles—essentially compost heaps—where they sit and gently rot for 35-40 days. The fermentation mellows the flavor of the leaf and reduces the amount of tar and nicotine (which in Cuba is already low due to a quirk of soil and climate). Most good cigar tobaccos are doubly fermented, while the flagship Cohiba brand is fermented three times, lending a uniquely mild yet rich flavor to the cigars. After fermentation, the leaves are warehoused and may wait up to two years before being sent to the cigar factory.

Cigar factories dot Cuba from Pinar del Río City in the west to Baracoa in the east, but for export cigars all the best leaf goes to five factories in Havana: Romeo y Julieta, La Corona, H. Upmann, Partagas and El Laguito. Five kinds of leaves go into a good cigar; four for the filler and one for the wrapper, which not only holds it together but gives flavor and even burn. In the first step of the process, the dry

continues

leaves are separated and sprayed with a fine mist of water to add moisture and soften them. Next the vein running down the wrapper leaf is stripped with a jerk. The wrapper and filler leaves are once again sorted, the fillers are mixed according to the recipe of the cigar type and they are all sent into the rolling gallery.

This is a long hall with rows of tables and dozens of cigar rollers, both men and women, bent over their work. The entertainment is provided by a reader, called the *lector*, who reads the daily paper in the morning and in the afternoon turns to literature. On average, a roller makes about 90 cigars a day, depending on adeptness and the shape of the cigar (there are over 60 shapes, and some are more difficult than others). First the filler is rolled and placed in a press so it keeps its form. Then the wrapper is trimmed to one side straight and the other curved and rolled around the filler. All-natural vegetable glue and water hold it in place. After trimming the loose pieces of leaf, the cigar is ready to smoke. (Rollers can smoke as many as they want on the job.)

The process does not end here, however. The cigars go to quality control, where a percentage are measured for size and opened to check the blend. Next they are sorted by color and packed in a scale with the darkest on the left and the lightest on the right. In order to insure that the aesthetic experience of opening a box is perfect, the cigars are rotated so their best faces are pointing up. Finally, labels are wrapped around the cigars, and the boxes are sealed with all the necessary symbols to indicate that they are indeed real Havana cigars.

In addition to Cohiba, now considered the top brand, the main export labels are Montecristo, Partagas, H. Upmann, Hoyo de Monterrey, Punch, Ramon Allones, Bolivar and Romeo y Julieta. Not every cigar of a brand tastes the same, because the recipes for each shape are different. Experiment and find your favorite. Cigar fanciers generally prefer the fuller-flavored large sizes, such as the *corona* or the short but stout *robusto*. The *piramide,* which tapers to a point, and its smaller cousin the *torpedo,* are currently in vogue. The hotter-burning small cigars—*panetelas* and the like—are usually damned with faint praise such as 'perfect for a morning smoke'.

Cigars are sold everywhere in Cuba, from the fanciest tourist hotels to the back alleys of Old Havana. Unfortunately, the quality is not always consistent. The stock of some hotels and tourist shops is antiquated or poorly stored. Most hotels have a cigar roller demonstrating his trade in the lobby; their products—cigars the size of a small baseball bat, etc.—have more novelty value than quality.

Nearly every tourist will encounter touts trying to sell black-market 'Cohibas' and other brands at drastic discounts (usually $25-35 a box). These are almost always phonies, made from fourth-rate tobacco tasting like barnyard sweepings. You can usually tell that the cigars are bad, because they are sloppily rolled and irregularly sized, and the box lacks the official marks on the bottom. These include the stamps saying 'Cubatabaco', 'Hecho en Cuba' and 'Totalmente a Mano' as well as the code indicating the factory of manufacture (EL for El Laguito, for example). Black-market cigars may have been stolen from factories but more likely were rolled at home or in small workshops. Your best bet is to buy at a cigar specialty shop, such as the one in the Partagas factory (which you can also tour) near the Capitolio or the Casa del Tabaco at Calle 16 and Quinta Avenida in Miramar.

If you are bringing a quantity of good cigars back to a cold and dry climate, you should protect your investment by buying a humidor to keep them moist. In Cuba you do not need one, because the tropical island is one giant humidor. Good humidors should be lined with cedar and keep the cigars at a constant humidity of about 71 per cent. You can tell if a cigar is properly moist if the end you light has a bit of give when you squeeze it.

Once you own a real Havana cigar, how do you smoke it? A fine cigar should be enjoyed at repose, classically accompanied by strong, sweet Cuban coffee or a glass of good rum. Using a sharp knife or a cigar cutter, snip off enough of the rounded end of the cigar to give a good draw. You can remove the label or leave it on if you want to impress your friends. Light the cigar with a wooden match or gas lighter (wax matches or fluid lighters impart an unpleasant taste), ensuring that the end is evenly burning. Savor. A cigar should be enjoyed not just for taste but for smell, touch and the sight of white clouds curling slowly heavenward.

Bloom, Soroa

PINAR DEL RÍO

This city (pop. 125,000) is a typical provincial capital, with enough sights to make a visit worthwhile. It was named for the pine trees that lined the river on the city's founding in 1774. Just west of town you can see the first tin-roofed *casas de tabaco,* the drying sheds for the harvested leaf. The Autopista becomes Calle Martí, the city's main street. At the entrance to town stands the Soviet-style **Hotel Pinar del Río** (1979), whose grounds are adorned with a jaw-dropping sculpture in memory of two brothers killed by the Batista regime.

Two blocks ahead on the left, you come to the eccentric one-storey mansion (1914) housing the **Natural History Museum** ($1). The aesthetic principle behind this construction, built by a Spanish doctor, is 'The Harmony of Disorder': Gothic spires jut from the roof, sea horses and gryphons line the facade, and Egyptian motifs adorn the corner columns. The interior houses displays on the present and past natural history of the province. Rooms hold collections of shells, birds, fish and mammals, but the real attraction is the courtyard, which is filled with two concrete dinosaurs and a concrete megalon, an enormous extinct rodent endemic to Cuba. Here you can also see an example of the rare cork palm, a scraggly palm with a fuzzy trunk said to have originated during the Jurassic era.

Continuing west on Martí a block and a half, you pass the **Provincial Museum** and, across Calle Colón, come to the **José Jacinto Milanés Theatre** (try to see the beautiful late 19th-century interior) and the **Historical Museum**. The latter contains archaeological and historical collections as well as personal effects and musical scores belonging to Enrique Jorrín, a Pinareño (Pinar del Río native) who invented the cha-cha-cha.

At Calle Rubio take a left and head three blocks to the **Casa Garay** liquor factory. Here they make *guayabita,* an alcoholic beverage made from wild guava unique to the province. You can tour the plant and in their tasting room sample the dry and sweet versions of this slightly spicy liqueur. Returning to Martí, just west of Calle Rubio, stands the Hotel Globo (1917), a cheaper and more charming choice for lodging than the Pinar del Río.

Orchids, Soroa

Three blocks farther west, a right on Calle Morales and the first left will take you to the 1853 **Tobacco Factory** ($2), housed in an ex-jail. Here you can watch the cigar-making process, including rolling, leaf sorting and label gluing, as the workers make six brands for national consumption. A small shop sells local brands as well as smoother export cigars. A half block north of the factory opens the **Parque Independencia.** The African-motif **Restaurant Rumayor** on the northern outskirts of town is the city's best, specializing in smoked chicken.

VALLE DE VIÑALES

A two-lane road heads 27 kilometres (17 miles) north from Pinar del Río to the Valle de Viñales, an area of striking terrain that resembles a Chinese brush painting. Two mountain ranges, the Sierra de los Organos and the Sierra del Rosario, meet here in a line of sugarloaf-shaped hills, called *mogotes,* with clifflike sides and green, vegetation-topped summits. These fossil-filled geological formations are the oldest in Cuba, dating back to the Jurassic era (150 million years ago). Mainly limestone karst formations, they were shaped when underground water currents cut through the soft rock, forming caves and cliffs.

The hills teem with unique plant and animal life; this is the home of the archaic cork palm and the pygmy boa constrictor that lives in the cliffs. Caves riddle the area; the Santo Tomás and Los Portales caverns run many kilometres and contain underground ponds and rivers that are home to blind cave fish (speleology tours can be organized). Below, the boxlike flat valleys, called *hoyos,* are filled with rich reddish soil on which *campesinos* grow tobacco used for cigarette and national (as opposed to export) cigar manufacture.

The beautiful town of Viñales, now a national monument, is the main settlement in the area. Rows of pine trees shade the main street, which is lined with one-storey, red-tile-roofed buildings with columned porches mainly built between 1875 and 1910. Viñales' oldest house, the 1822 **Casa de Don Tomás**, has been recently converted into a charming restaurant and bar that specializes in a drink made from sugarcane. A block east, the main square is lined with a simple 19th-century church and the Casa de Cultura, and a statue of José Martí stands in the centre.

Viñales's two hotels lie in the hills overlooking the town from the south. The nearest is **La Ermita**, with 64 rooms built vaguely in the style of the town. The recently renovated **Las Jazmines** also has a tourist overlook with a gift shop and snack bar. Both hotels have stunning views of the valley and the hills beyond. Aside from the paved road, dirt paths lead from the hotels through pastures and tobacco fields into town. The walk is worth it: the adventurous will see the relatively prosperous life of the Cuban *campesino* and, in season (January through April), smell the distinctive aroma of tobacco leaves. During the off-season they grow corn and beans.

Follow the road west of town and then take a right turn five kilometres (three miles) to the Valle de Dos Hermanas ('Two Sisters Valley') and the Mural of Prehistory, a gigantic artwork on a cliff designed by

Leovigilda González, a student of the Mexican muralist Diego Rivera. Begun in 1959, finished in 1966 and now being repainted, the mural depicts the course of evolution, from snail to dinosaur to megalon to *Homo sapiens*. If you approach the mural, you see that the painting is actually made of thin, horizontal lines of black between which the color is added. The artist directed the painting with a megaphone, while *campesinos* suspended from the clifftop by ropes followed her instructions. Although the work is aesthetically of dubious value, it certainly is impressive, and the narrow valley that is its setting possesses enough beauty to compensate. For some, the real attraction may be the restaurant at the foot of the cliff. Featuring a 'typical Cuban lunch', the restaurant serves delicious roast pork, as well as the usual rice, beans and *yuca* to huge tour groups. Entertainment is provided by a unique, wooden, hand-cranked player organ that adds a circus aura.

North of Viñales town a road winds between the hills to the coast. After a few kilometres, on the left you see the **Las Cuevas cabaret**, a bar and disco built in a dripping cave; it is open in the evening provided there is electricity. Of more interest is the **Cueva del Indio**, a few kilometres ahead on the right. It takes its name from the Indian bones that were found here. 1600 meters in length, the cave runs to an underground river (watch the slippery walkway), where you take a small boat on a five-minute trip to its exit from the hillside. The **Cueva del Indio** restaurant here features excellent charcoal-grilled chicken and ajiaco, a meat and vegetable stew.

Continuing north, in the heart of the hills stands **Rancho San Vicente**, a spa-hotel catering mainly to Cubans, with a pool fed by thermal springs and individual sulfur baths. You emerge from the looming line of hills into an area of rolling hills covered with palm trees. From here you can head west to Cayo Levisa (near the town of Santa Lucia), a small resort specializing in diving and watersports located on an island 1.2 kilometres (.7 miles) off the coast. In the opposite direction lies Havana, along a two-lane road that runs between interminable sugarcane fields.

WEST OF PINAR DEL RÍO

About 25 kilometres (16 miles) west of Pinar del Río, the road passes through the famous tobacco-growing area of Vuelta Abajo, centered around the towns of San Juan and San Luis. During the winter and early spring growing season, the tobacco plants are protected from direct sunlight by fabric shades suspended from poles covering many square hectares. After harvest, the tobacco is dried in the barns before being shipped to the factories in Havana to be made into world-famous cigars. The road ends at the **Guanahacabibes Peninsula**, the spit of land that is Cuba's westernmost point. Largely flat and covered with forest, the peninsula is now Cuba's largest national park and a UNESCO Biosphere Reserve. The forest, filled with endemic plant and animal species, is also an important way station for migrating birds. The southern side of the peninsula wraps around the **Bahía de Corrientes**, along which stretches an excellent beach. The **Villa Maria la Gorda** diving resort here runs divers out to prodigious coral reefs and shipwrecks offshore. According to legend, Maria la Gorda ('Mary the Fat') was a Venezuelan woman captured by pirates whoj abandoned here after a shipwreck. Destitute, she turned to selling fresh water, and her large body, to passing sailors and enjoyed a long and comfortable life.

■ ISLA DE JUVENTUD

Fifty kilometres (30 miles) south of the mainland, the Archipelago of the Canaries is an island group surrounded by the blue Caribbean. The largest of these is Isla de Juventud ('Island of Youth,' and once the Isle of Pines), which is not a province but a special municipality. The easiest way to reach it is by air from Havana; the main carrier is Cubana. There are also daily ferries that leave from near the town of Batabanó due south of Havana; the hydrofoil takes a little over two hours, while the car and truck ferry takes seven. For both planes and ferries you should book in advance. Roughly circular and at its widest point 58 kilometres across, Isla de Juventud is mostly flat, except for some hills in the central portion, and covered with forests, scrub and

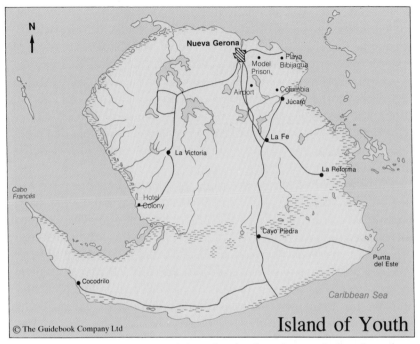

N

Nueva Gerona

Model
Prison

Playa
Bibijagua

Airport

Columbia

Júcaro

La Fe

La Victoria

La Reforma

Cabo
Francés

Hotel
Colony

Cayo Piedra

Punta
del Este

Cocodrilo

Caribbean Sea

© The Guidebook Company Ltd

Island of Youth

farmlands. The south part of the island is largely uninhabited, with a broad swamp and lots of dry, scrubby forest.

Isla de Juventud's first inhabitants were the Ciboney, who left a series of elaborate cave paintings, the best in Cuba, in a cave in Punta del Este at the island's southeastern point. Columbus landed on the island during his second voyage—1994 is the 500th anniversary of his visit—but for the following century it was largely forgotten. The Spanish established a small fort at Nueva Gerona in order to counter the mainly English buccaneers in the area. Its earliest industry was a large cattle plantation. The pirates blithely used the island's south coast as a base from which to attack the Spanish Treasure Fleet and as a suitably empty spot to bury stolen treasure. Legend has it that this was the 'Treasure Island' in the Robert Louis Stevenson novel. Aside from the fort and a mango plantation to the south, the island was ignored, home to runaway slaves and smugglers.

In 1826, the Spanish finally decided to establish a colony here, called Reina Amalia, with its capital Nueva Gerona. For the next 70 years, the Isle of Pines, as it became known, was Cuba's equivalent of Siberia, where they could ship political prisoners and be sure they were not heard from again. José Martí was interned here while still in his teens. In the 1898 Treaty of Paris ending Spain's domination of Cuba, the status of Isle of Pines was left undefined. The 1902 Hay-Quesada Treaty between the United States and Cuba stated that it belonged to Cuba, but the U.S. Congress did not get around to ratifying it until 1925.

In the meantime, savvy real estate speculators bought up most of the island's north end and began marketing it as a 'Lost Paradise', mainly to gullible buyers in the American Midwest. They arrived here expecting to be able to reach out their windows and pluck fruit from the trees. What they found was that they would have to work on their little farms to survive. The vast majority left after a couple of years; those who stayed founded towns with names like McKinley and Westport and managed to eke out a comfortable if simple living farming grapefruit and oranges. English became the primary language, the dollar the currency and American customs the rule. Some Americans left after the ratification of the treaty in 1925, and a devastating hurricane the following year chased away many more.

In 1925, President Gerardo Machado completed his massive Model Prison here, and any further immigration was discouraged by its menacing presence. World War II brought an American base here, and following the war many rich Cubans, including Batista, bought up huge tracts of land to sell to Americans for vacation homes. At the same time, the Model Prison became home to Fidel Castro and the rest of the Moncada conspirators as they planned the next step of their rebellion. During the 1950s there were over ten flights daily bringing vacationers and retirees from Havana and Florida. The baseball star Ted Williams had a house on the river near Nueva Gerona from which he used to embark on fishing expeditions. The crown of the tourist colony was to be the Hotel Colony, which was almost finished in 1959 when the Revolution brought the tourist trade to an abrupt end. The last of the remaining handful of Americans died a few years ago, but you can still see American-style houses, their cemetery and the American School, now in ruins.

After the Revolution, the Isle of Pines remained a center of citrus cultivation, and thousands of Cubans came here for 'voluntary labor' on the plantations. In 1971, at the peak of Cuba's internationalist phase, the government built the first school for foreign students to come here and learn the Cuban way of doing things and also work on the citrus plantations. They built over 60 schools, naming them for Cuban and internationalist heroes (such as Peruvian Indian rebel Tupac Amaru), dead cosmonauts and important dates. At their peak, 18,000 students studied here, the majority from Africa but also many from Latin America (Nicaragua) and Asia (North Korea). To celebrate this new role for the island, in 1978 it was renamed the Island of Youth. Since the onset of the Special Period, the international schools have fallen on hard times. Only 8,000 students study here at this writing, and many of the schools appear to be abandoned.

NUEVA GERONA

Isla de Juventud's administrative center and largest town is Nueva Gerona (pop. 14,000). It is not particularly attractive, with lots of industry about and marble quarries in the nearby hills. The main body of town lies immediately west of the Río Las Casas. Nueva Gerona is laid out on a grid pattern; odd-numbered streets run north-south and the even east-west. The **ferry landing** lies between Calles 22 and 24. The enormous white boat beached just to the south is **El Pinero**, the ferry that carried Fidel and the other Moncada conspirators to freedom after their sentences were commuted by Batista.

Calle 39, four blocks inland, is Nueva Gerona's main street. Starting at Calle 16 at the north end of town, Calle 39 heading south possesses the **Cubana office** and the **Hotel La Cubana**, the best hotel in town (hard for foreigners to get in). The **La Cochinita Restaurant** stands at the corner of Calles 39 and 18. Continuing south five blocks, you pass the **Intur office** and various restaurants and snack bars before coming to the **Parque Guerrillero Heróico**, Nueva Gerona's rather

sterile main square. A left on Calle 32 a block south of the park will take you to the Coppelia ice cream parlor at the corner of Calle 37.

Heading east on Calle 32, in one block you come to the town's small **Municipal History Museum** (nine miles) followed a block later by the one and only bridge over the Río Las Casas. A right turn after the bridge will take you to the airport, about 15 kilometres south of town. The road due east of town heads to the Model Prison. A road running southwest of town runs to the Hotel Colony on the island's west coast. Along this road, just on the outskirts of Nueva Gerona, stands the **El Abra farm**, where the youthful José Martí lived after the owner convinced authorities to release the rebel into his custody. The house is now a museum, preserving some of Martí's personal effects. The crafts specialty of Nueva Gerona, for sale in local galleries, is colorful ceramic tiles with striking relief decorations. The closest foreign tourist hotel is the **Rancho El Tesoro**, on the banks of the river southeast of town.

MODEL PRISON

In 1931, Gerardo Machado decided to build a prison for all of Cuba's most dangerous criminals and political prisoners. This prison was to embody all the latest advances in prison theory and design, specifically the panopticon plan, in which the authorities could see and regulate every aspect of the prisoners' lives. The Model Prison was directly copied from the Joliet, Illinois, penitentiary, with its massive circular prison buildings. Fittingly, the Model Prison was built using prisoners as laborers. After the Revolution, it continued as a penitentiary until 1966; today it is largely abandoned except for a museum.

You enter the complex by the heroically columned administration building. The little houses on either side were officers' quarters. Behind the administration building you pass two rectangular buildings for short-term prisoners and then see the first of four enormous circular edifices that housed long-term inmates. The prison's maximum capacity was 8,000; it frequently held more.

Although the buildings are closed, you can look through the windows and see the layout: In the center stood a watchtower with slits so

Marble Quarry, Isla de Juventud

the guards could watch the prisoners while remaining invisible to their charges. The tiers of cells, which lined the circular walls, had no doors, so privacy was nil. To make matters worse, the outside windows had no glass, only bars—the winter winds froze inmates to the bone. The lower tiers were occupied by the trustees, the prisoners who imposed a brutal discipline on their fellow inmates and committed many murders which the administration at best ignored. The four circular buildings are grouped around the lower, circular dining hall, known as 'The Place of 3,000 Silences', because talking was forbidden. At the far end of the complex stands the hospital building, which is now a **museum**.

From October 1953 until May 1955, the Moncada conspirators, including Fidel and his brother Raúl, were held here in order to keep them from influencing the other prisoners. If you speak Spanish, a guide will narrate a detailed history of this incarceration, from the school which they set up to teach and learn Cuban history and politics to the many methods they used to smuggle Fidel's speeches to their supporters in Havana.

SOUTH OF NUEVA GERONA

A network of two-lane roads, some in very poor condition, connects the various settlements on the island. South of the Model Prison (near Júcaro, ask for directions), you can see the remains—a few chimneys and foundations—of the American town of **Columbia** and the now-swampy **American Cemetery**. Heading southwest of Nueva Gerona, a road runs by many international schools—and students waiting desperately for a ride—down to the **Hotel Colony** on the west coast. This is one of Cuba's premiere diving resorts (watch out for over-booking), with its own hyperbaric chamber and fully equipped dive shop. From here, boats head out to **Punta El Cayuelo**, the island's southwestern tip, whose offshore waters are lined with spectacular dive spots. Closer to the hotel, the beach is narrow and the bay too shallow for swimming except at the end of the pier. On the opposite coast of the island, the **Indian paintings** at Punta del Este are reachable by a road from Cayo Piedra. Many of the turns are unmarked; it is best to go there with a guide.

■ Cayo Largo

A long strip of sand and trees, Cayo Largo is the easternmost island of the Archipelago of the Canaries. Unless you have your own boat, it is only reachable by air, directly from Canada and Europe via charters or with Aerocaribbean from Havana, Varadero, Isla de Juventud, Cienfuegos and Santiago. The majority of visitors are European tourists. Until 15 years ago, this flat, 27-kilometre-long (17-mile) island was uninhabited, populated only by a variety of bird life. Since then, it has slowly been developed as a tourist resort, taking care not to build too much, too fast. They have carefully preserved the finest beach in Cuba, Playa Sirena, and you can take excursions to islands populated by iguanas and flocks of migrating birds.

Cayo Largo is a free port, with full customs facilities and duty-free shops in the hotels. It is also one of the least Cuban places in Cuba: national tourists are not allowed to come, and Cuban workers lead heavily restricted lives here. According to the authorities, the island is crime-free. Cuban ecologists say that to avoid destroying the balance of nature on Cayo Largo the maximum hotel development is 3,000 rooms. Visit soon, before they approach that number.

No matter how early in the morning, on arrival you are greeted by a salsa band at the airport (the terminal doubles as the Blue Lake Disco at night). A new terminal was recently built to accommodate greater traffic. If you are staying the night, buses or minivans take you to one of six hotels on the island, all east of the airport. Bring mosquito repellent, because during the rainy season, the insects can be a plague. The hotels are overly fond of fumigating. The oldest and one of the most comfortable is the **Hotel Isla de Sur**, built in 1982 and renovated in 1992. The rooms at the **Villa Capricho**, the last hotel to the east, are rustic, thatched cabins. All the hotels feature modern conveniences like air conditioning, cable TV and satellite telephones.

Activities center on the water, including sailing, fishing and diving to the coral reef offshore. The island is ringed by 25 kilometres of beach, including the 7.5-kilometre-long **Playa Blanca** east of the **Villa Capricho** and **Playa Lindamar** in front of the new **Hotel Pelicano** to the west. **Playa Tortuga** at the east end of the island is a nursery for sea turtles.

Regular open-air buses (free) pick up tourists at the hotels and drive them eight kilometres to **Isla del Sol**, the Cuban workers' village, where there are a handful of shops and two restaurants. The **Casa de los Orishas** sells souvenirs of Santería, the Afro-Cuban religion. From the pier here—equipped with a bar and restaurant to make the wait easier—a ferry leaves (departures 8:30 am, 10:30 am and 2:30 pm) for **Playa Sirena**, a peninsula of white sand that juts out from Cayo Largo. This is the destination of the many day-trips from Havana and Varadero that come here. There is no finer beach in Cuba; locals claim that the sand's unique crystalline structure keeps it from getting too hot in the sun. Near the ferry dock are a bar and restaurant under a thatched roof and changing rooms. Topless sunbathing is allowed, although it is against Cuban law. The ferry returns to Isla del Sol at 1:30 pm, 3 pm and 5 pm. You can also take excursions to islands west of Cayo Largo. These include **Cayo Rico**, a perfect little island that just happens to possess a lobster restaurant; **Cayo Iguana**, which is appropriately crawling with the nearly tame lizards; and **Cayo Cantiles**, home to a population of monkeys.

■ MATANZAS PROVINCE

The province of Matanzas, which means 'slaughter', lies immediately east of Havana Province. Before the arrival of the Spanish, the coastal regions were settled by the Taíno Indians, and there is evidence of human habitation as early as 3,000 years ago. The province takes its name from the city of Matanzas on the north coast. There are at least three legends to explain the city's naming; the most proximate concerns a perhaps mythic incident on Matanzas Bay in which 32 Spaniards escaping from a shipwreck were attacked by Indians from the nearby village of Yucayo. Only four survived; the only woman became a wife of the chieftain. After the destruction of the Indians, the Spanish renamed the settlement Matanzas, and eventually that name was given to the province as a whole.

Since the earliest days of the colony, Matanzas has always been in the shadow of Havana. In the 16th century cattle were the principal industry, followed by tobacco in the 17th century and sugar after the 1762 English invasion. Recognizing the value of the Bay of Matanzas, which is Cuba's deepest port, in 1693 the Spanish Crown refounded the settlement of Matanzas as a city and administrative centre. In the 19th century it was home to many renowned artists and intellectuals and became known as the 'Athens of Cuba'. The surrounding country-side was an important center of sugar production, worked by thousands of African slaves. In 1825 and 1843, the slaves revolted and attacked the plantation owners. Spanish authorities decided that the latter revolt was the product of a conspiracy and, in order to eradicate it, they tortured and killed upward of a thousand blacks in a particularly brutal manner. Banned from openly worshiping their gods, Matanzas's slaves were adept at developing Christian disguises for their native beliefs. Ever since, Matanzas and other provincial cities have been known as centres of Afro-Cuban religion.

In 1850, a group of rebels raised Cuba's national flag for the first time in the city of Cárdenas. The province was racked by the Wars of Independence in the second half of the 19th century; an American general touring the area in 1898 saw nothing but ruin and starvation. In the 1920s, a number of American millionaires, led by the Du Ponts, discovered the Hicacos Peninsula just east of Matanzas city. They built palatial vacation homes there and renamed it after its beach, Playa Varadero. As tourism gradually became more important, the value of sugar to the province declined. Today the city of Matanzas is slightly run-down, while Varadero is a boomtown, the most important resort area in Cuba and a major generator of foreign currency.

In April 1961, a beach called Playa Girón on Matanzas's forgotten south coast was the scene of one of the most notorious events in Cuban history. A force of anti-Castro Cuban exiles backed by the United States landed here determined to force the downfall of the Revolutionary regime. The invasion was overly optimistic, poorly planned and lacked the total support of President Kennedy. When the U.S. government saw that the Cuban resistance was far fiercer than expected, the U.S. Navy ships backed off, allowing the capture of the exiles. The repercussions from this event still continue today.

MATANZAS

Matanzas, now semi-industrialized, is not the most alluring city in Cuba. However, there are enough sights to fill a few leisurely hours. For those staying in Varadero, it might be a welcome glimpse of the real Cuba. The principal approach to Matanzas is via the Vía Blanca, the four-lane highway from East Havana. Shortly before entering Matanzas Province you come to the **Bacunayagua Bridge**, the tallest in Cuba. It is worth stopping at the mirador to enjoy the spectacular view of the mouth of the river to the North and the **Valle de Yumurí** to the South. The highway then drops down to Matanzas Bay and enters the city from the west. Matanzas is located at the confluence of two rivers, the San Juan and the Yumurí; between them lies the city center. The terminal of the Hershey railway lies three blocks northeast of the Río Yumurí bridge.

Two street-naming systems confuse the traveler in Matanzas; we will use the old street names, which are still in use, rather than the new and overly complicated numbered streets system. After crossing

Sunset ride

the first bridge, spanning the Río Yumurí, in two blocks you see on the left the 19th-century **Palacio Junco**, containing the **Museum of History** and a locally popular mummy. The imposing, 1863 edifice that occupies the following block is the **Teatro Sauto**, a fine old theatre restored in the 1960s that has seen performances by legends such as Sarah Bernhardt. Next door stands the handsome **fire station**. If you head east of the theatre on Calle Milanés, in two blocks you come to the **cathedral**, a 1693 structure that was expanded in the late 19th century. A block and a half east opens the **Parque Libertad**, the center of town, surrounded by the city hall, the Casa de Cultura and a number of old hotels. Just east of the charming **Hotel Louvre** on the park's south side stands the 1882 **French Pharmacy**, now a museum. The **Bellamar Caves**, the largest open to the nonspeleologist public in Cuba, lie eight kilometres (five miles) south of Matanzas. To reach them, take a right on the Varadero road opposite the city beach on the south side of the bay. The caves were discovered in 1861 and are filled with dramatic formations given appropriately tacky names.

Blonde sands

VARADERO

Varadero is the Cancún of Cuba. It is built on a glorified sandbar called the Hicacos Peninsula jutting out into the sea between the cities of Matanzas and Cárdenas. For 20 kilometres (12.5 miles) the white sands of Varadero Beach face the seas to the west; the peninsula's east side encloses Cárdenas Bay. The citizens of Cárdenas began to use Varadero as an escape from summer heat in the late 19th century, eventually building vacation hofmes. The boom began in the 1920s, when a scion of the Du Pont munitions and chemicals fortune built a 'cottage' here and sold neighboring land to fellow American millionaires. Cuba's elite followed, including the dictator Batista. During the tourism explosion of the 1950s, American investors built the casino-equipped International Hotel. After the Revolution, Varadero was just as popular, if more proletariat, opening its doors to Cuban tourists and sunseekers from Eastern Europe.

Today, the resort is in the midst of another boom, as the Cuban government seeks new sources of foreign currency. Luxury hotels are popping up along the peninsula and the future will certainly bring many more. It remains to be seen whether the government can control the development or whether it will turn into a tourism disaster on the magnitude of Cancún.

The Vía Blanca, now a toll road, approaches Varadero from the west, passing at the base of the peninsula the **international airport**. Shortly, on the left across the lagoon you see the southern arm of the peninsula, which is actually an island. Just after the Cárdenas turnoff, the highway passes the **Varadero Amphitheatre** (featuring a popular Cabaret Varadero) and then crosses a bridge into Varadero proper. From here you can exit to the right for downtown Varadero or head north on the **Autopista Sur**, the highway that runs up the east side of the peninsula all the way to the end. The exit ramp enters Varadero on Calle Ocho. Moored at the inlet on the left is the **Calle Ocho floating bar**, ironically with the same name as Miami's famous Cuban exile neighborhood. A right will take you onto **Avenida Primera**, Varadero's main street; the cross streets are numbered, beginning with Calle 1 in the south. To the left lie two villa hotels,

Kawama and **Punta Blanca,** and, at the southern end, the **Paradiso-Puntarenas Hotel Complex.**

The layout of downtown Varadero is simple. On the beach side of Avenida Primera stand the cheaper hotels and villas, catering to both Cubans and foreigners, as well as restaurants and shops. Aside from a few small rocky spots, the white-sand beach stretches uninterrupted along this side of the peninsula. The bay side of the avenue is lined with shops and services for the Cuban population, who live along the east side of the peninsula. A few of the older hotels, like the Bellamar and the Acuazul, also stand here.

Varadero's **Coppelia ice cream parlor** lies in the **Parque Central** between Calles 44 and 46. The **Hotel Quatro Palmas,** between Calles 60 and 62, is built on the grounds of Fulgencio Batista's summer house; the dictator's mansion now houses the game rooms on the beach. Just to the south across the avenue, the **Retiro Josone** is a picturesque mini-mall of small shops and restaurants built around a small lake. Opposite, at the beach end of Calle 57, stands the Municipal Museum, Varadero's least frivolous cultural attraction.

Avenida Primera ends at the **Hotel Varadero International,** built in the 1950s with a casino to amuse and lighten the pockets of American tourists. From here north lies the luxury hotel zone, reachable on Av Las Américas or the Autopista Sur. The new hotel complexes include the pyramid-like **Tuxpan,** the all-inclusive **Club Varadero,** the luxurious **Meliá Las Américas** (suites and golf resort) and **Meliá Varadero,** the **Sol Palmeras,** and the brand new **Arenas Doradas, Club Med** and **Gran Hotel.** The best shopping is found at plaza **Las Américas,** between Meliá Varadero and Sol Palmeras hotels, with brand-name stores, restaurants and a well-stocked supermarket. Most of this land was originally the Du Pont estate. The old Du Pont mansion, modestly called 'Xanadu', is now the **Restaurant Las Américas** perched on a low cliff by the **golf course** just south of the Meliá America. Inside it is all marble, dark wood and heavy curtains, not most people's idea of a beachfront house. The restaurant serves expensive continental food—steaks and seafood—but you can also prowl around the mansion without eating.

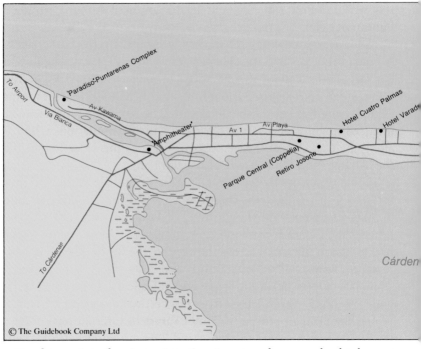

By this point, the Autopista Sur is a two-lane road which runs through undeveloped brush to the peninsula's northern end. Here you find the **Marina Gaviota** for sportfishing boats (the larger La Dórsena marina is at the south end of the island) and the **Frontier Guard** base, whose personnel are immortalized to the left of the road by a statue of a guard with his dog. You may also see in dry dock a few cigarette boats captured from drug smugglers.

If the beaches and nightlife begin to cloy, escape to the city of **Cárdenas**, 16 kilometres (10 miles) to the southeast. Here you can see the picturesque decrepitude that infects the rest of Cuba. Laid out on a grid plan, the city is filled with run-down colonial buildings and bicycles and horse carriages that have replaced cars. Aside from the atmosphere, the main sight is the **Oscar Maria de Rojas Museum** (Calzada #4), featuring an elegant 19th-century hearse and costumes for a pair of dancing fleas.

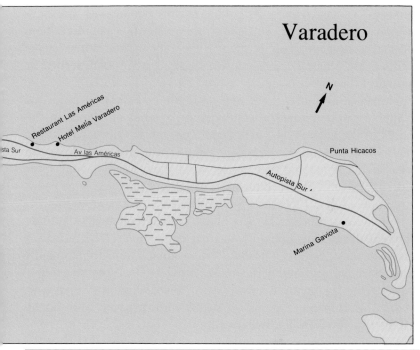

Varadero

N

Restaurant Las Américas

Hotel Melía Varadero

sta Sur

Av las Américas

Punta Hicacos

Autopista Sur

Marina Gaviota

GUAMÁ AND PLAYA GIRÓN

The sparsely populated south coast of Matanzas Province is covered with forest, swamp and a rich array of plant and animal life. The easiest way to enter this region is via the Playa Girón exit from the Autopista Nacional. Just inside the exit, air-conditioned buses stop at the **Fiesta Campesina**, a tourist trap with a restaurant, gift shop and small zoo. A few kilometres to the south stands the **Central Australia**, a large sugar refinery that was used as a headquarters by Fidel and the Revolutionary Armed Forces during the Bay of Pigs invasion. That victory is commemorated by a small museum in the refinery and by a series monuments along the road south in memory of soldiers killed in the battle.

Eighteen kilometres (11 miles) south of the highway stands the entrance to the mosquito-ridden **Laguna del Tesoro** (Treasure Lagoon). Here you find a tourist restaurant and gift shop and the **Crocodile**

Nursery, 20 huge circular pens holding over 40,000 reptiles. The crocodiles originally lived in the lagoon—they claim they captured them all—and were moved here to prepare them for their eventual fate as handbags and shoes. Feeding is twice weekly, but you can eat them at a grill near the nursery.

Behind the restaurant, the marina is the embarkation point for **Guamá**, a resort dramatically situated on a series of islands in the middle of the lagoon. The area greatly resembles Louisiana's bayou region. The ride takes you east a couple of kilometres along the Canal de la Laguna and then across the shallow, weedy lagoon itself to the islands of Guamá. Built from wood and thatched with palm, the complex (early 1960s) is supposedly a copy of a Taíno Indian village. Wooden sculptures by Rita Longa scattered about the grounds represent the Indians going about their daily chores. The reception area, restaurant, bar and 45 cabins (all needing renovation) are built on ten islands connected with wooden bridges. The espresso-colored waters of the lagoon are filled with bass, tilapia and other underwater life. Unfortunately, Guamá is plagued with voracious mosquitoes that distract you from the area's beauty.

Fourteen kilometres (nine miles) south of the Crocodile Nursery you come to **Playa Larga**, a beach and simple resort hotel on the beautiful **Bahía de Cochinos** ('Bay of Pigs'). The brilliantly blue water here is crystal clear and teeming with marine life. Playa Larga is also the entry point to the **Zapata Peninsula**, a vast swamp that is Cuba's most important bird sanctuary. Specialized bird-watching tours can be arranged. The limestone of the peninsula is punctured by numerous underwater caves that are refuge for crocodiles, manatees and an endemic species of alligator gar. Thirty-three kilometres (21 miles) east of Playa Larga on the eastern shore of the bay lies the famous **Playa Girón**. During the May and June rainy season, thousands of crabs cross this road in the early morning and evening, making driving messy, if not dangerous. To the left of the road, **El Cenote** is a limestone sinkhole filled with blue water in which you can dive or snorkel.

Playa Girón is the site of the April 17, 1961, invasion by 1,300 Cuban exile soldiers calling themselves Brigade 2506, trained and financed by the CIA. Within 24 hours they were surrounded by 20,000 Cuban troops personally led by Fidel, and by 5:30 pm on April 19 the vast majority of the exiles had been captured. The **Museo Girón** ($2) displays the remains of a Brigade 2506 aircraft and an intact Cuban fighter. Inside, the museum documents the day-by-day and hour-by-hour unfolding of the attack, called Plan Pluto, and its defeat. Here are photos and mementos of the 150 Revolutionary soldiers who died and documentation of the mass trial of the invaders. Before the Revolution, the Girón area's only occupants were dirt-poor charcoal-makers. Their resistance to the invasion earned them greatly improved living conditions and new schools and homes. The beach side of this little town is occupied by the **Villa Playa Girón**, 100 simple cabins mainly catering to Cuban tourists. The beaches here are excellent and there is good diving in the area.

Central Cuba

■ INTRODUCTION

MUCH OF CENTRAL CUBA IS FLY-OVER COUNTRY, bypassed by tourists as they travel between Havana and Santiago. However, there are enough interesting colonial cities, beautiful beaches and verdant mountain retreats to make a more leisurely visit worthwhile. And the colonial jewel of Trinidad is a must for every visitor to Cuba.

Cienfuegos and Santa Clara are two provincial capitals with a modicum of sights worth stopping for on the way somewhere else. Built on the north shore of Jagua Bay, Cienfuegos is a clean, 19th-century city possessing an attractive main plaza and a striking Moorish fantasy palace right on the water. To the south you find excellent beaches and three resort hotels. Santa Clara's attractions are colonial palaces flanking the central square and the massive Plaza de la Revolución monument to Che Guevara's 1958 victory here. In the lush green mountains nearby, Lake Hanabanilla has a resort hotel specializing in relaxation and bass fishing.

Trinidad, on the south coast of Sancti Spíritus Province, is one of the finest colonial cities in Latin America and a photographer's delight. Largely untouched since the mid-19th century, it possesses cobblestone streets, a citizenry mindful of its traditions and a wealth of fine architecture. Many of the old mansions have been converted into good museums. Most of the tourist hotels are down by the beach, Playa Ancón. The Escambray Mountains rising to the north of Trinidad are the site of Topes de Collantes, a mountain health resort that is rapidly becoming a magnet for visitors interested in wildlife and the ecosystem. A lush rain forest covers the hills and is home to an incredible variety of plant and animal species.

East of the Sierra de Escambray, the island of Cuba becomes flat and covered with vast sugar plantations and cattle ranches. Ciego de Avila Province has little to offer—except to sportsmen looking for prime bird shooting and fishing (both bass and saltwater) and those wanting to discover newly opened beaches. On the north coast, Cayo

Coco and Cayo Guillermo are now being developed as resort areas. Visit now, while the kilometres of beaches are still relatively virgin.

Camagüey, Cuba's largest province, is largely flat, agricultural and uninteresting. However, Camagüey City hides a trove of colonial riches: winding streets, centuries-old churches and gracious plazas. On the north coast, Santa Lucia Beach is home to five popular resort hotels.

■ CIENFUEGOS PROVINCE

The main sight in this largely agricultural province is the provincial capital, the city of Cienfuegos. It sits on the north shore of Jagua Bay, one of southern Cuba's finest harbors, which Columbus visited in 1494 on his second voyage to the island. During the colony's early years, this coast was a haunt of pirates and smugglers. In order to guard against pirate attacks, early in the 18th-century Jagua Castle was built at the mouth of the bay. In 1819, the city of Cienfuegos

Cathedral, Cienfuegos

was founded by emigrés from Florida, which Spain had ceded to the United States. Its first name was Fernandina de Jagua but it was quickly renamed Cienfuegos in honor of the captain-general governing Cuba at the time. Many of the early settlers were of French and Spanish descent, and the city quickly became a center of the sugar industry that flourished in the area. It was relatively untouched by the Wars of Independence, so many of the fine late colonial buildings are intact.

In 1957, a group of young navy officers and sailors allied with Fidel's 26th of July Movement rose up in arms and captured their base and a number of other military installations. With the help of American-supplied bombers, Batista's army struck back and squashed the rebellion after a day-long battle. Some of the captive rebels were summarily executed, while others were imprisoned until the end of the war.

Cuba's first nuclear power plant is now being built with Russian help on the Caribbean to the south of the city; due to the lack of funds and technical problems the work is progressing very slowly. Today Cienfuegos is relatively clean and prosperous and possesses enough sights for a half-day visit.

CIENFUEGOS CITY

From Havana, the main road to Cienfuegos City (1981 pop. 103,000) is the Autopista Nacional to the Cienfuegos-Trinidad exit, where there is a tourist restaurant on the north side of the highway, and then a two-lane road about 60 kilometres (38 miles) down to Cienfuegos. Shortly before the city limits, the road becomes a four-lane highway that enters the city via a hilltop zone of new residential skyscrapers. Cienfuegos's north-south streets are odd-numbered, while the east-west streets are even.

For the city centre, you turn south on Calle 37, better known as the Prado, which is the local Champs-Elysées. Numerous police usually cruise here looking for minor traffic offenders. The Prado is lined with colonnades below two- and three-storey shops and houses mainly built in the early part of this century. A left on Calle 54 will take you four blocks to the **Parque Martí**, Cienfuegos's main square, with a statue of the patriotic hero and a bandstand (concerts Sundays at 8 pm) in the centre. If you are on foot, you should try Calle 56, which between the park and the Prado is pedestrian-only and normally filled with people. The shops all have attractive windows but, except for the dollar stores, little to sell. The recently renovated **Hotel San Carlos** at the corner of the Prado and Calle 56 is the city's best peso hotel. The east side of the Parque Martí is occupied by the **Catedral de la Purísima Concepción** (1831-69), with a plain, yellow exterior and a single-vaulted nave. On sunny days the interior glows from light cast by stained-glass windows depicting the 12 Apostles.

The **Teatro Tomás Terry** (1889) dominates the north side of the park; the caretaker will show you around. This building, one of the finest theatres in Cuba at the time of its completion, was built by a wealthy *cienfueguero* in honor of his father (his statue sits in the lobby), who built his fortune on slaves and sugar. Caruso and many other famous performers appeared on its stage. Today, the theatre is desperately in need of renovation and new technical equipment. The lobby ceiling is adorned by lush, romantic murals; within, the three tiers of seats are held up by thin iron columns. From the roof, there is an excellent view of the city, the bay and, looming in the distance to the south, the smokestacks of the nuclear power plant under construction.

Cienfuegos has a two excellent museums: the **Museo Provincial** on the north side of the park (next to El Palatino Bar) with exhibits or pre-Hispanic archaeology, decorative arts and history of the city; and the **Museo Histórico Naval**, on the corner of Ave. 60 and Calle 21, dedicated to naval history.

At the southwest corner of the park stands the slightly fantastic mansion housing the **Casa de Cultura**. Originally the home of Don José Ferrer, another sugar millionaire, it boasts a tower adorned with blue tiles from which there is a fine view of the park. To the west of the park are many port facilities and a neighborhood that was once Cienfuegos's Chinatown.

The Prado continues south, passing the local Coppelia ice cream

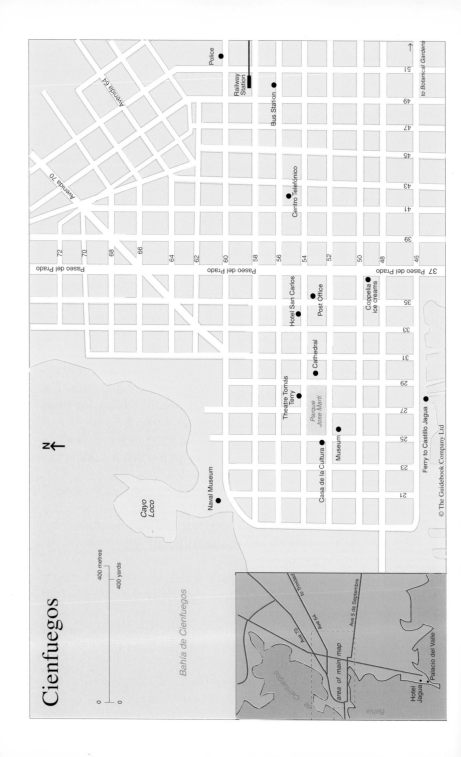

Cienfuegos

Bahía de Cienfuegos

Cayo Loco

400 metres
400 yards

N↑

Police

Railway Station

Bus Station

Avenida 64

Avenida 70

Centro Telefónico

Paseo del Prado

Paseo del Prado

Paseo del Prado

72
70
68
66
64
62
60
58
56
54
52
50
48
46

51
49
47
45
43
41
39

37

35
33
31
29
27
25
23
21

Hotel San Carlos

Post Office

Coppelia ice creams

Cathedral

Theatre Tomás Terry

Parque José Martí

Museum

Casa de la Cultura

Naval Museum

Ferry to Castillo Jagua

to Botanical Gardens

© The Guidebook Company Ltd

area of main map

Ave 70

Ave 64

to Trinidad

Ave 5 de Septiembre

Bahía de Cienfuegos

Hotel Jagua

Palacio del Valle

parlor at Calle 52, and two kilometres (1.25 miles) from the center reaches a terminus at a small peninsula jutting out into Jagua Bay. Here stands the **Hotel Jagua**, the city's main tourist hotel, catering mainly to bus tours. Immediately to the south is Cienfuegos's most interesting edifice, the Moorish-wedding-cake-style **Palacio del Valle**. Originally a country house on the shores of the bay, it was renovated in the Arab style between 1913 and 1917 for the Valle family. Today the palace is a tourist restaurant, but you can wander through it without eating, admiring the incredible mass of detailing and the view from the rooftop bar. The street immediately to the south is lined with charming summer homes built by the turn-of-the-century wealthy.

Fifteen kilometres (nine miles) east of town on the Trinidad road —take Calle 46 east—is the entrance to the **Botanical Gardens**. These were founded in 1901 by Harvard University and, although somewhat run-down today, still contain over 2,000 species, including cacti and every Cuban palm.

In order to reach the sights at the south of the bay, you must head east on Calle 46 and follow the signs to **Hotel Rancho Luna**. (There is also a ferry that departs thrice daily from the end of Calle 29 due south of the Parque Martí.) The resort is one of three at the east side to the bay entrance; all are on or near Playa Rancho Luna, the best beach in the area. The east side of the entrance is guarded by the **Castillo de Jagua**, a small, square fort built in 1745. A museum is in the works, but you can still clamber around the semi-ruins. The small village here is populated mainly by fishermen. The nuclear power plant is being built near Juraguá on the west side of the entrance.

■ VILLA CLARA PROVINCE

In a way, Villa Clara is the birthplace of Cuba. The provincial capital of Santa Clara occupies the site of Cubanacan, an Indian town whose first two syllables became the name of the entire country. Although no great ruins have been found here, Columbus believed that the island's Indian ruler—or was it the emperor of China?—governed from Cubanacan. In 1514, the Spanish settled at San Juan de los Remedios, near the coast. Cattle were the first industry, followed in the 17th century by tobacco and later by sugar. The region around Santa Clara is second only to Pinar del Río for high-quality tobacco.

In 1689, after years of pirate attacks, the provincial capital was moved inland from Remedios to Santa Clara. Like the rest of central Cuba, Villa Clara suffered greatly during the Wars of Independence. In Revolutionary Cuba, Santa Clara is best known as the site of a key victory against Batista's army.

After a short battle on December 28, 1958, forces under the command of Che Guevara captured an armored troop train that was trying to escape the city. Many of the captured soldiers asked to join the Revolutionary army. Over the next three days, fighting spread into the city, and by the evening of December 31 Batista's forces knew they had lost. When word filtered back to Havana, Batista realized that the end had come and he headed to an airfield where planes were waiting to take him into exile.

SANTA CLARA

Rolling cigars at home

Most travellers speed by Santa Clara City (1981 pop. 172,000) on their way to somewhere else. Just to the south and east begin the hills that eventually become the Sierra de Escambray. The city contains a few sights worth visiting, and is, a perfect example of a typical Cuban provincial city. Its major industry is the **INPUD Factory**, founded by

Street weaver

Che Guevara, which, the Special Period permitting, makes housewares and appliances for domestic consumption. In 1997, the remains of Che Guevara were unearthed and returned to Cuba, where they were interred in Santa Clara's Plaza de la Revolucíon.

Santa Clara's main square, around which most of the sights are found, is the **Parque Vidal**, named after a patriot who died here in 1898. The north side of the plaza is dominated by the **Teatro de la Caridad**, a gift of Doña Marta Abreu, a beloved local philanthropist whose statue graces the center of the plaza (facing the gazebo). Due east, at the northeast corner of the plaza, an old mansion now houses the **Museum of Decorative Arts**, containing a large collection of 18th- and 19th-century furnishings for the colonial upper classes. On the east side of the plaza stands the austere 1922 **Palacio Provincial**, behind two rows of Ionic columns. Across the plaza, the **Hotel Santa Clara Libre** is the best downtown hotel.

One block north of the plaza, Blvd Independencia runs a few blocks east, across the bridge to the Armored Train Monument.

These carriages were the goal of Che Guevara's 1958 attack and now house a museum commemorating the event. More on this subject may be seen at the Plaza de la Revolución southwest of the Plaza Vidal. The focus of this massive ceremonial space is an enormous sculpture of Che holding a machine gun to the right of a relief showing the Sierra Maestra mountains, from which the Revolutionary Army emerged, and the destroyed train. The podium supporting this sculpture houses the Museum of the Revolution and the remains of Che Guevara and other members of his Bolivian guerrilla group.

West of town in a parklike setting stands the Motel Los Caneyes, the main tourist hotel, with rooms in faux-Indian huts. East of Santa Clara, the Autopista Nacional eventually shrinks to three lanes and then disappears altogether as it merges with the two-lane Carretera Central.

LAKE HANABANILLA

A two-lane road heads due south of Santa Clara through the town of Manicaragua and over a rolling, lush landscape dotted with tobacco barns to Lake Hanabanilla, one of Cuba's most renowned bass fishing lakes. The lake is roughly equidistant—48 kilometres (30 miles)—from both Santa Clara and Cienfuegos. A hydroelectric dam blocks the lake's north end, behind which the waters stretch through many twists and turns 32 kilometres (20 miles) to the south end. The lake is framed by steep green hills that are home only to a few subsistence farmers, who use the lake's ferryboat to reach town. For tourists, a popular excursion is to Río Negro, a rustic restaurant a short boat ride away. Near the dam stands the 1975 Hotel Hanabanilla, a big Soviet-style hotel catering mainly to Cuban tourists and fishermen. The lake record largemouth bass weighed 22 pounds.

REMEDIOS

Forty-three kilometres (27 miles) east of Santa Clara, Remedios (pop. 17,000) is one of the best-preserved colonial towns in Cuba. Red-tile roofs and single-storey houses are the rule, and cars and trucks have never displaced horsecarts and bicycles on its narrow streets. Remedios's centre is the scenic Plaza Martí, around which all the main buildings rise. The 18th-century Iglesia de San Juan Bautista on the east side of the square has a rather plain facade that conceals a tremendous gold altarpiece inside. This was the gift of a rich parishioner who helped restore the church after a 1939 earthquake. On the north side of the square, the Caturla Music Museum houses the instruments and personal effects of the town's most famous musician, Alejandro García Caturla, a composer and iconoclast. Opposite stands the Hotel Mascotte, the town's only tourist hotel.

A few blocks away from the plaza, at Calle Máximo Gómez #71, you find the Museo de las Parrandas, dedicated to a unique local festival. Like Mardi Gras, the Parrandas are a celebration with music, parades and floats. For months prior to the day- and night-long festival, which takes place on the last Saturday of the year, two groups secretly construct their floats, which are then paraded through town accompanied by polka music (a local tradition). At nightfall the teams park their floats at opposite ends of the plaza and then attempt to outdo each other by opening cunningly constructed doors in the floats to shoot off fireworks and expose banners, figures and other surprises. The biggest surprise is kept for just before dawn. Unfortunately, the Parrandas have been cancelled during the Special Period. You can get an idea of the festival from the museum's exhibits of costumes and models of the floats.

Eight kilometres (five miles) east of Remedios you arrive at the port town of Caibarién on the Atlantic. Once again, the main square is called the Plaza Martí, notable for the parish church with its stark interior and ornate main altar. Caibarién is the embarkation point for Cayo Conuco, an island with a popular campground a kilometre or two offshore.

■ SANCTI SPÍRITUS PROVINCE

Occupying the geographical center of Cuba, Sancti Spíritus Province possesses some stunning landscapes in the Escambray Mountains and two of Cuba's oldest towns: the eponymous provincial capital and the

(following pages) Valle de los Ingenios

colonial jewel of Trinidad. In January of 1514, the conquistador Diego Velásquez founded Trinidad on the site of an Indian village named Guamuhaya and the following May founded the city of Sancti Spíritus. The latter quickly became the most important settlement in central Cuba. In 1518, Hernán Cortés landed his fleet at the harbor near Trinidad and offered vast rewards to any man who joined his expedition to conquer Mexico. Many accepted, drastically reducing the local population. During the 17th and early 18th centuries, both cities were repeatedly sacked by pirates, generally the English.

The San Luís Valley east of Trinidad was Cuba's most important center of sugarcane production during the 18th and early 19th centuries. Money poured into Trinidad, where the plantation owners, many of them of French ancestry, resided in palatial mansions. During the first half of the19th century, Trinidad's wealth and beauty attracted many visitors, beginning with the German explorer Alexander von Humboldt in 1804 and continuing almost uninterrupted to this day. Trinidad's decline into genteel poverty began with the economic crisis of the 1850s and was sped by the 1880s collapse of world sugar prices. Meanwhile, the more centrally located city of Sancti Spíritus flourished as an agricultural and trading center. Spanish and Cuban forces clashed frequently in this province during the Wars of Independence.

After 1900, Trinidad gradually became isolated from the Cuban economic mainstream; this was exacerbated by the construction of the Carretera Central on the other side of the mountains and the decline of maritime shipping. The 1959 Triumph of the Revolution drove many anti-Castro rebels, dubbed 'bandidos', to the Escambray Mountains, from which they harassed Revolutionary forces until they were finally eliminated in 1965. The Trinidad area was also one of the alternate landing areas proposed for the invasion that eventually arrived at the Bay of Pigs. In 1988, Trinidad joined Old Havana on UNESCO's list of treasures of world heritage.

SANCTI SPÍRITUS CITY

Few tourists stop in Sancti Spíritus (pop. 190,000); most bypass it on their way to or from Trinidad. If the Autopista Nacional is ever completed on its planned route to the north of the city, this exclusion will be made even more permanent. As it stands today, the Carretera Central runs straight through the city.

Although economics in the form of large paper and sugar mills have overwhelmed the colonial charm, there are a few sights to make a short visit worthwhile. The main square, and centre of the colonial district, is the Parque Central, on which you find the Hotel Perla del Sur, the best hotel in town. A block to the southeast of the square stands the Iglesia Mayor, considered Cuba's oldest church, although only the foundations date from its earliest incarnation. First constructed in 1522, it was completely rebuilt twice in the 17th century, and the tower and cupola were added in the 18th and 19th centuries, respectively.

From the church, Av Jesús Menéndez heads southwest two blocks to the Río Yayabo. If you take the first right, on Calle Placido, on the right at #64 you will see the Palacio Valle-Iznaga, built by sugar barons, which is now the Museo Colonial, with the usual display of period furniture. Av Menéndez crosses the river on the three medieval-looking arches of the Yayabo Bridge, built between 1817 and 1825. Sancti Spíritus's southeastern suburbs border on the Zaza Reservoir, home to many largemouth bass and the three-star Hotel Zaza. Another hotel, Rancho Hatuey, is located on the main highway out of town.

TRINIDAD

The distance of Trinidad (pop. 69,000) from the Central Highway has protected its charms from overdevelopment. It lies on the occasionally rough two-lane road that runs 73 kilometres (47 miles) from Cienfuegos to Trinidad and then 67 kilometres (42 miles) east to Sancti Spíritus. There is still sugarcane production in the nearby San Luís Valley, and a fishing cooperative down at the port, but the major industry by far is tourism. Despite the heavy tourist presence, there seems to be a dearth of certain necessities, like soap and matches, for which tourists are continuously importuned, particularly around the Parque Central.

The old, colonial section of narrow, cobblestone streets and brightly colored one-storey houses lies in the more elevated, north section of town, while the newer neighborhoods spread out to the south. Many of the streets in the old section are blocked from automobile traffic with old cannons jammed barrel-down in the middle of the cobblestone paving. According to legend, the gutters run down the centres of the streets because one of Trinidad's governors had a right leg shorter than the other, so he designed the streets so he would be level when strolling down the right-hand side.

The centre of the old town is the lovely, palm-tree-bedecked **Parque Martí**, guarded by bronze sculptures of greyhounds, around which Trinidad's main families, among them the Iznagas, Ortizes and Brunets, built their mansions. At the northeast corner stands the **Iglesia de la Santísima Trinidad** (1884-92), with a Gothic altar made from 18 different woods and 14 retables along the side walls. On the left side, the second chapel from the front contains El Cristo de Veracruz, a figure of Christ that was bound from Spain to Mexico on a boat that stopped in Trinidad's harbor. Three times the boat left to complete the final leg of the journey, and each time it was blown back to port by a huge storm. By then it became obvious that the icon was meant for Trinidad, where it has stayed ever since. Many of the church's statues came from the nearby Franciscan convent.

Immediately to the south stands the **Museo de Arquitectura Colonial**, exhibiting in a one-storey 1738 mansion the changing local architectural styles, with many pieces of detailing such as doors, ceilings and tiles. The patio is particularly pleasant. Just to the west of the church rises the two-storey Palacio Brunet, whose first floor was finished in 1740 and second, with its fine cedar ceiling, in 1808. Since 1974, it has been the **Museo Romántico de Artes Decorativas**, containing a large and good collection of furniture amassed by the Trinidadian wealthy—although not the Brunet family—notably a mother-of-pearl-encrusted bedframe. There is an excellent view of the square from the second floor balcony.

On the west side of the square you find the Museo de Arqueología, another mansion housing a collection of Indian artifacts—tools,

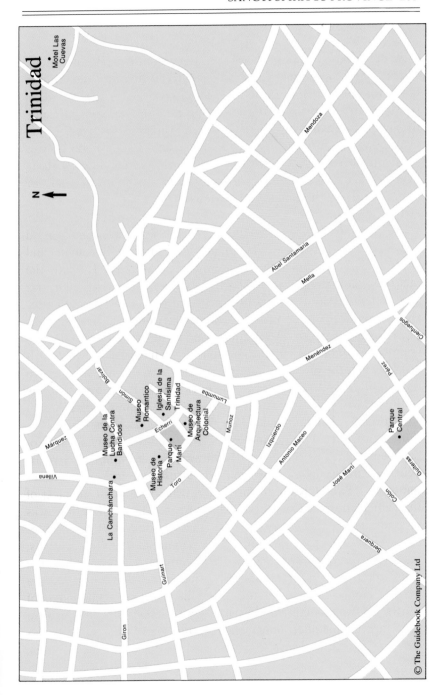

Trinidad

N

Motel Las Cuevas

Mendoza

Abel Santamaria

Mella

Cienfuegos

Menéndez

Pérez

Bolivar

Simón

Museo Romantico

Iglesia de la Santísima Trinidad

Echerri

Lumumba

Museo de la Lucha Contra Bandidos

Museo de Arquitectura Colonial

Muñoz

Parque Central

Márquez

Museo de Historia

Parque Martí

Izquierdo

Antonio Maceo

Güiteras

La Canchánchara

Toro

José Martí

Colón

Villena

Serquera

Guinart

Giron

shell decorations, ceramics—as well as skeletons from an African slaves' cemetery on the nearby Iznaga sugar plantation. Before this building's construction, Hernán Cortés's house supposedly stood on this spot. In a mansion at the south end of the plaza, the Galeria de Arte Universal exhibits works by modern Trinidadian artists.

Heading south from this side of the square, Calle Simón Bolívar passes the entrance to Calle Toro, a pedestrian-only block along which local artists and craftsmen show their wares. Just beyond you find the **Museo Municipal de História** in the ornate Cantero Palace (1827-30). Its owner was not only a plantation owner but a poet, writer, doctor and lover of luxury. The house contained a marble bath with one cherub spouting gin and the other eau de cologne. Beyond the main entrance, the first set of rooms were the family living quarters, with painted walls designed by imported artists. Here you find an exhibition of typical furniture of the period. The rooms beyond, around the large patio, house exhibits on local history since 1514, weapons, sugar, slavery, the Wars of Independence, carriages and the Revolution. A spiral staircase leads up to a watchtower with a good view of the plaza and the surrounding city. From it you can see on the hill to the north of town the **Iglesia de la Popa**, a small 18th-century church now in ruins (five blocks uphill from the plaza).

Returning to the north end of the plaza, one block to the west of the Museo Romantico you come to the 18th-century Franciscan convent, notable for its four-storey belltower. The convent now has the decidedly nonreligious function as the **Museo de la Lucha Contra Bandidos** ('The Museum of the Battle Against Bandits'). Inside you find explanations of the various stages of the fight against anti-Revolutionary rebels in central Cuba, memorials to dozens of Revolutionary soldiers killed in the fighting, pieces of a U-2 spy plane and a hammock used by Che Guevara. The belltower is occasionally open; from atop it there is a stunning view of Trinidad. Around the corner from the museum entrance on Calle Villena is **La Canchánchara**, a tourist bar specializing in a drink of the same name made from aguardiente, lime juice, honey and ice.

Trinidad's other sights are more far-flung. Nontourist life is centered on the Parque Central about ten blocks south of the Parque Martí (south on Calle Bolívar to Calle Martí and then to the left four blocks). Here you find the government offices, the Iglesia San Francisco de Paula and a number of peso stores. Calle Pérez at the east side of the plaza runs eight blocks north to the ruined Iglesia de Santa Ana. It then continues up the hill to the **Motel Las Cuevas**, the closest tourist lodging to town.

The other attractions you should discover on your own. For example, yellow, blue, pink and green stucco-faced one-storey houses line various cobblestone streets between the Iglesia de Santa Ana and the **Parque Martí**. Behind iron grilles, the interiors are half-hidden by drapery, which does not keep the life of the street from invading the house and vice versa. The iron bars seem to encourage rather than block gossip, the touch of lovers and eager children using them as a jungle gym. Every curve of the street brings a new surprise: a craftsman at work on his stoop, the toot of a horn or a taxi driver feeding his one-mulepower engine a bag of hay.

TRINIDAD'S BEACHES

Paseo Agramonte leads south of town to Casilda, a small port town on Casilda Bay. The bay is protected from the Caribbean by a sandy peninsula on which rise two beachfront resorts, the **Costa Sur** and the popular and crowded **Ancón**.

THE VALLE DE LOS INGENIOS

East of town, the Cienfuegos road enters the scenic San Luís Valley, also known as the Valle de los Ingenios ('The Valley of Sugarmills'). The valley was the source of Trinidad's sugar wealth, riches that could not have existed without the sweat of thousands of African slaves. In the heart of the valley, the impoverished town of Manacas Iznaga is built around the old **Hacienda Iznaga**, from which the Iznaga family oversaw its plantations. The hacienda house has been converted into a museum of the local sugar industry. The steps into the garden at the back descend over five arched different-sized niches that were appar-

Museo de Historia

Colonial interior

ently used to punish slaves. The slaves were chained here for days at a time; the smaller the niche, the greater the punishment.

You can climb to an excellent view of the valley atop the nearby **Torre Iznaga** ($1 entrance), a baroque, seven-storey rocket-ship-like structure soaring 45 metres (150 feet). The plantation owners apparently used the tower to oversee the slaves working in the cane fields.

TOPES DE COLLANTES

A few kilometres west of Trinidad, a road winds up hairpin turns and precipitous grades into the Escambray Mountains. This region is the rainiest in Cuba, especially during the May-October rainy season, but even during the 'dry' season you must anticipate sudden downpours. The humidity is always over 80 per cent, and the climate nurtures a mountain rain-forest ecosystem in which hundreds of plant and animal species thrive. The road is lined with two wildly successful botanical imports: towering eucalyptus trees and Caribbean pines. The highest peak is the Pico San Juán (1,140 metres, 3,800 feet); the lower Pico de Potrerillo (931 meters, 3,103 feet) is more popular with hikers.

Runaway Slave

One of the funny things about those days was courting. When a young man had his eye on a girl he would use thousands of tricks. They didn't set about these things the way they do now, quite openly. There was more mystery; and tricks, all sorts of tricks. If I wanted to make a respectable woman fall for me, I dressed myself in white and walked right by her without looking at her. I did this several days running until the time came when I decided to ask her something. The women liked seeing men dressed in white. A black man like me in white was something which caught the eye. A hat was an essential piece of equipment, because you could do a thousand and one things with it: put it on, take it off, raise it to a woman and ask, 'Well, how are you, then?'

If a courting couple, but particularly the girl, had parents, they courted each other with little stones and grains of corn. The girl would stand at the front door and as the man went by he would say, 'Psss-pss,' or whistle, and when she looked round he would smile and start throwing the little stones one by one. She responded by picking them up and keeping them. If she didn't keep them it meant she didn't fancy him. Haughty, conceited women would probably throw the stones right back.

The couple would meet later at some evening entertainment, at a wake or one of the fiestas or carnivals. If the girl had accepted his advances she would say, 'Listen, I've still got that corn you threw at me, here it is.' Then he would hold her hand or kiss her. She would ask, "Are you coming round to my house?" he would say yes, and the next day he would be round there to speak to her parents. The girl would pretend, because women always do, that she didn't know anything about this, and she might even say, 'I have to think it over.' The house would be made ready days before the wedding and the girl's mother helped in all the to-do. The couple would already own a dozen stools, a big bed, a Saratoga trunk and all the cooking things they needed. The poor didn't know about cupboards in those day. The rich had them, but without glass windows, tall cupboards like horses of cedarwood.

The custom was for the girl's parents and the couple's godparents to give the groom half a dozen chickens, a large sow, a young heifer, a milch cow and the wedding dress, which had to have a train because she was not allowed to show her ankles. Any woman who did was not religious or respectable. The man provided for the home; he was the head of the household. She carried out his orders and to begin with did no outside work except perhaps a little washing for some family or other. Once they were settled in their routine they began receiving visitors, and they would talk about the wedding reception and the beer and food they had served there. Every morning the girl's mother or her old man would come round and pay a duty-call.

The priest might call round too, although they were more concerned about visiting the rich people. All those saintly types were after was cash. When people were married they had to pay six or seven pesos, rich and poor alike. Poor people, plantatioin workers, were married in the chapel, which was at the back of the church. Rich people were married right in the middle, in front of the main altar, and they had benches with cushioins on them, whereas the poor sat on wooden stools in the chapel or sacristy, as is sometimes called.

—*The Autobiography of a Runaway Slave*, by Miguel Barnet

The main settlement in this area is Topes de Collantes (elevation 771 metres, 2,570 feet), a centre for nature lovers and those visiting for health reasons. In 1954, the Batista regime opened the massive, battleshiplike **Kurhotel** here as a sanatorium for tuberculosis patients. After the Revolution it became a school; in the mid-1970s it returned to its original use as a health center. Today it is a modern rest and rehabilitation center for postoperative patients and those in

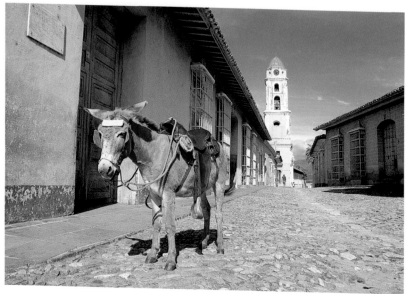

For hire

need of various kinds of therapy, such as medicinal herb treatments, a local specialty. You can try various herb teas at the tourism desk building by the enormous sundial just downhill from the Kurhotel. The hotel, which attracts patients from around the world (mainly other Latin American countries), has 210 rooms and almost 800 works of art, many by Cuba's most famous artists, scattered around the building. A small town for workers has sprung up in the valley below, where there are also some very comfortable hotels, such as the **Hotel Los Helechos**, catering to regular tourists (mostly Cubans).

Nature is the great attraction here. Aside from Pico de Potrerillo, one of the most popular hikes is to the **Caburní Falls**, which are three kilometres (two miles) downhill (remember you have to go climb up again) to the falls zigzagging down a rock face. The trail departs east from the Aparthotel north of the Kurhotel. Another, less rigorous, excursion is by Soviet truck 6.5 kilometres (four miles) on a rough dirt road to the **Finca Codina**. Originally the 1910 hacienda of a Catalán coffee grower, it has been converted into a paradise for bird-watchers

Downtown Trinidad

and nature lovers. An easy trail makes a loop through the hills—and one cave—where you can see butterflies, hummingbirds and hundred of species of plants, including the mariposa, Cuba's national flower. Bring rain gear!

Back at the hacienda you can sample their special cocktail made from ginger root, honey and rum, and when tour groups appear they also will roast a pig under a nearby overhanging rock. The dammed-up pond next door is supposed to contain medicinal mud. Caves, few of which have been explored, riddle the nearby hills.

■ CIEGO DE AVILA PROVINCE

The pancake-flat landscape of Ciego de Avila Province was always dominated by the neighboring cities of Sancti Spíritus and Camagüey. In 1538, a farm was founded at the site of Ciego de Avila City, and the region's early economy was based on cattle. Within 50 years, more cattle enclosures were established around the province, including one at Morón, and during the 17th century these developed into settlements. Ciego de Avila Province is also the narrowest point in central Cuba, a feature exploited by the Spanish military during the two Wars of Independence. In the early 1870s, the Spanish constructed a 50-kilometre (31-mile) fortified line known as the Trocha ('Path') from the Júcaro on the Caribbean coast to Morón near the Atlantic. Despite a double wooden fence and 43 blockhouses, forts and watchtowers, forces under General Máximo Gómez succeeded in breeching the Trocha in January of 1875. Still enamored of the idea, during the second War of Independence, the Spanish general Valeriano Weyler refortified the line with more watchtowers and forts, a wire fence, a mud ditch and 20,000 troops. In late 1895, two separate rebel armies burst through the Trocha and reunited in the west to advance on Havana.

In times of peace, Ciego de Avila Province has been an agricultural center, producing cattle, sugarcane and pineapples. There are few sights of historical interest here; rather, tourists should focus on the natural attractions, such as the islands off the north and south coasts and on Cuba's best bass-fishing lakes.

CIEGO DE AVILA CITY AND MORÓN

The provincial capital (pop. 75,000) lies on the Carretera Central 76 kilometres (48 miles) east of Sancti Spíritus and 108 kilometres (68 miles) west of Camagüey. Ciego is a glorified farm town, with streets laid out on a grid pattern and many early 20th-century buildings. Horse carriages outnumber automobiles. The main tourist lodging is the **Hotel Ciego de Avila** north of town. Those who overnight here are generally on their way to fishing and hunting to the north or south. All fishing or diving excursions to the Jardines de la Reina, the string of keys off the south coast, begin in Ciego de Avila. These trips may be arranged in advance or at the local tourism office.

Thirty-five kilometres (22 miles) north of Ciego, through the bright red dirt of sugarcane fields and orchards, you find Morón, an agricultural town that still has vestiges of the 'clean, handsome, well-cared-for, American appearing place' described by a 1920s guidebook. Opposite the entrance to the Soviet-style **Hotel Morón** stands a large metal rooster that crows at 6 am and 6 pm. At the nearby **Laguna de la Leche** and **Laguna Redonda**, fishermen will find some of Cuba's finest bass waters. The best season is May through November.

CAYO COCO AND CAYO GUILLERMO

North of Morón, the road passes by some isolated rock formations around which spreads a vast ranch teeming with Santa Gertrudis cattle. The farm workers live in the Comunidad Celia Sánchez, named after Fidel's longtime secretary. She fell in love with Dutch-style houses in Holland and organized the construction of a small community of them, their peaked roofs and chimneys looking rather out of place in the tropical sun.

Across the shallow flats between the mainland and the keys to the north, the government in 1989 completed a 34-kilometre-long (21-mile) stone causeway—half of it on water—called the Pedraplen. Before, boats were the only way onto the islands. Unfortunately, this engineering marvel only has a few pipes through which the current can pass, so the waters to the east of the causeway have become nutrient-starved, causing damage all the way up the food change. Nevertheless, you can still see flocks of bright flamingos wading across the flats. These keys are one of Cuba's most important sanctuaries for the birds and also shelter the remarkable *zunzuncito,* or bee hummingbird, one of the smallest birds in existence.

The Pedraplen hits land at Cayo Coco, a large island made up mostly of mangrove and brush. Although largely untouched—it is an important stop from migratory birds and also shelters many year-round species—the Cuban government plans to make it the next Varadero. At this writing, the island has two hotels, the **Hotel Cayo Coco** and the new **Club Cayo Coco**, comprising almost 1,000 rooms. Since 1991, the Academy of Sciences has had a branch here (visitors are welcome), with a team of 15 scientists, including biologists and environmentalists. They have told the government that developers could construct a maximum of 16,000 hotel rooms here without harming the ecosystem. Given the harm to wildlife caused by the Pedraplen, it is hard to trust this advice. An airport is on hold while they decide whether the migratory birds will be spooked (Ciego de Avila is the nearest airport). The Atlantic side of the island is lined with excellent beaches.

The Pedraplen continues across many mangrove islands to Cayo Guillermo just to the west of Cayo Coco. Modest tourist development began here in 1986, when visitors were shipped in by boat. Back then they stayed in the now-dilapidated Floating Hotel moored to the dock. Today the principal hotels are the low-key, attractive **Villa Cojímar** (jointly run by Italy's Venta Club) and the equally upscale **Villa Vigía**. You can either enjoy the sand in front of the hotel or take an excursion to Playa Pilar, a broad, white beach to the east. The dictator Batista had a hideaway on the now-deserted Cayo Media Luna just offshore, and Ernest Hemingway used to fish here. These waters were also the site of the writer's famous 'battle' with a German submarine. Dolphin and kingfish abound.

■ CAMAGÜEY PROVINCE

Camagüey is the largest and least populated province in Cuba. Mostly flat plains, it is perfect for cattle ranches and sugar plantations, which abound. Despite these agricultural riches, there are few natural lakes or streams in the province, and this lack of water has probably slowed the pace of development here. The only hills are the Sierra de Cubitas, which lie due north of the provincial capital.

On February 2, 1514, the city of Camagüey, originally called Santa María de Puerto Príncipe, was founded by Diego Velásquez near the present site of Nuevitas on the north coast. Fourteen years later the city was moved to its present site, where an Indian settlement called Camagüey had once thrived (the Indian name was restored in 1903). During the 17th century, the city was burned once, by slaves, and sacked by pirates twice, first by the English and then the French. The English pirates, led by Henry Morgan, locked the most prominent townspeople in the Iglesia de San Francisco until hunger forced them to give up their riches.

To adapt to the lack of water, the colonial *camagüeyanos* (residents of Camagüey) began building enormous clay pots, called *tinajones*, in order to store rainwater. A family's wealth could be measured by the number of *tinajones* in their possession, and the pots became the symbol of the city. A 1974 census found 18,000 *tinajones* in the city, all from the 19th century, but the art of making them had disappeared. Since then a local ceramics artist has reinvented the process, and they are again being manufactured.

During the 19th century, Camagüey was a centre of the rebellion against Spain. The most famous native son is General Ignacio Agramonte (1841-73), renowned for many feats of bravery, including the

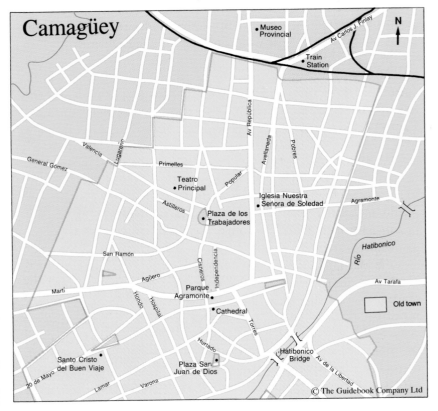

Camagüey

Museo Provincial

Av Carlos J. Finlay

N

Train Station

Valencia

Lugareño

Av República

Avellaneda

Popular

General Gómez

Primelles

Teatro Principal

Popular

Iglesia Nuestra Señora de Soledad

Agramonte

Astilleros

Plaza de los Trabajadores

Hatibonico

Río

San Ramón

Cisneros

Independencia

Av Tarafa

Agüero

Parque Agramonte

Old town

Marti

Hondo

Hospital

Cathedral

Torres

Hurtado

Hatibonico Bridge

Santo Cristo del Buen Viaje

20 de Mayo

Plaza San Juan de Dios

Av de la Libertad

Lamar

Varona

© The Guidebook Company Ltd

daring rescue of a captured comrade while armed only with a machete. In 1895, Jimaguayú, the town where he was killed, was the site of a constitutional assembly in which the rebel generals Maceo and Gómez asserted the primacy of the military over the civilian administration in fighting the war. Camagüey was also the birthplace of Carlos Finlay, the doctor who first linked the mosquito with the yellow fever germ. The city's rebellious nature continued in the early 20th century, when there were numerous strikes by students and workers. In order to quell political unrest, U.S. Marines occupied Camagüey in 1917 and 1921.

Development of the rest of Camagüey Province only took off with the completion of the Havana-Santiago railway line. The volume of sugar production increased many times, and farms and orchards profitably exported a wide variety of fruits and vegetables.

CAMAGÜEY CITY

Today Camagüey (pop. 275,000) is the third-largest city in Cuba and the most under-appreciated by foreign tourists. It lies on the Carretera Central between Ciego de Avila and Las Tunas. Although thriving, with many modern buildings on the outskirts, the city has protected a large colonial core—recently named a national monument—containing more old buildings than any other city save Havana.

Downtown Camagüey is a labyrinth of one-way streets running off at odd angles. Foot power is the easiest way to navigate. As in many provincial Cuban towns and cities, there are few cars and buses but many horse carriages.

Calle Martí bisects the heart of the city from east to west and is a good reference point for the disoriented. The **Parque Agramonte**, on Martí between Calles Independencia and Cisneros, occupies the center of the colonial core. The focus of this park is the equestrian statue of Ignacio Agramonte (1916) brandishing a sword and galloping atop a pedestal surrounded by a relief of charging cavalry soldiers. The palm trees at each corner of the square commemorate four early Cuban patriots who were executed by the Spanish in 1851. The colonial authorities forbade any monuments to the four; instead, under the guise of obtaining a little shade, locals planted the four palms with their secret patriotic significance.

At the south side of the square stands Camagüey's cathedral, sanctuary of **Nuestra Señora de la Candelaria**. The first church was built on this site in 1530; since then it has burned and been rebuilt, collapsed and been rebuilt, and used as military quarters during the Wars of Independence. The simple, single-naved interior contains an early beamed roof, and the altar guards the figure of Nuestra Señora de la Candelaria. The street heading west from the cathedral's main door ends in seven blocks at the Iglesia de Santo Cristo del Buen Viaje (1844), behind which opens Camagüey's cemetery, a little city of ornate marble tombs.

Returning to Parque Agramonte, if you head north on Calle Cisneros in three blocks you will come to Calle Agramonte and the **Plaza de los Trabajadores** ('Workers' Plaza'). In the 19th century, this was the site of circuses and later bullfights. At the corner of Calles Agramonte and Candelaria stands the **Casa Natal de Ignacio Agramonte**, the birthplace of the patriotic hero and the mansion where his family lived for many years. It is notable for the third-floor balcony that runs the length of the facade and around the corner. Now a museum, the house preserves the original furniture, enormous *tinajones* in the courtyard, and exhibits on the life of Ignacio Agramonte. The Plaza de los Trabajadores is dominated by the fortresslike **Iglesia Nuestra Señora de la Merced**, built in 1748 and restored after a 1906 fire. The ornate wood, silver and marble altar was donated by a local philanthropist and houses a statue of the church's patroness. At this writing, the church is closed for restoration, but it still is possible to peek inside. To the left, a chapel shelters a silver altar and the image of the Infant Jesus of Prague, the object of much local reveration.

Calle Valencia heads west of the square two blocks to the **Teatro Principal** (1850). This is the home of the Ballet de Camagüey, the most respected Cuban dance group after the Ballet Nacional. They are almost always on tour abroad.

Two blocks east of the church on Agramonte, you come to Calle República, the major north-south street, across which stands the

1756 Iglesia Nuestra Señora de la Soledad. The elaborate wooden ceiling of this spacious church is suspended above rows of massive, square pillars. If you head north on República, in seven blocks you will come to the train station. The recently restored **Hotel Plaza** nearby is the best downtown hotel.

A block to the north stands the imposing white **Museo Provincial Ignacio Agramonte** (1848). The building was originally constructed as the local headquarters for the cavalry. After independence, this castlelike structure was purchased by a railway company and converted into what became the most famous hotel in Cuba, the Hotel Camagüey, featuring a tropical jungle in the courtyard. A 1920s guidebook advertised: 'The hotel is an ideal place in which to loaf, or read, or drowse or dream or do literary work that requires an atmosphere of undiluted romance.' Today, more practically, it is a museum containing exhibits on local history, zoology and art.

Returning to the Parque Agramonte, a short walk three blocks south on Calle Cisneros and then left on Calle Hurtado will take you to the **Plaza San Juan de Dios**. Constructed in the 18th century, this cobblestone square, with its red tiles, bright paints and one-storey houses, preserves a colonial atmosphere undiluted by modern life. Next door to the 1728 Iglesia San Juan de Dios (open only on Mondays) stands an early hospital with a Moorish facade. Two Spanish restaurants, the **Parador de los Tres Reyes** and the **Meson La Campaña de Toledo**, also occupy the square. The local specialty is *ajiaco* Camagüeyano, a kind of stew with a little bit of everything, especially corn. The local brand of beer, Tínima, is refreshing but low in alcohol.

Three blocks east of the square, the **Hatibonico Bridge** (1773) crosses the Río Hatibonico and enters La Caridad. This neighborhood boasts many attractive, early 20th-century buildings and colonnades running along both sides of Avenida de la Libertad, the main street. Seven blocks to the southeast, the simple, yellow **Iglesia de la Caridad** guards an icon of Our Lady of Charity, the patroness of the city. A festival in her honor is celebrated on September 8. Never having undergone significant reconstruction, this red-tile-roofed 1734 building is one of the few that preserves a pure 18th-century style.

Two blocks to the east, Av Libertad merges with the Carretera Central and heads four kilometres (2.5 miles) to the Soviet-style **Hotel Camagüey** (1976), whose atmosphere is a far cry from 'undiluted romance'. The bus station is on the same road a little closer to town.

PLAYA SANTA LUCIA

From Camagüey, a road heads northeast through kilometres of pancake-flat cattle ranches tended by *vaqueros* ('cowboys'), egrets and buzzards. Rather than heading straight to the ugly, industrial port of Nuevitas, branch to the right to reach the beach resort of Santa Lucia. Five resort hotels very popular with European tourists line the rather narrow beach here. Offshore there lie excellent reefs for diving. On the lagoon side of town are the works of a large salt-manufacturing facility. The nearest airport is in Holguín, from which it is a three-and-a-half-hour bus ride.

For calmer waters and a broad strip of fine, white sand, visitors usually take a bus six kilometres (four miles) west to the **Playa Coco** at the mouth of Nuevitas Bay. Protected from the ocean, this beach lies in a small bay with tiny waves and soup-warm water. The fishing village Los Cocos lies just next door. For better beaches, you can take an excursion by boat to **Cayo Sabinal**, a large key at the west side of the bay. Here you will also find casual restaurants, campgrounds catering mainly to Cubans and excellent diving offshore.

Another recreation option is horseback riding at **Rancho King**, 26 kilometres (16 miles) southwest of Santa Lucia on the road back to Camagüey. This cattle ranch was built by the owners of Texas's famous King Ranch and expropriated after the Triumph of the Revolution. (Before the Revolution, the north coast of Camagüey was home to many U.S.-owned ranches and plantations.) You can also enjoy roast meats at the open-air restaurant and watch a Cuban rodeo. The ranch house, once a government guest house, can now be rented for overnight stays.

A Poem

Yo soy un hombre sincero
De donde crece la palma,
Y antes de morirme quiero
Echar mis versos del alma.

Yo vengo de todas partes,
Y hacia todas partes voy:
Arte soy entre las artes,
En los montes, monte soy.

Yo sé los nombres extraños
De las yerbas y las flores,
Y de mortales engaños,
Y de sublimes dolores.

Yo he visto en la noche oscura
Llover sobre mi cabeza
Los rayos de lumbre pura
De la divina belleza.

Alas nacer vi enlos hombros
De las mujeres hermosas:
Y salir de los escombros,
Volando las mariposas.

He visto vivir a un hombre
Con el puñal al costado,
Sin Decir jamás el nombre
De aquella que lo ha matado

Rápida, como un reflejo,
Dos veces vi el alma, dos:
Cuando murió el pobre viejo,
Cuando ella me dijo adiós.

I am an honest man
From where the palms grow;
Before I die I want my soul
To shed its poetry.

I come from everywhere,
To everywhere I'm bound:
An art among the arts,
A mountain among mountains.

I know that unfamiliar names
Of grasses and of flowers,
Of fatal deceptions
And exalted sorrows.

On darkest nights I've seen
Rays of the purest splendor
Raining upon my head
From heavenly beauty.

I've seen wings sprout
From handsome women's shoulders,
Seen butterflies fly out
Of rubbish heaps.

I've seen a man who lives
With a dagger at his side,
Never uttering the name
Of his murderess.

Twice, quick as a wink, I've seen
the soul: once when a poor
Old man succumbed, once when
She said goodby.

Temblé una vez—en la reja,
A la entrada de la viña,—
Cuando la bárbara abeja
Picó en la frente a mi niña.

Once I shook with anger
At the vineyard's iron gate
When a savage bee attacked
My daughter's forehead.

Gocé una vez, de tal suerte
Que gocé cual nunca:—cuando
La sentencia de me muerte
Leyó el alcaide llorando.

Once I rejoiced as I
Had never done before,
When the warden, weeping, read
My sentence of death.

Oigo un suspiro, a través
De las tierras y la mar,
Y no es un suspiro,—es
Que mi hijo va a despertar.

I hear a sigh across
The land and sea; it is
No sigh: it is my son
Waking from asleep.

Si dicen que del joyero
Tome la joya mejor,
Tomo a un amigo sincero
Y pongo a un lado el amor.

If I am said to take
A jeweler's finest gem,
I take an honest friend,
Put love aside.

Yo he visto al águila herido
Valar al azul sereno
Y morir en su guarida
La víbora del veneno.

I've seen a wounded eagle
Fly to the tranquil blue,
And seen a snake die in its
Hole, of venom.

Yo sé bien que cuando el mundo
Cede, lívido, al descanso,
Sobre el silencio profundo
Murmura el arroyo manso.

Well do I know that when
The livid world yields to repose,
The gentle brook will ripple on
In deepest silence.

Yo he puesto la mano osada,
De horror y júbilo yerta,
Sobre la estralla apagada
Que cayó frente a mi puerta.

I've laid a daring hand,
Rigid from joy and horror,
Upon the burnt-out star that fell
Before my door.

continues

Oculto en mi pecho bravo
La pena que me lo hiere:
El hijo de un pueblo esclavo
Vive por él, calla y muere.

Todo es hermoso y constante,
Todo es música y razón,
Y todo, como el diamente,
Antes que luz es carbón.

Yo sé que el necio se entierra
con gran lujo y con gran llanto—
Y que no hay fruta en la tierra
Como la del camposanto.

Callo , y entiendo, y me quito
La pompa del rimador:
Cuelgo de un árbol marchito
Mi muceta de doctor.

My manly heart conceals
The pain it suffers; sons of
A land enslaved live for it
Silently, and die.

All is permanence and beauty,
And all is melody and reason,
And all, like diamonds rather
Than light, is coal.

I know that fools are buried
Spendidly, with floods of teas,
And that no fruit on earth
Is like that graveyard's.

I understand, keep still,
Cast off the versifier's pomp,
And hang my doctoral robes upon
A withered tree.

—*Major Poems* by José Martí

Oriente (Guantanamo)

■ INTRODUCTION

ORIENTE, CONSISTING OF CUBA'S FOUR EASTERN PROVINCES, is the cradle of independence (all of Cuba's revolutions began here) and a fount of Cuban culture. The region's rich traditions of dance, music and festival —largely based in the Afro-Cuban population—are famous worldwide.

Skipping over Las Tunas Province, which has little to offer tourists, you come to Holguín Province, whose capital is interesting more for its history than for any colonial charm. To the north, in a region of lush hills, the beach town of Guardalavaca is one of the fastest-growing resorts in Cuba. Due south lies Granma Province, locale of flat sugarcane fields and the Sierra Maestra, Cuba's largest mountain range. Bayamo, the provincial capital, is a friendly colonial town with many interesting monuments and a citizenry proud of its role as birthplace of the 1868 War of Independence. From here you can head south up into the Sierra Maestra or down to the arid coast and Marea del Portillo, with two good resort hotels.

Santiago Province is home to Santiago de Cuba, the island's second most important city and a fascinating place to visit. Here you see important colonial buildings and monuments to key events in the Wars of Independence and in the Revolutionary fight against Batista. You can also meet the sociable, spirited *santiagueros*, heirs to a rich Afro-Cuban tradition of dance, music and religion. A few kilometres out of town stands the shrine to the Virgen de la Caridad del Cobre, the patroness of Cuba. The Parque Baconao along the coast to the east is a sprawling zone of beaches, resort hotels, wildlife preserves and amusement parks that has something for every taste.

At the easternmost tip of Cuba lies Guantánamo Province, one of Cuba's most isolated and beautiful areas. The mouth of Guantánamo Bay is occupied by the notorious U.S. naval base, a thorn in the side of U.S.-Cuban relations. Across a range of mountains you find Baracoa, Cuba's first settlement and one of the most captivating colonial towns on the island. Once you visit this lush region filled with palm trees and fruit groves, you may never want to leave.

■ LAS TUNAS PROVINCE

Las Tunas Province is known for having the fewest tourist attractions in Cuba. In 1510, an early conquistador named Alonso de Ojeda gave a statue of the Virgin to a local Indian chief in thanks for the image's help in crossing a dangerous swamp. The sanctuary constructed by the chief is considered Cuba's first church. According to legend, this same statue is the Virgin of Charity worshipped in Santiago Province as the patroness of Cuba.

Development of the province proceeded slowly, and it was not until 1847 that Las Tunas City was officially founded. During the Wars for Independence, a number of fierce battles were fought in and around Las Tunas, culminating in the torching of the city by rebel forces in 1897. As a result, Las Tunas has very few colonial buildings. Today Las Tunas Province's main industries are sugar and chemicals; many of the latter factories are located in Las Tunas City. Most tourists speed through on their way to more picturesque locations. If you must stop, the best hotel is the **Hotel Las Tunas** on the outskirts.

■ HOLGUÍN PROVINCE

Holguín Province covers the north coast of Oriente from the Camagüey border almost all the way to Cuba's eastern tip. Most tourist installations are concentrated in the northwest of the province. After the monotony of central Cuba, it is a relief to find rolling hills and three small mountain ranges here. Lush and dotted with palm trees, this varied landscape is one of the most pleasing in Cuba.

Before the arrival of Europeans, this coast was a centre of the Taíno Indian population. Important discoveries, such as gold figurines and elaborate burials, have been made near Banes and Guardalavaca. Somewhere on this same coast Columbus took his first step on Cuba in late October of 1492. The beauty of the region (and the occasional gold ornament on a native) seduced him into believing that the island was a trove of riches. In 1525, Captain García Holguín founded a settlement at the site of Maguanes, an Indian village, which he modestly renamed San Isidoro de Holguín; it's now the provincial capital. Development of the region proceeded slowly; Oriente's economy struggled during the first centuries of the colony, and most of the population was concentrated on the south coast.

In 1608, two Indians and a young slave found the statue of the Virgin of Charity, Cuba's patroness, floating in the waters of Nipe Bay on the north coast. She now presides at El Cobre near Santiago.

During the 19th century, the province became a centre of agriculture, mainly sugar, tobacco and fruit cultivation. U.S. business interests entered the area after the downturn of the 1850s and gradually came to dominate the region's economic life. Like the rest of Oriente, Holguín was a hotbed of rebel support during the Wars of Independence. Within days of the Grito de Yara call to arms in October 1868, a hastily organized rebel militia attacked Holguín. They forced the Spanish infantry there to hole up in a house nicknamed 'La Periquera' ('The Parrot Cage') after the sight of the brightly uniformed soldiers hiding behind bars. They were only freed two months later when a Spanish army retook the city. After the 1878 signing of the Pact of Zanjón, General Antonio Maceo led his troops in one last battle against the Spanish in Mayarí east of Holguín as a mark of his contempt for the treaty. On February 24, 1895, Holguín Province was one of the sites of the abortive start of the Second War of Independence as rebels struck at Spanish targets. Holguín's most famous son was General Calixto García, the principal rebel commander by the end of the war.

After independence, Holguín—and particularly its coastal region—became an outpost of the United States. All the large sugar estates were owned by U.S. companies, and the United Fruit Company purchased an enormous banana plantation around Nipe Bay. Originally, the U.S. Navy wanted to establish its base in this excellent harbor but later decided on Guantanamo Bay on the south coast. U.S. mining companies also found iron ore in the inland mountains and later discovered nickel ore near Moa. (Today nickel processed in Moa produces 15 per cent of Cuba's export income.) The U.S. workers lived in American-style towns like Banes with modern schools, hospitals, country clubs and a lifestyle that few Cubans in the area could approach.

For the roughly raised son of a local plantation owner, the American presence only bred bitterness that eventually turned into a life-long loathing. Fidel Castro's father Angel had been a United Fruit Company employee who through brute force and cunning had amassed enough land for his own prosperous sugar estate; despite his success he always resented his ex-employers. Fidel's wife, the long-suffering Mirta Diaz-Ballart, was the daughter of the mayor of Banes, the American idyll in the tropics. Her middle-class pretensions and family connections to the Batista regime did not mix with his chaotic lifestyle and revolutionary aspirations; they soon divorced. Another mark against the Americans.

Since the Revolution, Holguín Province has thrived. In addition to the nickel-processing plants in Moa, there are ten sugar refineries here as well as huge factory making mechanical sugarcane harvesters in Holguín City.

HOLGUÍN CITY

The Carretera Central enters Holguín Province from Las Tunas and at Holguín makes a sharp turn southwest to Bayamo. The fourth-largest city in Cuba, Holguín (pop. 190,000) has expanded rapidly in recent years, diluting any colonial charm. The city is laid out on a grid plan, making it relatively easy to navigate, at least in the city's centre.

Downtown, most sights, including five parks, lie between the parallel streets of Libertad and Maceo. One of these parks, the **Parque Calixto García** between Calles Frexes and Martí, is the city's commercial and cultural centre. On weekend evenings in years past, the whole population used to perambulate here, the men in one direction, the women in the other. At the north side stands the **Museo Provincial**, built between 1862 and 1868 as the Casino Español, where the Spanish aristocracy used to entertain. At the outbreak of the First War of

Independence, rebel forces besieged the Spanish infantry inside, and the building took on its nickname as 'La Periquera'—the 'Parrot Cage'. It has also acted as the seat of local government and as a clothing store. Today the museum guards good archaeological and historical exhibits about Holguín. The star artifact is the Holguín ax, a figure of the man in the shape of a wide blade found near the city. You will also find the local **art gallery** and the **Casa de la Trova** on this square.

Just south of the park on Calle Maceo stands the **Museo de Historia Natural**, which contains the usual stuffed animals exhibited with a 19th-century charm. The exhibit of thousands of brightly colored *polymita* snail shells is stunning. Maceo then enters the **Parque de San Isidoro** at the south end of which stands the **Iglesia de San Isidoro** (1720), Holguín's most important church. The interior displays a mix of architectural styles, an old wooden ceiling and a couple of statues of San Isidoro, the city's patron. His day is celebrated on April 4. In 1869, slaves voluntarily carried the altar here from Bayamo after its original church burned. In the centre of the plaza stands a **statue of Karl Marx**. Six or seven blocks to the south, Calle Maceo ends at the **train station**.

Holguín's new quarter lies to the east of town on the road to Guarda-lavaca. The centrepiece is the **Plaza de la Revolución**, with a huge 1980 mausoleum for Calixto García's remains. Nearby stand the hospital, stadium and the **Hotel Pernik**, Holguín's best tourist accommodation, which is named after the birthplace of the first leader of communist Bulgaria. Another hotel, **Villa Cocal**, is located near Holguín's airport.

If you are feeling energetic, you can head due north on Calle Maceo to the **Loma de la Cruz** on Holguín's northern outskirts. Four hundred and fifty steps climb this hill up to a **lookout** and a cross that was erected here in 1790. Every May 3, locals celebrate the Day of the Cross with a pilgrimage up the staircase.

Southeast of town on the road to Santiago stands the pride of the Revolution: the enormous factory where they make sugarcane har-vesters. Farther to the south rises another hill topped by the **Mayabe Lookout**, a tourist restaurant complex. The feature attraction is a

Cuba, 1926

The Average Cubano is a happy helpful, songful, tuneful, whistling, pleasure-loving person, non-vicious, of cleanly habits, and at peace with himself and the world. He is of medium size; weighs about 150 lbs.; carries himself well; is lithe; manly; with small hands and feet; has the true American sense of humor; and is naturally urbane. A commendable trait is truthfulness. Customarily he will promptly confess ignorance if he does not know a thing, and this often saves the tourist time and confusion. When asked for specific information the native will sometimes say, *No estoy fuerte en eso,* I'm not strong on that; or *soy muy bruto en tales cosas,* I'm a lunkhead in such matters! His distate for sustained hard work is not constitutional, but rather the result of climate and class distinction, for when he has to work he does it well. Many Cubans work as hard and as steadily as certain Americans, and not unfrequently the visitor to a Cuban's office will note above the executive desk printed signs of the following tenor: *Hágalo breve, el tiempo vuelo*—make it brief, time flies! Or *hágalo ahora,* do it now; or *el tiempo es dinero,* time is money. Of the countryman it is said that he works Tuesdays, Wednesday and Thursdays, plays the guitar, dances and attends cockfights the rest of the week.

Unlike many Latin Americans the Cuban is slow to anger. Personal quarrels are rare. Malice, envy, contumacy and destructiveness seem lacking in his character. One sees little wrangling, despite the fact that in social matters the people are as ceremonious as the French. The visitor cannot fail to note that patience and good humor with which traffic-jams in Havana's narrow streets are untangled. It is a recognized fact that the taxi-chofers drive too fast. Because of this they often get into a snarl that would warp the philosophy of the most optimistic policemen. But such *enredos* are unraveled with skill and forbearance, and with a notable absence of the profanity that often garnishes such encounters elsewhere.

—*Terry's Guide To Cuba,* by T. Philip Terry

burro addicted to the good local Mayabe beer; obviously, you must buy the beer before you pour it down the donkey's throat.

On the coast 30 kilometres (19 miles) due north of Holguín lies the fishing town of Gibara, also called Villa Blanca, with narrow streets and many simple 19th-century houses. Historians believe that Columbus probably landed in one of the bays immediately to the east. Somewhere offshore lies **Cayo Saetía**, an island that does not appear on any maps because it until recently was a rest-and-relaxation retreat for top officials. Today, tourists can stay in the small **Villa Cayo Saetía** and enjoy miles of empty beaches and excellent fishing and bird hunting.

GUARDALAVACA AND BANES

A road runs 54 kilometres (34 miles) northeast of Holguín through a beautiful landscape of hills and palm trees down to the beach resort of Guardalavaca. This is the third most popular resort in Cuba (after Havana and Varadero), with five hotels and plans for more. But, aside from a rather narrow beach, excellent diving on the reefs and two good seafood restaurants, there is little else.

Just south of the Banes road five kilometres (three miles) east of Guardalavaca lies the **Chorro de Maita** archaeological site. A large building covers the excavation of a Taíno Indian graveyard dated between 1490 and 1540. One hundred and eight skeletons were found here, making it the largest Inidan burial site yet found in Cuba. One of the dead was apparently a male Caucasian, perhaps a conquistador who died here. Exhibits around the walls display artifacts buried as offerings with the dead.

It is a beautiful drive through country villages with thatched huts and cactus fences and over lush palm tree-covered hills and banana groves to the town of Banes, 32 kilometres (20 miles) southeast of Guardalavaca. This was a centre of the American influence in Cuba in the years between 1900 and 1959, but there is little hint of that today. During the early 20th-century sugar booms, thousands of Jamaican workers were imported to cut cane in the region, and many still live around Banes. The only tourist sight downtown is the

Museo Indocubano ($1), one of Cuba's best archaeological museums. On display are stone, shell and ceramic artifacts, mainly pottery and ornaments, found at Chorro de Maita and other sites in the region. The most famous object is a tiny gold idol in the shape of a woman with a large headdress found near Yaguigay. (Some say that this is a copy and that the original languishes in a bank vault.) Banes's downtown streets are a pleasant place to stroll, with brightly painted buildings and bustling pedestrian traffic.

■ GRANMA PROVINCE

The province of Granma has two distinct landscapes: the flat flood-plain of the Río Cauto, Cuba's longest river, and the pine-covered peaks of the Sierra Maestra, the island's largest mountain range. At 1,974 metres (6,580 feet), Turquino Peak here is Cuba's highest point. The western spur of the Sierra becomes a peninsula jutting out into the Caribbean to form the Gulf of Guacanayabo, into which the Cauto drains.

This region has a long, glorious and bloody history as a main stage for three revolutionary wars. In November 1513, the conquistador Diego Velásquez founded San Salvador de Bayamo, the second Spanish settlement in Cuba, at the site of Indian villages. The economy was centred on agriculture—cattle, sugar and tobacco—and smuggling. In fact, Bayamo and the nearby port of Manzanillo were the centres of the contraband trade in Cuba, where tobacco and hides were exchanged for manufactured goods and slaves. In 1602, royal authorities arrested eight of the town's leading citizens for smuggling; in the first Cuban revolt against the crown, the rest of the townsfolk took up arms and forced their release.

Bayamo was also a centre of Cuban intellectual life. In 1607, a French pirate kidnapped the bishop; rather than pay the ransom, his rescuers attacked the pirate's band, killed the pirate and displayed his head on the main square. In honor of this illustrious event, a local worthy wrote what is considered the first Cuban poem, the 'Espejo de Paciencia' ('Mirror of Patience'), in which the heroic events are recounted in semimythic, or fantastic, form.

This intellectual tradition led to the outbreak of the First War of Independence. Living far from the centres of power and money, the owners of Bayamo's small- and medium-sized estates devoted themselves to literature, history and the radical new political ideas coming from abroad. They sent their sons to Europe and the United States for education, and the new generation came back with a burning desire for Cuban independence. Led by the Europe-educated Carlos Manuel de Céspedes, they gathered in the local Masonic lodge and began to plot revolution. They saw their chance in 1868 when Spain's Queen Isabella was toppled by a coup.

On October 10, 1868, Céspedes freed the slaves at La Demajagua, his plantation, and delivered an oration known as the 'Grito de Yara' ('Shout of Yara'—named after the neighboring town) espousing equality for all men and independence from Spain, 'or death!' With a force of 147 men, he marched on Bayamo and captured it on October 20. For these actions he is considered 'The Father of Our Country' and a close second to José Martí as a patriot. After the town's capture, a rebel named Perucho Figueredo composed a martial hymn called the Bayamo Anthem—'To the battle, Bayameses!'—that is now the national anthem. When Spanish troops menaced the freed city in January 1869, the rebels burned the town rather than let it fall into their hands. First employed here, this use of arson as a weapon was widespread in both Wars of Independence. Meanwhile, the flames of rebellion quickly spread through Oriente and only were extinguished after ten years of bloodshed. In 1874, Céspedes was killed in an ambush in the Sierra Maestra.

During the Second War of Independence, the Bayamo region was once again a hotbed of revolt. Shortly after that war began, the main instigator of the rebellion, José Martí, was killed in a skirmish at Dos Ríos, just east of Bayamo. According to one version, he was eager to prove himself a man of action, not just an orator, and rushed into the fray where he met the fatal bullet. On April 28, 1898, Spanish soldiers retreated from Bayamo for good, and the city was taken by

General Calixto García. After the fighting had stopped, historians counted and discovered that Bayamo had contributed 22 generals to both Wars of Independence.

Revolution returned to Bayamo during the 1950s, when Fulgencio Batista replaced the Spanish as the enemy. Early on the morning of July 26, 1953, 25 lightly armed men attacked the army barracks in Bayamo. Planned by Fidel Castro, this attack was coordinated with a larger attack on the Moncada barracks in Santiago and was supposed to signal a mass uprising against Batista. Both attacks failed. In Bayamo, the army's horses raised the first alarm, and when the smoke cleared 15 minutes later, ten of the attackers lay dead. A few escaped; those captured were brutally tortured before being executed.

Fidel persevered. After a jail term, he went into exile in Mexico, where he raised and trained an invasionary army. On December 2, 1956, the 26 July Movement force of 82 men landed in a swamp at Playa de las Coloradas in the southwestern corner of the province. Their transport was the pleasure boat Granma, whose name was given to the province after Cuba's 1976 re-division. Three days later, as they tramped toward sanctuary in the Sierra Maestra, they were ambushed in a sugarcane field. Only a few more than a dozen escaped capture and death. Somehow, that was enough.

With the support of the sierra's impoverished peasants, the fighters held on. When word filtered back to Havana that Fidel might have survived, recruits and weapons began to arrive. The revolutionaries had won some small skirmishes against Rural Guard post, when they got their big break. Herbert Matthews, a reporter for the New York Times, trekked up to the sierra to find out if Fidel was really alive. Using all his formidable powers of persuasion, Castro painted a rosy picture of the large and well-armed rebel army and their glorious conquests. When the rest of Cuba read Matthews's article, men and equipment poured into the mountains. The battles got bigger and so did the revolutionaries' victories. By May 1958, Batista was forced to strike back with his best forces and most advanced weapons. Accustomed to easy life in the barracks, Batista's soldiers were no match for Fidel's sierra-hardened men and widespread intelligence network.

Within months the offensive had collapsed, and many of the infantry had changed sides, bringing their weapons with them. In August, Castro's forces came out of the Sierra Maestra and began the liberation of the rest of Cuba.

Today Granma Province is largely agricultural, with most of the economy based on rice and sugar cultivation along the Río Cauto. Bayamo's principal industry is milk and milk products such as butter and cheese.

BAYAMO

The city of Bayamo (pop. 120,000) is built along the east side of the Río Bayamo, which drains into the Río Cauto. It lies on a zag of the Carretera Central between Holguín (the zig) and Santiago. For a shortcut between Santiago and central Cuba, take the occasionally rough two-lane road that runs directly to Bayamo from Las Tunas. The Sierra Maestra looms to the south.

The colonial town is the part closest to the river, and here you find all the tourist sights. There are few cars or buses here; horse carriages are the favored means of transportation. Bayameses are justly proud of their history, and the local tourist industry is pleasantly aggressive about sharing the city's attractions. Like much of southern Oriente, Bayamo is also a mulatto city. The local Bayamesas (women of Bayamo) are famed throughout Cuba for their beauty, even inspiring a famous love song, 'La Bayamesa'.

The centre of Bayamo is the **Plaza de la Revolucion**, lying on Calle General García, around which you find the majority of sights. In better times the townsfolk used to take their evening promenade here. In the centre stands a statue of Bayamo's favorite son, Carlos Manuel de Céspedes, and, opposite, a bust of Perucho Figueredo, the author of the national anthem. The words may be read below. Every October 20, the anniversary of its composition Bayameses stage a big celebration here.

Céspedes was born in a mansion at the north end of the square. It miraculously survived the fire that destroyed Bayamo and is now the **Museo Carlos Manuel de Céspedes**. On the ground floor you

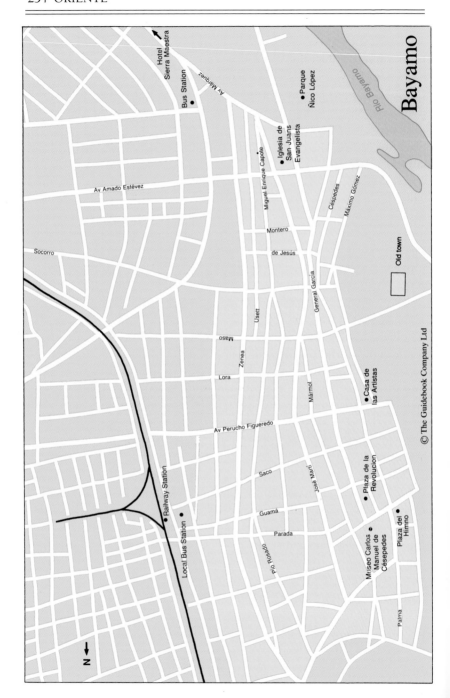

Bayamo

Río Bayamo

Hotel Sierra Maestra

Bus Station

Av Márquez

Parque Nico López

Iglesia de San Juans Evangelista

Miguel Enrique Capote

Av Amado Estévez

Céspedes

Máximo Gómez

Montero

de Jesús

Socorro

Old town

General García

Usett

Maso

Zenea

Lora

Mármol

Casa de las Artistas

Av Perucho Figueredo

Railway Station

Saco

José Martí

Plaza de la Revolución

Guamá

Local Bus Station

Parada

Pío Rosado

Museo Carlos Manuel de Céspedes

Plaza del Himno

Palma

N

© The Guidebook Company Ltd

find exhibits on the history of the building and on Céspedes's life, including the printing press on which he published El Cubano Libre, free Cuba's first newspaper. The floor above contains displays of period furniture. Next door stands the **Museo Provincial**, housing many interesting and weird displays. In the latter category are two objects made by a local shoemaker: a guitar made from hundreds of strips of different rare woods, and a picture frame constructed from 13,000 pieces of wood and containing a drawing of Antonio Maceo. There are also good exhibits on local archaeology, culture and natural history.

At the south side of the square stands a building housing **Poder Popular**, the local government. Here in 1869 Céspedes signed a document abolishing slavery in free Cuba. The **Casa de Cultura** occupies the southeast corner of the square. Along the west side you can find a movie theater and the local post and telegraph office.

One block west of the Museo Céspedes opens the **Plaza del Himno**, named in honor of the national anthem. This is the site of the **Templo del Santísimo Salvador de Bayamo** (1516), Cuba's second-oldest church. The church was gutted by the 1869 fire, but, miraculously, the **Capilla de la Dolorosa** (1733) to the left of the altar was spared, saving a beautiful baroque retable and a mudéjar ceiling. The image of the Virgin on the retable has dark skin and the features of a Bayamesa, say locals. The main arch over the nave is decorated with a fine painting depicting the blessing of Céspedes's rebel flag by a priest at the church door. A glass case displays a figure of Christ on the Via Dolorosa that was hidden from the Spanish by rebel soldiers. Céspedes was baptized in the church's ancient (1540s) wooden font, and an urn guards the ornaments worn by the priest while blessing the flag. Finally—as if you still doubt the church's patriotic significance—12 women gave the first performance of the national anthem here in 1868. Just west of the church, a 19th-century house has been converted into the **Casa de la Nacionalidad Cubana**, a centre for historical investigations. There is an excellent view of the river from the patio behind.

Five blocks south of the park on Calle Céspedes, you come to the **Casa de los Artistas**, an art gallery housed in one of Bayamo's oldest houses, with a large patio and beautiful ceilings. This was also the birthplace of Tomás Estrada Palma, Cuba's first president after independence. The old house next door was the site of the premiere performance of 'La Bayamesa' by a swain to a local beauty named Luz Vázquez. Carlos Manuel de Céspedes lived across the street, and a few steps to the south you find the local **theatre.**

A short walk south on Céspedes and then right on Calle Masó one block will take you back to Calle García. Just to the left stands the **Hotel Plaza,** Bayamo's best peso hotel. Four blocks to the south you come to Av Estévez; here you turn left and enter a square containing the ruined tower of the **Iglesia de San Juan Evangelista**. This church, destroyed by the 1869 fire, was the gateway to Cuba's first cemetery, which was also destroyed. The only remnant of the cemetery is a sculpture from a tomb placed in the base of the tower. Nearby stands the **Relief of the Heroes**, a sculpture featuring portraits of various Cuban patriots.

The street at the south end of the square is Av Marquéz, which begins a half block to the west at the **Parque ñico López**. Originally, this was Bayamo barracks, the army base attacked by Fidel's followers on July 26, 1953. The barracks' officers' club is now a museum celebrating the failed attack and the subsequent bravery and frequent martyrdom of the Revolutionary fighters against Batista. Ñico López was a participant in the Bayamo attack and later in the *Granma* landing. Despite the mosquitoes, the grounds of the barracks have been converted into a very pleasant park, a favorite spot for spooning couples.

In the opposite direction, Av Marquéz heads southeast and merges with the Carretera Central to Santiago (here called Av Cedeño) just before the bus station. Four blocks to the south, Cedeño passes the Soviet-style **Hotel Sierra Maestra,** the best in town. The lobby furniture was donated by Daniel Ortega when he was president of Nicaragua. Two typical Bayamese dishes are *rosquilla* and *matahambre* ('hunger killer'), both sweets, the latter made with yuca.

THE SIERRA MAESTRA

The stunning landscapes and lush mountainsides of the sierra have barely been developed as a tourist destination. From the agricultural town of Yara (as in the Grito de **Yara**; locals say that the Indian chief Hatuey, the 'first rebel' was burned here) 41 kilometres west of Bayamo, a road heads up the Río Yara into the sierra. The only hotel here is the **Villa Turistica Santo Domingo**, with 20 cabins, from which you can take expeditions into the mountains and hike among large virgin forests now protected by a national park. You can also organize visits to Fidel's pre-1959 headquarters and climb Turquino Peak (1,974 metres, 6,580 feet) to see the patriotic monuments there. Militants of the Revolution often ascend the peak to 'reconnect' with the spirit of Fidel and his men. On the north side of the sierra, the forests are lush and humid, with giant ferns and hundreds of species of birds. The south side is dryer, particularly down near the coast, where it is a near desert.

FROM MANZANILLO TO MAREA DEL PORTILLO

Twenty kilometres (13 miles) west of Yara lies the sun-baked and weather-worn port city of Manzanillo overlooking the Gulf of Guacanayabo. For tourists, there is little to recommend here except for lots of yellow 19th-century buildings, ubiquitous potholes and an aura of better days gone past. Manzanillo's glory days were the 1920s, when it was the port for the U.S.-owned manganese mines in the sierra. Today sugar is the major cargo load, and there is also a large fishing cooperative on the grubby Malecón. The main square (on Calle Martí) is notable for an ornate Moorish-style gazebo. The only tourist accommodation is the recently renovated, Soviet-style **Hotel Guacanayabo**, on the hill just west of downtown; the view is its best feature.

From Manzanillo the road heads southwest along the gulf. A few kilometres out of town, you come to the turnoff for **La Demajagua**, Carlos Manuel de Céspedes's sugar plantation. The house is now a museum with displays on his epochal October 10, 1868 oration that sparked a rebellion.

Fifty kilometres (31 miles) from Manzanillo, the sleepy town of Media Luna was the birthplace of Celia Sánchez, a revolutionary and Fidel's devoted secretary until her death in 1980. The family house is now a museum. Eleven kilometres beyond Media Luna, a turnoff to the right takes you to **Playa Las Coloradas.** Now a national park, this was where Fidel and his men landed from the yacht *Granma* in December 1956. A pathway helps you reenact their first steps toward the sierra, and for mass meetings there is also a large square. The bright blue water here is crystal clear, and there is good diving offshore. The region also shelters many endemic species of snails and cacti.

The main road turns south and heads over the western foothills of the Sierra to **Marea del Portillo.** As you descend to the Caribbean, the landscape turns arid, palm trees becoming dry scrub, before ending up at a near-desert along the shore. Like a mirage, rising from the black-sand beaches in the middle of nowhere are three luxurious resort hotels, the **Marea del Portillo**, the **Farallon del Marea** and the **Punta Piedra.** The main customers are Canadians, who fly directly into Manzanillo's airport. You can take excursions to a nearby oyster farm or out to some offshore keys with white-sand beaches. If you get the chance, drive the south coast; you won't regret it. It's one of the most magnificent in all of Cuba. But drive carefully: It can be a real endurance course. As you head east from Marea del Portillo, you hug teal-blue sea on your right and slide past steep cliffs on the left. You'll pass beaches of varying colours, from the dark gray Marea del Portillo to the stark white Playa Hicaco.

■ SANTIAGO DE CUBA PROVINCE

Santiago is one of the smaller provinces of Cuba, but in population it is second only to Havana. It lies on the south coast of Oriente at the east end of the Sierra Maestra. Lush mountains and hills rise from the coast, while to the north are rolling plains covered with sugarcane.

Historians debate whether Columbus actually saw Santiago's large and excellent harbor. Two decades later its value was immediately recognized by the indefatigable Diego Velásquez; on June 28, 1515,

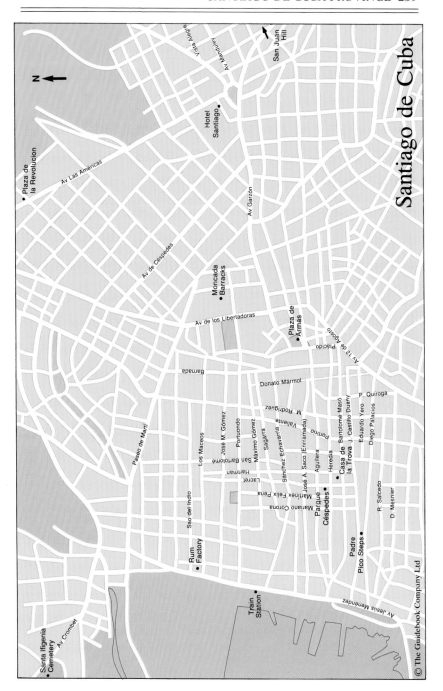

N

Santiago de Cuba

Plaza de
la Revolución

Av Las Américas

Av de Céspedes

Av Manduley

Vista Alegre

San Juan
Hill

Hotel
Santiago

Av Garzón

Moncada
Barracks

Av de los Libertadoras

Plaza de
Armas

Plácido

AV 12 de Agosto

Barnada

Donato Mármol

M. Rodríguez

Valiente

Portirio

José A. Saco (Enrramada)

Casa de
la Trova

Bartolomé Masó

J. Castillo Duany

P. Quiroga

Eduardo Yero

Diego Palacios

Paseo de Martí

Los Maceos

José M. Gómez

Portuondo

Máximo Gómez

San Bartolomé

Sánchez Echavarría

Sagarra

Aguilera

Heredia

Hartman

Lacret

Martínez Félix Peña

Mariano Corona

Parque
Céspedes

R. Salcedo

D. Mesnier

Sao del Indio

Rum
Factory

Padre
Pico Steps

Train
Station

Av Jesús Menéndez

Santa Ifigenia
Cemetery

Av Crombet

© The Guidebook Company Ltd

he founded Santiago de Cuba, the fifth Spanish settlement on Cuba. In 1518, Velásquez sent Hernán Cortés from Santiago on a mission to explore the American mainland. In the meantime, Spanish authorities had named the city the island's capital. This status only lasted until 1553, when the governors moved to Havana, the port of the Treasure Fleet. By this time, Santiago's Spanish population had shrunk to 150; the rest had gone to Mexico and other new colonies to make their fortunes.

Semi-abandoned by the colonial government, Santiago was at the mercy of French, English and Dutch pirates. The worst of these numerous raids came in 1662, when 900 pirates under Henry Morgan captured and burned the town and blew up Morro Castle, which was supposed to defend against these assaults. Between pirate raids, earthquakes shook the region, most severely in 1580.

Santiago's fortunes began to turn around with the discovery of new veins in a nearby copper mine first worked in 1547. The labor was provided by African slaves, who rebelled in 1731 to protest against the inhuman work conditions. Santiago had been the first Cuban city to receive African slaves, and by the 18th century it was well on its way to becoming the mulatto city of today. Next to the copper mine, devout slaves built a small sanctuary to a statuette of the Virgin of Charity found floating in Nipe Bay. Today it is housed in a stately church that draws the faithful from all over Cuba and other countries.

In the late 18th century, travellers were still complaining about the miserable conditions in Santiago—streets knee-deep in mud, ragged natives—but the economy was growing rapidly. Escaping from Haiti's 1791-96 slave uprising, around 3,000 French plantation owners and their families arrived in this city of 10,000 and used their knowledge to found modern sugar and coffee estates. French traditions, such as the *contredanse,* mingled with African and Cuban culture to form a new and unique *santiaguero* culture that became one of the richest in Cuba. From here, new dance forms, musical styles, festivals (such as carnival) and religious practices spread throughout the island.

As with the rest of Oriente, Santiago was a hotbed of rebellion during both Wars of Independence. The local Masonic lodge was a

Santeria: Oshun, orisha of water and love

centre of the conspiracy, and a native son, Antonio Maceo, 'The Bronze Titan', rose to become a leading general and the first Cuban of mixed African and Spanish descent to achieve renown. At the end of the First War of Independence, Maceo met with the Spanish General Martínez de Campos at Baraguá north of Santiago to discuss peace. When the Spaniard read him the terms in the Pact of Zanjón, Maceo rejected them because they did not mention freeing the slaves. Maceo and Martínez de Campos then politely agreed that the war would be resumed, giving Maceo a week to organize his army. Maceo's refusal, known as the 'Protest of Baraguá', is revered as one of the key moments in Cuba's fight for independence. Unfortunately, many whites on the rebel side distrusted Maceo, and he could not rally support. After one or two skirmishes, the 1879 'Guerra Chiquita' ('Little War') around Santiago petered out.

Maceo was also a prime mover in the Second War of Independence. After Martí's death, he was one of the military leaders who took power. In October 1895, symbolically beginning at Baraguá, Maceo began a brilliant campaign in which his forces crossed Cuba all the way to Pinar del Río, burning and destroying as they marched. The Spanish fought back, and Maceo was killed near Havana in December 1896. Despite his victories, a Spanish garrison still controlled the city of Santiago, which it converted into a fortress surrounded by acres of barbed wire. In early 1898, the United States entered the deadlocked conflict, and Santiago was its main target.

With a sense of impending doom, the Spanish fleet assembled at Santiago to await the arrival of the U.S. Navy. Previously, the Americans had secretly conferred with rebel General Calixto García and he had agreed to provide intelligence and support troops. On June 20, 6,000 U.S. soldiers landed unopposed at Daiquirí Beach east of the city. Suffering from dysentery and malaria, they force-marched toward the city and on June 30 finally arrived at the foot of San Juan Hill on its eastern outskirts. Early the next morning they attacked; led in part by future-president Teddy Roosevelt, they charged up the hill in the face of withering fire. They took it, but at a severe cost: 223 U.S. soldiers and 102 Spanish lay dead and many more were wounded. Santiago's eastern defenses were shattered. Smaller Spanish garrisons outside the city were wiped up by the Cuban rebel forces.

Meanwhile, the U.S. fleet had the Spanish navy bottled up in Santiago's harbor. On July 3, the Spanish decided to escape. Some ships were sunk immediately; others made a run for it up the coast to the west and were run aground. The Spanish admiral had to swim ashore. The U.S. asked the Santiago garrison to surrender, and after days of dickering they agreed. On July 17 the Spanish flag was lowered and the U.S. flag—not the Cuban—rose in its place. Not only that, General Calixto García refused to attend the ceremony because Cuban city officials were also present. The U.S. snub of the Cuban rebels still echoes today.

After the war, the U.S. military government went to work rebuilding the city's infrastructure and constructing many new public buildings, including schools and hospitals. In 1912, Cuban blacks began a nationwide series of strikes and demonstrations that hit hardest in Santiago and Guantánamo. In May a force of U.S. Marines landed at Daiquirí Beach, ostensibly to protect U.S. interests, and stood by as the local army killed thousands of blacks.

In the decades before 1959, there were a number of antigovernment conspiracies hatched in Santiago—most notably by a young left-wing activist named Antonio Guiteras—but none was so ambitious as the plans of Fidel Castro. Castro had lived in Santiago from the late 1930s to the early 1940s, attending two Catholic schools there. A decade later in Havana, Fidel hatched a seemingly suicidal plot to attack the Moncada army barracks in Santiago, seize the weapons and use them to topple the government. Beyond the desire to strike a blow at the Batista regime, the plan was designed to unite the fractured opposition behind one man, Fidel Castro.

The Moncada attack was timed to coincide with another raid on the military barracks in Bayamo. In late July of 1953, 134 conspirators gathered at a small farm in Siboney east of Santiago. It was the season of carnival, when Santiago's streets were sure to be chaotic and Batista's soldiers drunk. Armed with a motley selection of rifles and pistols, the revolutionaries set out from Siboney early on the morning of July 26. They broke into three groups; two smaller ones struck at a nearby hospital and the Palace of Justice, while the main body attacked the barracks.

The attack was a disaster; 100 poorly trained men found themselves facing 1,000 soldiers with rifles and machine guns. After an hour-long battle, the revolutionaries fled. Within days, over 80 of them had been captured and most were tortured and then killed. After Fidel's capture, he managed to escape death when the officer in charge disobeyed orders and sent him to the regular jail rather than giving him to the army (for this, the officer was himself jailed and was one of the first released—by Castro himself—at the Triumph of the Revolution). In the subsequent furor, Fidel reached one of his goals: he was now the acknowledged leader of the anti-Batista forces.

Fidel returned to Oriente aboard the yacht *Granma* in early December 1956. In order to distract Batista's forces, the young and brilliant head of the 26 July Movement's Action Section in Oriente, Frank País,

Matching colors

organized a series of daring, highly successful raids in Santiago. They attacked the police station, customs and harbor offices and a number of other buildings, effectively controlling the city for two days before withdrawing with only three of their men dead. País kept the pressure on in Santiago until July 30, 1958, when he was captured in a police raid and summarily executed in the street. His funeral turned into a massive protest demonstration headed by Santiago's mothers, whose sons were being killed indiscriminately by the police. After the funeral, *santiagueros* went on strike, and they were followed by sympathy protests across Cuba.

After Batista fled on January 1, 1959, Fidel Castro appeared in Santiago's Parque Céspedes and gave his first speech (of thousands) as the new leader of Cuba. In honor of Santiago's past, in 1984 it was bestowed the title of 'Hero City of the Republic of Cuba'.

Since the Revolution, rural Santiago has remained largely agricultural, with cattle and sugarcane in the north and coffee in the hills. The city has grown by leaps and bounds, thanks to large-scale industrial

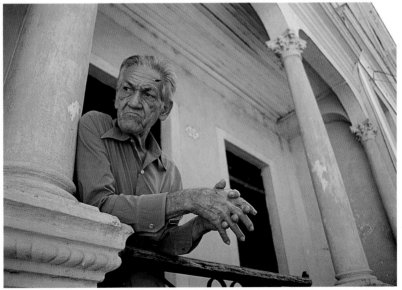

The face of Santiago

development around the harbor. With the help of the Soviets, they have built a huge power plant, an oil refinery, a cement factory and the largest textile mill in Latin America. Luckily, these installations are far enough from downtown not to ruin the city's charm. During the Special Period, Santiago has suffered compared to Havana, and at this writing there are severe shortages of everything from rice to matches.

SANTIAGO DE CUBA CITY

The Sierra Maestra runs along the south coast of Santiago Province from east to west. About halfway along its length, a break in the mountain range forms a bowl in which lies the city of Santiago (pop. 370,000) on the eastern side of Santiago Harbor. The hills protect the city from the prevailing breezes, causing temperatures to rise to stifling levels during the summertime hot season. The rest of the year the climate is usually warm and comfortable. Substantial earthquakes rattle the city two or three times every century; the last big one was in 1942. Near the town of San Luis 21 kilometres northwest of Santiago, the Autopista Nacional miraculously reappears, giving you a six-lane highway on which to make your triumphal entry into the city

Downtown Santiago, which is based on a rough grid pattern, rises from the east side of the harbor. For almost five centuries, the centre of town has been the **Parque Céspedes**, lying seven blocks east of the waterfront between Calles Aguilera and Heredia. Cultural, political, religious and social Santiago all meet here, and tourists can expect to be greeted by a variety of touts and locals curious about the world beyond. For children, the traditional amusement is a ride in a little carriage hitched to a large billy goat.

The square is dominated by Santiago's often-rebuilt **cathedral** occupying the south end. The first church on this site was begun in 1516, and its successive incarnations were repeatedly burned, looted and shaken by temblors and then rebuilt bigger than before. The yellow facade of the current structure was completed in 1922, while the nave is held up by walls erected in 1810. Between the twin towers is a large sculpture of an angel blowing a horn. The main door opens on the

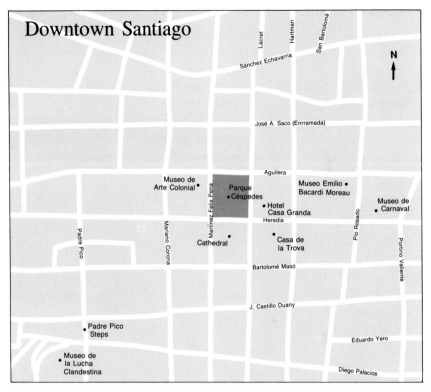

Downtown Santiago

Lacret

Hartman

San Bartolomé

Sánchez Echavarría

N

José A. Saco (Enrramada)

Aguilera

Museo de Arte Colonial

Martínez Félix Peña

Parque Céspedes

Museo Emilio Bacardi Moreau

Mariano Corona

Hotel Casa Granda

Heredia

Museo de Carnaval

Pío Rosado

Cathedral

Casa de la Trova

Padre Pico

Portirio Valiente

Bartolomé Masó

J. Castillo Duany

Padre Pico Steps

Eduardo Yero

Museo de la Lucha Clandestina

Diego Palacios

square, but on the second floor, so you have to enter from the side. Most of the interior decoration, including many paintings, date from the early part of this century. Here you find four neo-classical retables, an elaborate wood choir and an old organ in a state of disrepair. From the balcony outside the main door, there is an excellent view of the square. At street level, the cathedral foundations are occupied by a **bookstore, tourist office, crafts shop** and **ice cream parlor.** Tourist taxis (much less expensive than in Havana) have their stand at the curbside here.

On the east side of the square rises the famous old **Hotel Casa Granda,** now finally restored. In the early part of the century, it was the best hotel in town, 'an admirable blend of American comfort and Castilian charm.' Graham Greene used it as a setting in his *Our*

Man in Havana. Its terrace is a pleasant place to have drinks and watch the action on the plaza. The building next door houses the local Casa de Cultura, with a ground-floor art gallery. Above is the Casa de Matrimonio, where couples recite their civil vows.

The antiquated-looking Ayuntamiento at the north end of the square is actually a 1940s reconstruction of a reconstruction, both of which were destroyed in earthquakes. The Spanish Crown and the American military government made their headquarters here, and today it houses the Poder Popular (the city government). On January 1, 1959, the building's second-floor balcony was the platform for Fidel Castro's first speech as leader of Cuba to thousands assembled in the park and millions listening by radio. Fidel returned here on January 1, 1994, to celebrate 35 years of the Revolution. Inside the entrance, there is a beautiful tiled patio with a well and trees.

The **Museo de Arte Colonial** at the northwest corner of the park is the oldest house in Cuba. It was built in 1516 as the home of Cuba's conqueror, Diego Velásquez. Along the second story runs a

Ayuntamiento, Parque Céspedes

balcony built with a Moorish-style wooden grille to shield its delicate aristocratic occupants from prying eyes. Inside, the old portion of the house contains a large collection of 16th- and 17th-century furniture. Originally, the ground floor contained the smelter where gold was turned into ingots before it was shipped to Spain. Across the patio is a 19th-century addition filled with more period furniture. The modern building next door is the local office of the **Partido Comunista de Cuba**.

The three blocks of **Calle Heredia** east of the square are well worth a stroll. On weekend evenings a stage is constructed here, closing the street to traffic and opening it to a dance party. A few doors east of the park stands Cuba's best-known **Casa de la Trova**. The trova is an indigenous ballad style that began as a form for romantic songs and became politicized with the *nueva trova* movement of the late 1960s. The Casa de la Trova is a combination club house and theater where local troubadours come to show their art. Everyone is welcome, and the performances often run continuously from late morning into the evening. The walls are covered with portraits of renowned local musicians, most famously the members of the Trio Matamoros. At the bar in back you can buy tapes of the local music. At the next corner the Casa de Vino is a bar serving some unique local 'wines', including one made from grapefruit.

The **Casa Heredia** on the next block, is the birthplace of Santiago's most famous poet, José María Heredia (1803-39). His best-known poem, the 'Ode to Niagara', imaginatively places palm trees at the side of the waterfall at the U.S.-Canadian border. The interior contains 19th-century furniture and a pleasant patio. The library opposite was founded by Emilio Bacardí Moreau, the heir to the rum fortune and a revered philanthropist and patriot.

Across Calle Pio Rosado, the north side of the following block is occupied by an old prison now housing the **Museo de Carnaval**. Originally called the Fiesta de las Mamarrachos (roughly, *Festival of the Nincompoops)*, Santiago's carnival—the most famous in Cuba—was founded by three Afro-Cuban social and religious organizations, the Carabalí Izuama, Carabalí Olugo and La Tumba Francesa. These groups practice year-round for the late July celebration, in which huge floats with large papier-mâche figures and costumed dancers in ornate capes take over the city. Each year the celebration has a theme, usually another Latin American or Caribbean country, on which the costumes and floats are based. The parade entrants are judged on originality and popularity—those who attract the most onlookers to their congas win. The sounds of drums beating a rumba rhythm and the wailing *corneta China* ('Chinese cornet') fill the city late into the night, and the entire town takes to the streets, dancing, eating special holiday snacks and drinking gallons of rum and beer. Unfortunately, Santiago's carnival has been cancelled since the onset of the Special Period, and only a dramatic reversal in the local economy will bring it back. A block to the east stands the old **Jesuit college** where Fidel Castro attended high school.

One block north of Heredia on Calle Pio Rosado stands the imposing **Museo Emilio Bacardí Moreau.** In the past this has held a large collection of paintings and objects relevant to local history as well as Bacardí's collection of European art and Egyptian and South American antiquities. One hopes they will be returned if and when the building's restoration is finished—the work has dragged on for years. The **Cafeteria Isabelica** at the corner of Calvario one block to the east is Santiago's most famous coffee shop, with many types of flavored and spiked coffees.

On a rise three blocks south of the Parque Céspedes on Calle Félix Peña and then three blocks west on Calle Palacios (also known as Santa Rita) stands the **Old Police Station.** On November 30, 1958, revolutionaries led by Frank País attacked and burned this building in order to distract attention from the landing of Fidel and his forces aboard the yacht *Granma*. Completely rebuilt, it is now the **Museo de la Lucha Clandestina**, with a large and good exhibition on the underground struggle against the Batista regime. From the second-floor balcony you have an excellent view of the port.

Just below the building are the famous **steps of Padre Pico.** Automobile traffic was impossible on the steepest street in Cuba, so they substituted a picturesque stairway on which children like to play.

One block north of Parque Céspedes, Calle Jose A. Saco—better known as Enramadas—is Santiago's main commercial street. Although the stores have little to offer, the colorful 1950s style signs hanging above the doorways—and the pre-1959 cars that fill the city—give the street the atmosphere of decades past. Enramadas climbs about seven blocks to the Plaza de Armas, a square flanked by two peso hotels, the Rex and the Libertad. Heading east from the north side of the plaza, Av Garzón is the main boulevard to the newer districts—and many of the tourist hotels—spreading to the east.

Two blocks east on Garzón, take a left (north) on Av Libertadores and then a right (east) in two blocks to arrive at the Moncada Barracks, now the 26th of July Historical Museum. This large yellow art deco structure was the target of the famous July 26, 1953, attack that launched Fidel Castro and his band of revolutionaries. The facade is pockmarked with bullet holes that are actually reconstructions based on historical photos (Batista's men had filled them in). The museum inside documents the attack, its causes (beginning with the evils of colonialism) and its bloody aftermath. You can see uniforms stained with the blood of captured revolutionaries and photographs of their corpses. There is also an exhibit on the 1956-58 battle in the Sierra Maestra, displaying among other objects Fidel's sharpshooter rifle. The museum only occupies about a third of the barracks; the rest houses the 26th of July School.

From the Plaza de Armas, Av Garzón runs east down the hill into Santiago's new neighborhoods. At a traffic circle about 1.5 kilometres east, Garzón meets Av Las Americas. Continuing straight, Garzón becomes the tree-lined Av Manduley, which is the main street for the **Vista Alegre**. This was the neighborhood of Santiago's nouveaux riches (the old rich still lived in mansions downtown) and U.S. businessmen in the early part of the century. Many of the beautiful art nouveau mansions have been converted into schools and government institutes; nevertheless, they are well preserved and surrounded by lush greenery. The huge mansion of the Young Pioneers has an old MiG fighter plane in the yard. The small but comfortable **Villa Gaviota** hotel stands at the east end of Av Manduley.

Life passes by, Santiago

From the Garzón traffic circle, Av Pujol runs up the south side of Vista Alegre to **San Juan Hill**. On the right you will see the **Hotel Villa San Juan** (until recently the Motel Leningrado) and a small vista with a memorial to those who fell in battle here. The hill is not particularly high or impressive; it is hard to picture this as the site of a bloody battle. One's historical imagination is not helped by the **26th of July Amusement Park** next door; it is now often idled by power cuts.

Returning to Av Las Americas, immediately to the north of the traffic circle towers the ultramodern, Canadian-designed **Hotel Santiago**, one of the best hotels in Cuba. Drinkers in the 15th-floor lounge have the best view of the city; unfortunately, at night many of the surrounding neighborhoods are blacked out by power outages. Across the avenue stands the **Hotel Las Americas**, which suffers in contrast but is nevertheless inexpensive and comfortable.

A few blocks to the north sprawls the **Plaza de la Revolución**, built for the 1991 Pan-American Games. Here are the Sala Polivalente

Yarayó Fort, Santiago

gymnasium and the Teatro Heredia, which is used for important events like Fidel's annual July 26th speech to the nation. The centre point of the plaza is the gigantic **statue of Antonio Maceo,** a masterpiece of socialist aesthetics. Constructed from bronze, of course, it shows the 'Bronze Titan' astride his rearing horse as if frozen in the instant of battle. He rides amid a field of 23 huge machetes of bronze that symbolize March 23, 1878, the day he vowed to continue the war against the Spanish. A marble-lined bowl is cut into the mound that acts as the statue's base; in it you find the eternal flame and the entrance to a **museum** ($1) containing a holographic portrait of the rebel hero.

Av Las Americas continues north past the **baseball stadium** and meets the entrance to the Carretera Central and, just beyond, the road to Cobre. In this direction lies the **Tropicana,** a huge cabaret that rivals the one in Havana.

Seven blocks west of the Parque Céspedes, Av Jesús Menéndez runs along Santiago's harbor. The water is blocked by docks, ware-

houses and the main **train station**, which turns into a madhouse at
the arrival of the Havana train. A block or two north of the station
stands the 1862 **rum factory** built by the now expatriate Bacardí
family. They now make Ron Caney here. The factory, with its aroma
of rum raisin ice cream, is open for tours. You can visit the factory
store to sample and purchase the excellent local brands, including
some expensive aged labels only for sale here. A **giant rum bottle**
hovering just inland is actually the water tower of the Hatuey brew-
ery, where they make one of Cuba's best beers.

Continuing north, Av Menéndez ends at Av Crombet, where you
take a left and in a few blocks arrive at the **Santa Ifigenia Cemetery**
(1868). This is one of the two most important cemeteries in Cuba
(the other is the Cementerio Colón in Havana). Many of the leading
figures in the various struggles for independence are buried here.
Like most Cuban cemeteries, this is a miniature city of marble tombs
topped with ornate sculptures of angels, Virgins and crosses. Just inside the entrance and to the left stands the 1951 art deco tomb of
José Martí, Cuba's most revered patriot. From ground level, you look
down on a small rotunda with a square stone topped with the Cuban
flag at its centre. The walls are lined with the coats of arms of the
American nations. Nearby are the tombs of Carlos Manuel de Céspedes (the 'Father of the Country'), Tomás Estrada Palma (Cuba's
first president) and a black monolith in memory of Emilio Bacardí
Moreau. A small castle contains the remains of heroes of the Wars of
Independence, and another mausoleum houses the martyrs of the
Moncada attack.

THE MORRO CASTLE

Santiago's fort, the Morro Castle, stands at the east entrance to Santiago Harbor about seven kilometres (four miles) south of town. You
can reach it by a number of roads. From the Parque Céspedes, head
eight blocks south to Trocha and then continue south on Av Chivás,
which turns into the Carretera del Morro. A kilometre before the
castle lies Santiago's airport. Via the industrial zone you can take Av
Menéndez south from the port and keep hugging the harbor all the

THE ISLAND OF RUM

It is hard to believe that rum was not always the most popular drink in Cuba. For many Cubans, a bottle of rum is an essential accessory. No fiesta is complete without it, and, once open, a bottle is never left unfinished. Nevertheless, this taste only appeared about 150 years ago, as a byproduct of the island's sugar boom.

For the Spanish, wine made a meal, and they had no penchant for hard liquor. Among the first crops planted by the Spanish settlers was sugarcane, but they only wanted its products (sugar and molasses) as sweeteners, not to make alcohol. They certainly knew this was possible—in India and the Arab world, alcohol had been made from sugar for over a millennium—but the grape ruled their European palates.

As the Cuban sugar industry slowly grew in the 17th and 18th centuries, so did the amount of residues from the manufacturing process. Those who had no access to expensive imported wines, such as slaves and poor whites, began to use these sugar residues to make liquor. Using homemade stills, they produced near-pure alcohol, which they then watered down to a still potent beverage called 'aguardiente', from *agua* and *ardiente* or 'burning water'. African slaves used aguardiente in religious rituals, and this practice continues today in Santería. Many aguardientes were essentially flavorless, but with experimentation distillers produced a tastier beverage. (Today you can still buy aguardiente, although it is not nearly as popular as rum.)

Meanwhile, Cuba's neighboring islands, English colonies such as Jamaica and Barbados, were doing a booming business in the rum trade. Rum is made from sugarcane juice, molasses and sugar residues mixed with yeast (for fermentation) and bacteria (for flavor) and then distilled into a flavorful, clear liquor. In order to mellow the bite of new rum, the liquor is blended and aged. The color should come from tannin in the oak barrels in which it is aged. Normally, only sugar products are used to make rum, but many distilleries add flavorings like almond extract or mashed fruits.

In 1655, the English Royal Navy decreed that rum was its official drink (beer was too hard to stock for far-flung missions), and its

continues

sailors were given a half pint of 160-proof liquor per day. When the sodden seamen got into too many accidents, the rum was cut fifty per cent by water, making grog. The craze for rum soon spread throughout the English-speaking world and (with molasses for rum making in English distilleries) became the English colonies' biggest export.

Cuba's sugar boom began in the late 18th century with the arrival of thousands of African slaves, the relaxation of trade rules and the immigration of French sugar experts from Haiti. One of the island's biggest markets became the newly independent United States, whose revolutionary spirit had been fired by vast quantities of rum. This potential spurred the nascent Cuban rum manufacturers, but their products were better known for their kick than for their flavor: the English called Cuban rum 'The Old Red-Eyed Brawler'. Far more Cuban molasses was sold to New England rum factories than rum to its drinkers.

The breakthrough for Cuban rum came at the hands of a Spanish immigrant named Don Facundo Bacardí. After settling in Santiago, he became a wine merchant, purchasing a shop that contained a small still for making rum. As a way of improving Cuban rum and selling more abroad, the colonial government had offered a prize to the distiller who produced the smoothest and lightest rum. Bacardí began to experiment with his still. Months of work led to a batch that everybody agreed was the best rum they had ever sampled. On February 4, 1862, Bacardí and Company was founded to manufacture the rum, and its fame quickly spread across the island and internationally.

Soon Cuban rum was being touted as the finest in the world, a perfect match to the island's other exceptional product, the Havana cigar. Competition sprang up throughout the island, and Cárdenas and Manacas joined Santiago as the largest centres of rum manufacture. Despite the Bacardí family's troubles with the Spanish government—his son, Emilio Bacardí Moreau, was a prominent rebel—the company thrived and became the toast of U.S. troops after independence. Perhaps apocryphally, U.S. soldiers are credited with creating the two most famous Cuban cocktails, the daiquiri and the Cuba Libre.

The rum industry boomed up until October 1960, when the Revolutionary government nationalized all distilleries, including Bacardí. From exile in the Bahamas, the Bacardí family began to rebuild their business as an international conglomerate. There are now Bacardí factories in numerous countries, including the Bahamas, Puerto Rico, Canada, Mexico and Spain. Through astute marketing, the company (now based in Bermuda) has made Bacardí rum the world's most popular brand of liquor.

In the 1960s, the government continued to manufacture rum under the Bacardí label in its old Santiago factory. When the state tried to sell the product abroad, though, where the Bacardí family had trademarked the name, the bottles were seized and a lawsuit was filed in the World Court. The government lost, and since then the Santiago factory has changed the name of its product to Caney.

Today, the Bacardí label is a guarantee of a smooth liquor with the same mild flavor wherever it is manufactured. However, it's best suited to mixing into weird concoctions like frozen strawberry daiquiris. For rums to sip and savor, you have to turn to Cuban products. Officially, Havana Club, the dry main export rum, is the top of the line. Most Cubans prefer Caribbean Club, which is slightly sweeter and smoother. But there are dozens of other brands, and nothing is more enjoyable than the hunt for your favorite. A good place to start is the Casa del Ron above the El Floridita Restaurant in Old Havana.

way to the end. About halfway there the road passes the parking area for the hilltop **Parque Frank País**, dedicated to the assassinated revolutionary leader. A path leads up to a big monument. Just inside the harbor entrance you will see **Cayo Granma** (known until the Revolution as Cayo Smith), a very picturesque island with a seafood restaurant and fishermen's houses.

The earliest incarnation of the **Morro Castle** was built around 1640 to ward off pirate attacks. This effort failed; in 1662 the pirate Henry Morgan stormed it and then blew it up. A more solid structure was begun in the late 18th century, and this is what you see today. During the colonial era it also doubled as a prison, holding many Cuban rebels, including Emilio Bacardí Moreau. You enter the fort ($1.50) on a drawbridge over a dry moat. From the battlements—acrawl with lizards basking in the sun—you have a spectacular view of the harbor and its bottleneck entrance. The fort's architecture is particularly interesting; the great stone walls and dramatic angles give you the impression of something that is ancient and at the same time utterly modern. The interior houses the **Museo de la Pirateria**, an exhibition of pirates during the colonial and modern eras. According to the displays, the principal modern pirates are the CIA. You can ponder a captured CIA rubber raft and various weapons.

On the cliffs east of the castle stand a lighthouse and the **Restaurante El Morro**, with tables under a grape arbor and a specialty of horsemeat criollo style. Next door lies the **Hotel Balcon del Caribe**, an older but well kept up resort hotel with a stunning view over the Caribbean. It caters mainly to European tour groups.

COBRE

In the hills 12 to 15 kilometres (7.5 to nine miles) west of town lie the copper-mining town of Cobre ('Copper') and the sanctuary of the **Virgen de la Caridad del Cobre**, or the Virgin of Charity, Cuba's most sacred image. The distance depends on which route you take— the old road or the turnoff from the Carretera Central—both of which begin at the north end of Av Las Americas.

In 1608 two Indians and a young slave named Juan Moreno found the statue of the Virgin, with the identifying inscription 'I am the Virgin of Charity', floating in the waters of Nipe Bay on the north coast. According to legend, this was the same statue given to the Indian chief by the conquistador Alonso de Ojeda in 1510; the chief set it adrift when his jealous enemies repeatedly tried to capture it. The Virgin was originally housed in Santiago's cathedral, but it was moved after being damaged in a 1677 earthquake. Its new home was in a small sanctuary next to the copper mines of Cobre, where it became the patroness of the slaves working below. Over the years, the sanctuary has been improved and expanded; the most recent church

Castillo del Morro

dates from the 1920s. The Virgin was named patroness of Cuba in 1916.

The three yellow towers of the church dominate the valley; it stands on a hilltop above the mineworker's town of Cobre. It is open daily 6:30 am-6 pm and masses are offered Monday to Saturday at 8 am and Sunday at 8 am, 10 am and 4:30 pm. In 1993, the church was briefly closed to foreigners after tourists forced their way inside to take photos during a religious service. Common decency dictates that you honour local customs and any restrictions.

If you get permission, the sanctuary is well worth a visit. Most enter the building from the parking lot at the rear. The room behind the altar is a small chapel with a fascinating collection of votive offerings to the Virgin in thanks for her intercession. Here are autographed baseballs, Revolutionary Armed Forces patches and photographs of rafts that made it to Florida with her help. Until recently, the star attractions were Ernest Hemingway's Nobel Prize medal and a Catholic amulet given to the sanctuary by Fidel's mother for the protection of her son. Both are now kept in a vault after the Nobel Prize medal was stolen (and subsequently recovered).

A stairway to one side leads up to a second-floor chapel immediately behind the main altar and the image of the Virgen del Cobre. Kept in a glass case, the Virgin wears a copper and gold cape and crown and holds an infant Jesus. During mass, the figure is rotated to face the congregation. From the main entrance a long flight of stairs leads down to town.

Even in this atheistic country, with a long tradition of distrust for the Catholic Church, few Cubans would be so foolish as to omit a prayer to the Virgen del Cobre in a time of trouble. In Santería, she is the image of Ochún, the goddess of eros, who is always dressed in yellow. Her festival is celebrated on September 8.

PARQUE BACONAO

East of San Juan Hill, Av Pujol heads out to Baconao Park, a 52-kilometre-long zone of resort hotels, beaches, restaurants and amusement areas built since the Revolution. This was also the route taken by two invading forces, first the Americans in 1898 and next Fidel Castro's revolutionaries in 1953. The road is lined with 26 memorials—for July 26, 1953—to the fighters who died in the Moncada assault. (Also, Fidel was born in 1926 and was 26 years old in 1953—numerology is very popular in Cuba.)

About 10 kilometres (six miles) east of town, a road heads left 14 kilometres (nine miles) up to **La Gran Piedra**, a peak of the Sierra Maestra mountains. The road is one of the steepest and windiest in Cuba, and you should watch out for livestock, cowboys, hikers and landslides. Near the cloud-wrapped summit, the forest turns to pines and the cool, sometimes chilly breeze is a respite from the Santiago heat. You can spend a night here at the Villa La Gran Piedra tourist cabins. La Gran Piedra is an immense rock whose 1,234-metre (4,113 foot) summit is reached by a trail with about 460 steps. Clouds permitting (mornings are clearer), you have an eagle's-eye view of the coast to the south and green valleys to the north. The neighboring rock holds a meteorological station.

During the early 19th century, many French refugees from Haiti built coffee estates up in these cool heights. The remains of the La Isabelica plantation, in a charming state of decay, may be seen about half a kilometre beyond the Gran Piedra. You enter via the coffee-drying floors. Its walls mottled with orange lichen, the main house takes on an aura of mystery when wrapped in clouds. It now contains a museum of the early coffee industry. A path to the right leads to the circular thatched hut where the coffee was ground.

Returning to earth and the road to Bacanao, shortly before the beach town of Siboney, you see on the right the Granjita Siboney. A few weeks before July 26, 1953, this farmhouse was rented by Abel Santamaria, Fidel's second-in-command, and the revolutionaries gathered here on the night before the Moncada attack. The weapons were hidden in the nearby well. After the assault, some of the revolutionaries were captured, tortured and killed here. The bullet holes in the walls are reconstructions. Inside is a small museum exhibiting the bloody uniforms of the martyrs and many of the same materials found in the Moncada museum. **Siboney's** beach is very popular with young *san-*

Iglesia del Cobre

tiagueros. A few kilometres to the east is the turn off for the **Hotel Bucanero**, a resort hotel built into the rocks next to a beautiful little cove.

About ten kilometres east of Siboney, the road passes through the Valley of Prehistory ($1). This park contains 169 painted concrete replicas of dinosaurs and prehistoric mammals and humans, all frozen in action poses. None of them were endemic to Cuba. They are all life-size except for the gigantic caveman threatening to use his club on the buses in the parking lot. Look for the caveman burial and the bear eating the cavewoman. Aside from tourists, the only live animals found here are a flock of goats calmly munching among the prehistoric beasts.

At the next intersection you find the **Museum of Transport** ($1), a collection of old cars donated to the Cuban government by a Spaniard. Among the attractions are the handmade smallest car in Cuba, Beny Moré's Cadillac and hundreds of toy cars inside the museum. A road to the right heads down to the **Daiquirí Beach**, site of the 1898 landing by U.S. troops and now home of **Villa Daiquirí** resort hotel. According to legend, the daiquiri cocktail was named by a U.S. soldier in honor of this beach.

The road continues east through a game preserve to the **Baconao Lagoon** at the end of the road. At this writing, the area is closed for reconstruction. When it reopens, it will contain a number of beachfront resorts, a crocodile nursery, a cactus garden, an amusement park, the largest aquarium in Cuba and an exhibition of Mesoamerican art donated by the Mexican government.

The virgin of Cobre, patroness of Cuba

■ GUANTÁNAMO PROVINCE

Occupying the easternmost end of Cuba, Guantánamo Province has long been one of the poorest and most remote areas of the island. Aside from a region of flat agricultural land around Guantánamo City, the province is largely mountainous, containing part of the Sagua-Baracoa group of ranges. Cuba's driest and wettest regions are found here. The south coast is a near-desert dotted with cacti, while the Baracoa region is humid and lush, the perfect climate for coconut trees and cacao plantations.

Before the arrival of the Europeans, Guantánamo was home to a Taíno people with advanced agricultural and artisan skills. According to archaeologists, they were recent arrivals themselves, having only landed here around AD 1450. One of the most interesting discoveries in the region is a ballcourt resembling the ones found in Mexico, raising the possibility of a Central American connection.

It is a matter of debate, but many historians believe that Columbus landed here on his 1492 voyage. He described a flat-topped mountain that could easily be El Yunque near Baracoa. The remnants of a cross he supposedly planted are now housed in Baracoa's church. On his second voyage in 1494, Columbus explored Guantánamo Bay on the region's south coast. This later became an important source of salt for the colony.

In late 1510 or early 1511, Diego Velásquez arrived at Baracoa from Hispañola. His mission was to conquer Cuba for the Spanish Crown. Baracoa was the capital of Cuba until 1515, when Velásquez moved his government to the more strategic port of Santiago. Since then Baracoa has fallen into obscurity, blocked from the main currents of Cuban history by the impassible mountains. At the beginning of the Second War of Independence, many of the rebel leaders, including José Martí and Antonio Maceo, made their landings here, because the area's remoteness concealed them from the Spanish army.

The rest of Guantánamo Province was not really settled until the late 18th century, when thousands of French from the nearby colony of Ste. Domingue (Haiti) moved here to escape the slave rebellion. The lowlands were converted into sugar plantations, and many coffee estates were established in the hills. The city of Guantánamo was founded in 1796. Thousands of African slaves were moved here in the early 19th century, and, after the abolition of slavery, the province attracted many plantation workers from Haiti, Jamaica and other Caribbean islands. As a result, the province's inhabitants have the highest percentage of African blood in Cuba.

In 1901, the American military government forced Cuba to indefinitely lease the land around Guantánamo Bay's entrance for a U.S. Navy base. (See the 'Guantánamo' special essay, page 268.) The U.S. only kept a small post here until World War II, when it was expanded into a major port and airbase. Between 1945 and 1959, the base was one of the area's largest employers in the area and extremely important to the local economy. This relationship changed after the Revolution, of course. After a number of years of high tension and military incidents along the border, the situation has cooled down to an uneasy and highly separate peace.

The Cuban Revolution also brought great changes to Baracoa. After centuries of only being accessible by sea, a winding road called La Farola ('The Beacon') was constructed across the mountains. Today it has an airport and modern schools and hospitals. Nevertheless, Havana seems very far away.

GUANTÁNAMO CITY

East from Santiago, a road winds through an inland valley and agricultural towns, such as La Maya, with a population largely of African ancestry. The south side of the valley is lined with the inland cliffs of the coastal range. About 25 kilometres (15 miles) west of Guantánamo City, the road turns into a four-lane highway with more cattle than cars as traffic.

You enter town from the north, via the **Plaza de la Revolucion**, with a large and ugly sculpture and some of the last billboards glorifying the achievements of Karl Marx and Friedrich Engels. Just to the left (west) is the Soviet-style **Hotel Guantánamo**, the town's best accommodation. Farther south you find the **Parque Martí**, Guantánamo's main square. Before 1959, this was a favorite gathering spot of U.S. sailors. The square is lined with some nice 19th-century buildings but little of tourist interest. In the residential neighborhoods, many of the houses have a cactus on the roof. According to Oriente custom (you also see them in Santiago), the cacti will repel the evil eye, but if it dies you will have one year of bad luck. Outside the city lies the **Stone Zoo**, a park filled with all kinds of animals carved by a self-taught local artist. Unfortunately, they are now in need of restoration.

A road southeast of town leads to the fishing and salt-refining village of **Caimanera** on the border of the naval base. This is a restricted zone—many Cubans have tried to swim into the base from here—and you must pass through two checkpoints to enter the town. Tourists can only enter if they have reservations at the Hotel

Caimanera (see below). After the police checkpoint, you pass across a couple of kilometres of salt flats on the south side of the Cuban watchtowers and fence surrounding the base. The American watchtowers are set back from the border to reduce the possibility of incidents. The largest minefield in the Western Hemisphere is here, invisible just belowground.

Shortly before the military checkpoint at the entrance to town, you see the picturesquely desolate local cemetery on the right. Caimanera is a somnolent seaside town with wooden houses, muddy streets and a few new apartment buildings. On a rise at the centre of town, the recently constructed Hotel **Caimanera** is well worth a stay, with 17 rooms built around a swimming pool and excellent food. At night you can see the bright lights of the naval base, blazing away like a small U.S. city.

THE GUANTÁNAMO NAVAL BASE

There is no transit between the rest of Cuba and the U.S. naval base. The latter is also off-limits to all but approved U.S. military personnel and their families, so it is even difficult to get there from the United States. However, you can enter the Cuban military zone and climb to a lookout on a hill above the base. You must arrange this with a hotel travel desk a couple of days in advance, either in Santiago or in Guantánamo City.

East of the city, a road runs through a dry plain along the east side of the harbor. At kilometre 24 (mile 15), you arrive at an intersection with a military checkpoint on the right. Unless you are with a military guide, you will not be allowed to enter the military zone. From here a road winds 10 kilometres (six miles) to the lookout through forests of cacti. Among these are the treelike *aguacate cimarron,* whose largest specimens may be over a century old. Many of the cacti were planted by the army as a natural fence, hence the 'Cactus Curtain'.

The road ends at a hill just northeast of the base. From here you enter a concrete bunker dug out from the hill. In times of conflict, this is a military command post equipped with meeting rooms and a kitchen. Here you can examine a large diorama of the base in order to get oriented. A stairway leads to the hilltop lookout covered with camouflage netting. Soldiers will lend you Soviet binoculars so you can spy on the base. It looks like nothing so much as an ideal suburban U.S. community, with split-level ranch houses, streetlights, offices and a mall. The base occupies 117 square kilometres of Cuban land and includes a port, two airfields and around 7,000 inhabitants, according to the soldiers. An American flag flies over the base entrance just below the hill. The only ones who ever pass between the two zones are a handful of aging Cuban workers; they have been working on the base since before 1959 but maintain their homes on the Cuban side. The lookout also contains a restaurant specializing in grilled chicken.

continues on page 272

Main gate, Guantánamo Bay Naval Base

GUANTÁNAMO BAY NAVAL BASE

By Natalie Coe

Guantánamo Bay Naval Base is the oldest U.S. military base on foreign soil, and the only U.S. base ever to be situated in a communist country. To the chagrin of the Cuban government, it is also the only U.S. military base with an infinite lease.

Toward the end of the 19th century, the United States was seeking to expand its spheres of political, economic and military influence. The Spanish-American War stemmed from such expansionist sentiment, and in 1898 the U.S. Marines seized Guantánamo Bay to aid in that campaign but also with an eye toward protecting the proposed Panama Canal.

Often described as one of the world's great natural harbors, Guantánamo Bay's natural assets—its deep harbors and ready access to major sea-lanes—were exploited in the U.S. campaign against the Spanish at Santiago de Cuba. The American troops, soon joined by Cubans, fought to secure the eastern part of Cuba and barricade the Spanish stronghold at Santiago. The U.S. government and the public, aided by glowing press reports, were soon convinced of Guantánamo's usefulness as a linchpin of U.S. naval power in the Caribbean.

In part to protect its new base, the U.S. obliged the Cuban Assembly to write the Platt Amendment into its own constitution of 1901. Although deeply resented by the Cuban Assembly and the Cuban public, the Platt Amendment was finally passed; it stated that 'to enable the United States to maintain the independence of Cuba, and to protect the people thereof, as well as for its own defense, the Cuban Government will sell or lease to the United States the lands necessary for coaling or naval stations, at certain specified points . . .' The U.S. was to pay an annual rent of $2,000 in gold coins. (This was changed to $4,085 in 1934, when gold coins were discontinued. Fidel Castro, not wishing to appear to accept the legality of the base's existence, has only cashed one of the annual checks, the first one. The U.S. continues to send a check each year, and while uncashed, they are all still valid.)

Even then, controversy surrounded Guantánamo's existence, and the thorny issues of ultimate sovereignty over the area and the lease's duration have been debated ever since. During the base's early years, other problems surfaced as well: The base, surrounded by hills, would be highly vulnerable to land attack. Water was another problem. The Navy had assumed deep wells would suffice, but no water was found, meaning that water would have to come from rivers several miles away, passing through Cuban territory and thus vulnerable to attack as well. The base at Guantánamo could defend Cuba from foreign attack, but the greater threat, then as now, came from just over the fenceline.

Although the base underwent some development, Guantánamo's only role in World War I was that of a refueling station. For the next 20 years, Guantánamo changed little in either size or function, and life at the base was quiet.

In 1934, Franklin D. Roosevelt's 'Good Neighbor' doctrine ushered in a less interventionist era in U.S.-Latin American relations. The U.S. abrogated the Platt Amendment, except, however, for the portion relating to Guantánamo Bay. A new U.S.-Cuban treaty in 1934 formalized the 1903 agreement on Guantánamo, adding that 'So long as the United States shall not abandon the said naval station of Guantánamo or the two Governments shall not agree to a modification of its present limits, the station shall continue to have the territorial area that it now has . . .' In effect, the lease of Guantánamo Bay is infinite. This status, as well as the fact that the original treaty was imposed on an unwilling Cuba, has led many to question the base's legality.

In the late 1930s, as the possibility of war with Europe grew, Guantánamo underwent extensive development, and some $34 million was invested toward that end. During World War II, the base's population reached a high of 10,000 personnel, who provided logistic services and support for the U.S. Atlantic Fleet, kept the bay free of mines, rescued survivors of ships torpedoed in the area, protected merchant shipping threatened by German submarines and patrolled for German U-boats themselves. After the war, the base's operations were greatly curtailed in the postwar military cutbacks.

continues

The base's position in Cuba, always somewhat tenuous, became more so as Fidel Castro and his guerrillas began operations in the Sierra Maestra, just west of Guantánamo Bay, in 1956. The U.S. government, in violation of the 1903 agreement on Guantánamo, supplied Batista with munitions from Guantánamo and allowed him to refuel his bombers there in the war against the guerrillas. In June of 1958, in retaliation, Raúl Castro seized a busload of Guantánamo personnel returning from leave. Their release was negotiated, but Cuban territory was declared off-limits to base personnel. The naval base closed its gates for good on January 1, 1959, except to select Cuban nationals working on the base. (No Cubans have been hired since, but a handful remaining from the pre-Castro era still commute to work on the U.S. base.)

Guantánamo Bay Naval Base posed an ideological dilemma for the new government of Fidel Castro. While the existence of an American military base was antithetical to Castro's revolutionary ideas, he was also wary of the possible consequences of provoking the U.S. over Guantánamo. With that in mind, Castro inveighed against the base, but made no move either to seize it or to officially approach the U.S. to change its status.

In 1961, Castro ordered a large number of cactuses of a species known for its particularly prickly spines to be planted along the northeastern section of the fenceline around the base, an area that came to be known as the 'Cactus Curtain'. This was to discourage any Cuban from fleeing to Guantánamo, by then a regular occurrence. Although under the terms of the lease the U.S. is obliged to return fugitives to Cuba, many Cubans continue to attempt their escapes via Guantánamo, usually by swimming to the base. The U.S. does not return them to the Cuban authorities, but, mindful of the lease, neither confirms nor denies the existence of such refugees.

The missile crisis in 1962 created obvious difficulties for Guantánamo. Dependents and civilian personnel were evacuated, but though the atmosphere was tense, the big showdown never came to pass. Tensions around the fenceline, however, continued unabated. The Cubans stepped up the patrols along their side of the fence, and tightened procedures for the Cuban employees of the base to pass to the other side. On its side, the U.S. laid down a 735-acre minefield, described as the largest active U.S. minefield in the free world.

In February of 1964, the Cuban government, in retaliation for a dispute over fishing rights, finally cut off the water supply to Guantánamo. Although the U.S. had long contemplated this possibility, the incident suddenly sparked off a national crisis. Guantánamo was ordered to become self-sufficient, and over $10 million was spent to transport a desalination plant to Guantánamo and assemble it. The costs of self-sufficiency are extremely high for the U.S.; absolutely everything must be flown or shipped in, save what can be grown on the base itself.

After the water crisis, hostilities over Guantánamo subsided and stabilized to the point of stalemate. There were numerous fenceline incidents, usually involving the U.S. guards shooting at the Cuban patrols; each side would then accuse the other of staging such incidents deliberately in order to provoke a larger confrontation or to distract the Cuban or American public from domestic problems.

In 1977, the debate over the Panama Canal Treaty and its goal of returning the canal to the Panamanians inevitably raised questions about the status of Guantánamo. The secretary of the Navy even proposed closing Guantánamo, but the recommendation was later reversed and the base merely consolidated.

Recently, Guantánamo served as a U.S. detention camp for Haitians fleeing turmoil in their country. Forty thousand Haitian boat people were detained at Guantánamo, 10,000 of whom were finally allowed to pursue their asylum claims in the United States. The remainder were repatriated to Haiti, and the detention camp at Guantánamo was closed in June of 1993. In 1995, in the depths of the economic crisis, hundreds and then thousands of rafters began to leave Cuba's shores every day, seekng a better life in the United States. Instead of deterring them, the Cuban government decided to relieve pressure and let them go. Unlike in the Mariel exodus of the early 1980s, however, the U.S. did not allow them in immediately but detained them for months on the Guantánamo base until new homes could be found for them and hardened criminals were weeded out. Since that episode, an agreement between the two countries allows the U.S. to immediately return to Cuba any Cubans trying to enter

continues

the country without the proper visa. At present, Guantánamo continues its normal duties of training the entire U.S. Atlantic Fleet.

Guantánamo Bay Naval Base has always seemed an anomaly, and seems even more out of place in the post-cold war world. Yet the United States seems unlikely to abandon the base given the financial and ideological capital it has sunk into it, and the base remains, an outpost of the United States in communist Cuba and another obstacle to improved relations between the two countries.

—A graduate of Oxford University,
Natalie Coe has travelled extensively in Cuba

BARACOA

The road to the easternmost point of Cuba heads from Guantánamo Bay over a range of dry hills and then along the empty southern coastline. On one side of the road are red, cactus-covered cliffs and on the other crashing waves. Low cliffs all along the coast make swimming impossible except for in a few coves with dark-sand beaches. The small towns here live off fruit orchards (the mangoes are excellent in July and August), fishing and salt.

Just after **Playitas de Cajobabo**, where José Martí landed shortly before his death in 1895, the road turns inland to become **La Farola** ('The Beacon'), the windingest road in Cuba. It runs over the mountains—the landscape gradually becomes lusher—49 kilometres (31 miles) to Baracoa. From a lookout at the summit, you can see the northern and southern coasts of Cuba. From here you drop down into Baracoa's lush coastal plain. This is the home of the polymite, a small land snail with a brightly colored shell that is one of the wonders of nature of Cuba.

For this writer, Baracoa is the most charming town on the island. It is the Cuban version of Macondo in Gabriel García Márquez's *One Hundred Years of Solitude*. Myths, and lies, abound. The Three Lies of Baracoa are: La Farola ('The Beacon'), the Río de Miel ('River of Honey') and El Yunque ('The Anvil' but also 'The Ship'), because the first has no light, the second no honey and the last is not a ship. Baracoa has no heavy industry; its inhabitants live off of tourism and agriculture, particularly coconuts and cacao, of which the area is the largest producer in Cuba.

After crossing the Río de Miel, the road enters town via the new section of modern apartment houses, luckily hidden by the ornamental shrubbery lining the road. It becomes the wave-battered **Malecón** by the waterfront baseball stadium. Shortly, on the left you see the **Fuerte Matachín** (1739-42), now the local museum. This contains good exhibits on local history and culture. It has particularly interesting displays on three local personalities who help make up the Baracoa Myth: El Pelu, La Rusa and Cayamba. Baracoa's historian, Alejandro Hartman, has his office in the museum and is a trove of information about the area.

About a kilometre (half mile) to the west stands the bright yellow **Hotel La Rusa**, originally the home of La Rusa, a Russian woman who became enamored of the town and the Revolution. Three blocks inland lies the **Parque Central**, Baracoa's main square (actually a triangle). The weathered **Iglesia de la Asunción** on the east side is Cuba's oldest

Hotel La Rusa, Baracoa

existing church, founded in 1512. It was destroyed by pirates in 1652; the present incarnation dates from the early 19th century. Unfortunately, the early interior decor was cleared out by a previous pastor. The church's one great relic is the gilt **Cruz de la Parra**. Locals believe that this was the cross planted here by Columbus in 1492. It was found buried along the shore in the 19th century. According to recent scientific tests, the wood in the cross dates from the mid-15th century, making the Columbus attribution possible. The church's pastor, Valentin Sanz, is another expert on the region and an avid photographer. In the centre of the plaza stands a bust of Hatuey, the Indian chief who asked to go to Hell rather than Heaven with all the Spaniards. A block east on Calle Maceo you find the **Casa de Chocolate**, where they sell locally made chocolate bars and ice cream.

On a hill overlooking the plaza stands the **Hotel Castillo**, built inside another 18th-century Spanish fort with an excellent view of the town. To the west you can see **El Yunque**, the flat-topped mountain that is one of the region's landmarks. The hotel has the best restaurant in the region; some guests stay for months at a time. There are few other sights downtown, but it is pleasant just to wander the streets looking in doorways and finding things like the jukebox repair shop and the cigar factory.

At the west side of town stands La Punta fort, now housing a restaurant, at the entrance to Baracoa's little harbor. The grounds of the **Hotel Portosanto** next to the **airport** on the opposite side of the harbor are the supposed site of Columbus's cross painting. A road here runs a couple of kilometres to the **Fabrica de Cucurucho**. This is the world's only factory for *cucurucho,* a delicious soft coconut and sugar candy that comes wrapped in triangular packages made from palm leaves. Stock up: it is only sold here in Baracoa. It is said that if you bathe in the nearby **Río Toa,** you will definitely return to Baracoa. The nearby hills, including El Yunque, are filled with wildlife and caves with Indian relics. **Excursions** can be arranged at the Hotel Castillo or through **Gaviotatours** in Havana (33-8808)

A couple of kilometres on the way back to Guantánamo, there is a turnoff left (east) to **Maisí**, a town and lighthouse at the easternmost tip of Cuba. Due to a collapsed bridge, you can not reach Maisí without the most rugged four-wheel-drive vehicle. Nevertheless, an abbreviated drive is worthwhile; the road passes along kilometres of deserted black-sand beaches. Cave paintings have been found in the hills. **Yumurí** is an impoverished fishing village at the mouth of the Río Yumurí. Locals will take you up river through a steep gorge to various swimming holes and catch and cook fish for you. Beyond Yumurí are some small towns where farmers grow coffee and vegetables in deep red soil that stains the landscape.

From the Diary of Columbus

Sunday 28 October

He went from there to the south-southwest looking for the nearest land of the island of Cuba and he entered a very beautiful river free of dangerous shoals or other obstacles. And the whole coast that he went along there was very deep and clear [of shallows] all the way to land. The mouth of the river had a depth of 12 *brazas* and was quite wide enough for tacking. He anchored a lombard shot, he says, inside. The Admiral says that he never saw such a beautiful thing, full of trees all surrounding the river, beautiful and green and different from ours, each one with its own kind of flowers and fruit. [There were] many birds, and some little birds that sang very sweetly. There were great numbers of palms, differing from those of Guinea and from ours: of medium height and the trunks without covering and the leaves very large. With them they cover their houses. And the land [is] very level. The Admiral got into the launch and went ashore and reached two houses which he thought belonged to fishermen who had fled in fear. In one of them he found a dog that never barked, and in both houses he found nets of palm thread and cords and a fishhook of horn and fish spears of bone and other fishing equipment and,

continues

inside, many fires; and he thought that each house was occupied by many persons jointly. He ordered that not a thing of all this was to be touched, and thus it was done. The grass was as tall as in Andalusia in April and May; he found much purslane and pigweed. He returned to the launch and went up the river for some time and it was, he says, a great pleasure to see those green plants and groves and the birds, for he could not leave to go back. He says that that island is the most beautiful that eyes have ever seen: full of good harbors and deep rivers, and the sea appears as if it must never rise, because the growth on the beach reaches almost to the water, which it usually does not where the sea is rough. Up until then they had not experienced rough seas in any of those islands. He says that the island is full of very beautiful mountains, although they are not great in length, but high, and all the other land is high after the manner of Sicily. It is full of streams of water according to what he could understand from the Indians whom he took in the island of Guanahani and has with him. They tell him by signs that there are ten big rivers: and that with their canoes they cannot circle it in 20 days. While he was going toward land with the ships, two dugouts or canoes came out. And when they saw that the sailors were getting into the launch and were rowing to go look at the depth of the river in order to know where they should anchor, the canoes fled. The Indians said that in that island there were gold mines and pearls, and the Admiral saw a likely place for pearls and clams, which are a sign of them. And the Admiral understood that large ships from the Grand Khan came there and that from there to *tierra firme* was a journey of ten days. The Admiral named that river and harbor San Salvador.

—*The Diario of Christopher Columbus's First Voyage to America, 1492-1493*

Castillo de la Real Fuerza, Old Havana

Hotels

CUBA'S HOTELS HAVE COME A LONG WAY in the decade since the Revolutionary government began developing tourism. Havana, Varadero, Santiago and some of the smaller beach resorts contain hotels that would be considered very good by any international standard. As the tourism industry learns how to better tend visitors' needs, and as they learn from the many foreign managers who have arrived in the last two years, you can be sure that accommodations will improve even more.

Hotels are rated by a star system—from one up to five—that is not always reliable, because the stars are given by the hotels themselves, not some independent organization. In April 1994, the old Cubatur organization was dissolved, and its hotels were divided into three new groups: Gran Caribe handling luxury hotels, and Horizontes for moderate- and budget-priced hotels. The third group, Isla Azul, is to be the parent organization for all of Cuba's peso-only hotels. Although it is possible for foreigners to stay in the latter hotels, it is technically illegal, and they are not included in the following list. You can also stay in a number of hotels belonging to Cubanacan, which has many new beach resorts, and Gaviota, specializing in smaller hotels, many in beautiful natural settings. Cuba's tourism year is divided into the more expensive high season—December 1 to April 30 and July 1 to August 31—and the cheaper low season (the rest of the year). You can generally get far better rates through package tour operators abroad than at the hotel desk in Cuba. Note that hotel telephone numbers are often changed, so what works one month may not the next.

PRICE RANGE OF HOTELS IN U.S. DOLLARS		
(For a single room, as of July 1998)		
	High Season	Low Season
★★★★★	$70 – 190	$60 – 155
★★★★	$50 – 80	$40 – 70
★★★	$30 – 40	$25 – 35
★★	$18 – 30	$15 – 25
★	$16	$14

HAVANA

COHIBA ★★★★ **Calle Paseo at 1st and the Malecon, Vedado, tel 333636.** The new Cohiba is the first Cuban hotel built expressly for international business travellers. The smoked glass building could fit into any major world city. Inside, you find every amenity, including meeting rooms, a gym, shops and the best hotel food in Havana. The 582 rooms contain all the modern conveniences, such as satellite TV and an up-to-date phone system.

HABANA LIBRE ★★★★★ **Calle L between Calles 23 and 25, Vedado, tel 334011, 606 rooms.** This tower was originally the Havana Hilton; after 1959 Revolutionaries disported here. Today the Hubana Libre is finally near the end of its top-to-bottom renovation. The ground floor is the place to meet in Vedado; it contains shops, airline offices, a post office, long-distance phone office and a sparkling new cafeteria.

NACIONAL ★★★★★ **Calles O and 21, Vedado, tel 333564, 495 rooms.** The Nacional is the *grande dame* of Havana hotels, a 1930 wedding cake that was designed by the same architect who built Palm Beach's Breakers and the Biltmore in Coral Gables. During the 1950s the mobster Meyer Lansky operated one of Cuba's most elegant casinos here. The Spanish tile interior was recently renovated and while the new furniture does not exactly match it, it still has much of the old aura. Its nightclub and restaurant are some of the classiest in Cuba, and it also contains a number of shops and a pool by the side of which mobsters used to play penny-ante poker.

RIVIERA ★★★★ **Avs Paseo and Malecón, Vedado, tel 334051, 383 rooms.** The Riviera happily preserves an authentic late-1950s Florida modernism decor. Meyer Lansky spent $14 million on its construction, the first hotel specifically designed with a casino. It is located right on the Malecón, with a saltwater pool, shops and a nightclub occupying the old casino. It is currently undergoing a much-needed renovation.

Cannon, Morro castle

SANTA ISABEL ★★★★★ **Calle Baratillo 9, Plaza de Armas, Old Havana, tel 338201, 27 rooms.** This colonial palace is now a small luxury hotel. Most rooms overlook Havana's beautiful Plaza de Armas. The restaurant claims to serve gourmet Spanish cuisine.

AMBOS MUNDOS ★★★★ **Calle Obisbo 153, Old Havana, tel 669529, 54 rooms.** Ernest Hemingway's favorite Havana hotel (his old room is now a museum), the Ambos Mundos recently reopened after a long renovation. The rooms are now modern and comfortable, and the rooftop bar and restaurant is a pleasant place to spend an evening.

CAPRI ★★★★ **Calles 21 and N, Vedado, tel 333747, 235 rooms.** The Capri was built to house Santo Traficante Jr.'s casino. It needs a renovation to return it to its sharp-edged 'Miami Beach mod' elegance. Rooftop pool and the Salon Rojo nightclub.

COPACABANA ★★★★ **Calle 3 at 84th, Miramar, tel 241037.** This small, comfortable beach-front hotel is a favorite with businessmen. The rooms are large and comfortable, and the services include meeting halls, tennis courts and a disco. Evenings, the hotel presents a free water ballet show in the pool.

COMODORO ★★★★ Av 1 and Calle 84, Miramar, tel 245541, 139 rooms. This modern resort hotel sprawls on the beach out in Miramar. You can go into town—a 15-minute drive— or stay here with three restaurants, a big pool and all the services.

INGLATERRA ★★★★ Calles Prado and San Rafael, Centro Havana, tel 627072, 86 rooms. In the 19th century, the Inglaterra was the flagship of Cuba's tourism industry. The atmosphere is charming, but the services and the food need to be brought into the late 20th century. On weekend nights, the rooms echo with loud music from the rooftop terrace.

NEPTUNO-TRITON ★★★★ Calles 3 and 70, Miramar, tel 241606, 556 rooms. Linked by a pool and a restaurant complex, these two towers are known as 'The Prince and the Pauper.' The poor relation, the Triton is now being renovated to bring it up to the same level as its sibling. The hotels are right on the beach in Miramar.

PANAMERICANO ★★★★ Calle A and Av Central, Cojímar, tel 684101, 103 rooms. The Panamericano was built near the beaches east of Havana to house athlete's for the games; today it is a comfortable resort hotel catering to the athletic-minded tourist— it is near many tennis courts and gymnasiums—and those needing physical therapy.

PLAZA ★★★★ Calle Ignacio Agramonte 267, Centro Havana, tel 338538, 206 rooms. In the 1920s this was one of the most elegant hotels in Old Havana, and some of that aura is preserved with the decor. The service could be more friendly and the food in the rooftop restaurant improved.

PRESIDENTE ★★★★ Calle G and Calzada, Vedado, tel 327521, 144 rooms. This 1928 tower rises near the Casa de los Americas and the Malecón. Slightly removed from the hurly-burly, it is preferred by those who like quiet and lots of antique furnishings. The hotel is currently under renovation.

SEVILLA ★★★★ Calle Trocadero between Zulueta and Prado, tel 338560. The Sevilla was just completely renovated to a level approaching that of the 1920s, when it was the Sevilla-Biltmore, featuring 'unexcelled comfort and faultless cuisine [attracting] the diplomatic life and the most exclusive society of Cuba's brilliant capital'. The ground floor has two restaurants and a number of handy shops.

COLINA ★★★ Calles L and 27, Vedado, tel 323535, 84 rooms. Fans of Soviet-style furnishings will enjoy the Colina. Others will agree that it needs a remodelling and new mattresses.

DEAUVILLE ★★★ Calle Galiano on the Malecón, Centro Havana, tel 628051, 142 rooms. Another 'Miami Beach mod' hotel, the recently renovated Deauville is one of the few near Old Havana with its own pool. During the winter, you can just walk out on the Malecón and let the waves crash over you.

HOSTAL VALENCIA ★★★ Calle Oficios at Obrapía, Old Havana, tel 623801, 14 rooms. An Old Havana mansion was recently converted into this charming, small, colonial-style hotel, with a good Spanish restaurant and a sunny courtyard.

LINCOLN ★★★ Calle Galiano at Virtudes, Centro Havana, tel 628061, 145 rooms. During the late 1950s, Revolutionaries kidnapped a famous foreign race-car driver from this hotel, ruining the Havana Grand Prix for Batista. The decor seems little changed since then, but the rooms are comfortable and pleasant.

LIDO ★★ Calle Consulado between Animas and Trocadero, tel 627000, 65 rooms. The great virtue of the Lido is that it is cheap. The plumbing is spartan—cold water only. Avoid the cavelike rooms that do not look over the street, which buzzes with black-market traffic. Some travellers complain of pilfering from the rooms.

CARIBBEAN ★ Calle Prado #164 at Colon, tel 622071, 36 rooms. The Caribbean is the cheapest tourist hotel in Havana, and you get what you pay for. Those who stay on the higher floor tend to return, while those nearer ground level rarely do.

PLAYAS DEL ESTE

ITABO ★★★ Laguna Itabo, Santa María del Mar, tel 2581, 204 rooms. This relatively new hotel with many services is a beachfront favorite, built on a lagoon.

TROPICOCO ★★★ **Av Sur at Av de las Terrazas, Santa Maria del Mar, tel 2531, 202 rooms.** The Tropicoco is a modern resort complex in the heart of the hotel zone.

VILLA BACURANAO ★★★ **Vía Blanca km 5.5, tel 656332, 49 rooms.** This small hotel features bungalows along the beach, lots of greenery and diving at a wreck offshore.

VILLA TROPICO ★★ **Arroyo Bermejo, Santa Cruz del Norte, tel 83555, 146 rooms.** At the east end of the beach zone, the Tropico's hotel and bungalows are surrounded by lush greenery.

PINAR DEL RÍO

LA ERMITA ★★★ **Carretera a la Ermita km 2, Viñales, tel 93208, 64 rooms.** Situated on a hilltop overlooking the beautiful Valle de Viñales, La Ermita features a pool, good restaurant and comfortable rooms.

LOS JAZMINES ★★★ **Carretera de Viñales km 25, tel 33404, 74 rooms.** Nearly every room in this recently renovated colonial-style hotel has a great view of the Valle de Viñales.

PINAR DEL RÍO ★★ **Calle Martí at the Autopista entrance, tel 5070, 136 rooms.** This is your usual Soviet-style hotel, the best in town, featuring a restaurant, small pool and shop.

ISLAND OF YOUTH

EL COLONY ★★★★ **Carretera de Siguanea km 16, tel 98181, 83 rooms.** On the southwest coast of the island, the Colony is Cuba's foremost dive resort. The decor dates from before the Revolution, when construction began, but it was only completed recently. It contains a good dive shop, a decompression chamber and a pool for practice dives. Watch out for overbooking.

CAYO LARGO

CORAL ★★★★ **Tel 48159, 66 rooms.** This new colonial-village-style resort complex is set a bit back from the beach and features a number of theme restaurants. It needs time to grow into its surroundings; now the atmosphere is a little stark.

ISLA DEL SUR ★★★★ **Tel 48159, 59 rooms.** The Isla del Sur

Pelican and flamingoes

was one of the first hotels on the island and remains one of the most comfortable and attractive. All rooms overlook the sea, and it also possesses a large circular pool.

VILLA CAPRICHO ★★★★ **Tel 48159, 60 bungalows.** Guests stay in charming thatched 'Indian' bungalows with all the comforts, including air conditioning and satellite TV. Right on the beach.

MATANZAS

VILLA GUAMA ★★★ **Laguna del Tesoro, Ciénaga de Zapata, tel 2979, 94 rooms.** This hotel is built on a series of islands in the middle of a lagoon near the south coast. Guests stay in thatched bungalows and can enjoy fishing or just cruising the waterways. Bring mosquito repellent.

VILLA PLAYA GIRÓN ★★ **Playa Girón, Ciénaga de Zapata, tel 4110, 303 rooms.** The scene of the notorious Bay of Pigs invasion is now the site of this low-key resort hotel situated among palm trees on the edge of this beautiful bay. Excellent diving and snorkeling offshore.

VARADERO

MELIÁ VARADERO ★★★★★ **Autopista Sur, Playa del las Américas, tel 667013, 497 rooms.** This enormous, star-shaped complex is one of the best hotels in Cuba, with attractive rooms, excellent restaurants, pools and a stunning jungle in the central atrium. The manager is known as 'El Exigente' ('The Demanding One'), and consequently the service is friendly and highly professional.

PARADISO-PUNTARENA ★★★★★ **Final de Kawama, tel 667120, 518 rooms.** These brand new twin towers rise at the south end of Varadero and share a restaurant-shopping-pool complex between them.

CUATRO PALMAS ★★★★ **Calle 1 between 61 and 62, tel 667040, 222 rooms.** The Cuatro Palmas is built on the beach at the north side of downtown Varadero. The hotel arcs around a large swimming pool, and you can also stay in one of their comfortable bungalows. The game room is housed in Batista's old summer house.

GAVIOTA TOURIST COMPLEX ★★★★ **Carretera de las Américas, tel 667194, 792 rooms.** This is a hotel and villas complex set among palm trees and gardens right on the beach.

INTERNACIONAL ★★★★ **Av las Américas, tel 667038, 165 rooms.** In the 1950s, the Internacional was the glittering jewel of Varadero hotels, featuring a casino, of course. The jet set rarely visits anymore, but there is still lots of charm to this five-storey Miami-beach-style resort with landscaped grounds.

KAWAMA TOURIST COMPLEX ★★★ **Calle O and Camino del Mar, tel 667156, 207 rooms.** Guests stay in pre-1959 vacation villas here with shared pools and a couple of restaurants. At the south side of town.

TUXPAN ★★★★ **Carretera las Morlas, Playa de las Américas, tel 667560, 234 rooms.** Cancún style, this new resort is built in the shape of a Mesoamerican pyramid. It is on the beach, of course, with every imaginable facility.

BELLAMAR ★★★ **Calle 17 between Avs 1 and 3, tel 63014, 290 rooms.** Situated in the heart of downtown a couple of blocks from the beach, this tower caters to budget tour groups who like to disport around the pool.

DOS MARES ★★★ **Calles 53 and Av 1, tel 62702, 38 rooms.** The Dos Mares is housed in a downtown colonial building a couple of blocks from the beach. No pool, but lots of atmosphere and friendly service—it doubles as a hotel school.

VARAZUL ★★★ **Av 1 between 14 and 15, tel 667132, 69 rooms.** The Varazul and its sister, the Acuazul, are two of the original downtown hotel towers. This one is quieter than its twin but has no pool.

VILLA CALETA ★★★ **Calle 19 between Av 1 and Playa, tel 667080, 42 rooms.** This is a small downtown resort built around a pool right on the beach. Some of the rooms are in pre-1959 vacation homes.

TORTUGA ★★★ **Calle 7 at Camino del Mar, tel 62243, 259 rooms.** The Tortuga is the less expensive part of the Kawama complex, with rooms in villas near the beach and a club for diving, fishing and other water activities.

PULLMAN ★★★ **Calle 49 at Av 1, tel 62575, 15 rooms.** Low-budget tourists enjoy this old downtown hotel with lots of Cuban atmosphere.

CIENFUEGOS

JAGUA ★★★★ **Calle 37, Punta Gorda, Cienfuegos, tel 3021, 154 rooms.** Built on a peninsula jutting into Jagua Bay, this modern hotel has a saltwater pool, restaurants and a nightclub. The Moorish fantasy Palacio del Valle next door is a city landmark.

RANCHO LUNA ★★★ **Carretera Rancho Luna km 16, tel 048120, 237 rooms.** This resort is built on a beach overlooking the Caribbean, with a large pool, gardens and good diving offshore. At the entrance to Jagua Bay.

VILLA CLARA

HANABANILLA ★★★ **Manicaragua, tel 86932, 126 rooms.** A Soviet-style resort, the Hotel Hanabanilla is built on the shores of the bass fishing lake of the same name. The atmosphere is cheerful and the food good. There are many excursions you can take across the lake or in the beautiful hills to the south.

LOS CANEYES ★★★ **Carretera de los Caneyes, tel 4512, 90 bungalows.** Just outside the city of Santa Clara, Los Caneyes is a complex of thatched huts, all with air conditioning and TV, built among the trees. Good food and service.

TRINIDAD

ANCON ★★★ **Trinidad, tel 4011, 216 rooms.** This resort complex on the beach south of town caters mostly to package tours. The water sports—swimming and diving—are excellent, but the food and service could be improved.

LAS CUEVAS ★★ **Trinidad, tel 3624, 124 rooms.** Built on the hill overlooking the city, Las Cuevas is the best lodging in town. It is an easy walk to the main square. The motel is named after some nearby caves.

TOPES DE COLLANTES

LOS HELECHOS ★★★ **Escambray, tel 40180, 49 rooms.** Los Helechos is located near the Kurhotel in this mountain resort. The hotel features excellent service, good food and a pool.

(top) Hotel La Ermita, Viñales, (above) Hotel Santiago de Cuba

CIEGO DE AVILA

CIEGO DE AVILA ★★★ **Carretera de Ceballos km 2.5, tel 28013, 138 rooms.** This Soviet-style hotel is the best in town, with a pool and restaurant.

MORÓN ★★★ **Av Tarafa, tel 3901, 144 rooms.** Another Soviet-style hotel, this accommodation is used mainly by fishermen and hunters as a base. Poor service.

CAYO COCO

CAYO COCO ★★★★ **Cayo Coco, tel 301311, 458 rooms.** This new village-like hotel complex offers all the modern amenities in a casual setting amid one of the north coast's most beautiful ecological areas. The beach is right out front, while the services include a half dozen restaurants and equipment for watersports from diving to sailing to fishing.

CAYO GUILLERMO

VILLA COJÍMAR ★★★★ **Cayo Guillermo, tel 301712, 90 rooms.** The Cojímar is a small, comfortable resort hotel built on a white-sand beach. It is a perfect spot to enjoy water sports—fishing charters leave from the dock—or just get away from it all.

CAMAGUEY

CAMAGUEY ★★ **Carretera Central, tel 72015, 142 rooms.** The Hotel Camaguey is another Soviet-style hotel with all the usual services, including restaurants, bars and a pool.

SANTA LUCIA

CUATRO VIENTOS ★★★★ **Playa Santa Lucía, Nuevitas, tel 36160, 214 rooms.** This casual Cuban- and Spanish-style hotel is just off the beach and offers all the usual watersports, a number of restaurants and nightly entertainment.

LAS TUNAS

LAS TUNAS ★★★ **Av 2 de Deciembre at Calle Finlay, tel 45014, 142 rooms.** Another product of the Eastern European cookie cutter, the Hotel Las Tunas is the best in town and where the elite meet.

HOLGUÍN

PERNIK ★★★ **Av Jorge Dimitrov and Plaza de la Revolucion, tel 481011, 202 rooms.** The Pernik was named in honor of Dimitrov, the hero of communist Bulgaria, so the decor is appropriately garish in an outdated socialist kind of way.

VILLA EL COCAL ★★ **Carretera Central to Bayamo km 7.5, tel 461902, 40 rooms.** This small new tourist hotel out by the airport is built around a nice swimming pool.

GUARDALAVACA

RÍO DE LUNA ★★★★ **Estero Ciego, tel 30030, 222 rooms.** Located on its own, excellent beach, the Río de Luna is surrounded by a lush garden. With pool and all the facilities.

ATLANTICO ★★★ **Playa Guardalavaca, tel 30180, 364 rooms and 133 bungalows.** This is a very comfortable resort right on the beach. Popular with European package tours.

BAYAMO

SIERRA MAESTRA ★★★★ **Carretera Central to Santiago, tel 481013, 228 rooms.** The Sierra Maestra is a cut above the usual Soviet-style hotel, with an elegant lobby (furniture donated by the Sandinistas) and good food and service.

MANZANILLO

GUACANAYABO ★★★ **Av Camilo Cienfuegos, tel 54012, 120 rooms.** The Hotel Guacanayabo was recently renovated but retains much weird socialist decor. It stands on a hill overlooking town and the bay.

MAREA DEL PORTILLO

FARALLON DE MAREA ★★★★ **Carretera Marea del Portillo km 15, tel 594201, 140 rooms.** This spanking-new resort hotel stands on a hill just above the coast's dark-sand beaches. It will cater mainly to Canadian package tourists, who get good food and friendly service.

MAREA DEL PORTILLO ★★★ **Carretera Marea del Portillo km 14, tel 594201, 122 rooms.** The first resort in the area, this hotel is now undergoing renovation. It is built among the palm trees right on the beach.

SANTIAGO DE CUBA

SANTIAGO DE CUBA ★★★★★ **Av de las Américas and Calle M, tel 42612, 322 rooms.** The Hotel Santiago occupies a sleek tower that unfortunately has no aesthetic connection to its surroundings or even to Cuban culture. Nevertheless, this is one of the most modern and best-equipped hotels on the island, with extremely comfortable rooms and lots of gadgets, including satellite TV. The ground floor contains shops, a Cubana office and a pool. It is a pity that regular Cubans can not enter.

CASA GRANDA ★★★★ **Calle Heredia #201, tel 86600.** Finally opened after a long renovation, the Casa Granda offers a return to Santiago's turn-of-the-century elegance. Its setting is inparalleled—right in the heart of town—and offers a great view of the central plaza.

BALCON DEL CARIBE ★★★ **Carretera del Morro km 7, tel 91011, 96 rooms.** The setting of this older resort hotel is spectacular: on the cliffs next to the Morro Castle overlooking the Caribbean. It is a long way down to the sea, but there is a pool on the grounds.

LAS AMÉRICAS ★★★ **Av las Américas and Calle Cebreco, tel 42011, 68 rooms.** The Hotel Las Américas pales beside the Hotel Santiago next door. However, the rooms are comfortable, and the service is friendly if somewhat disorganized.

VERSALLES ★★★ **Barrio Versalles, tel 91014, 60 rooms.** Located near the airport in the hills south of town, the Versalles has a great view of the city and rooms in a string of bungalows all with porches.

VILLA GAVIOTA ★★★ **Av Manduley #502, tel 41368, 53 rooms.** This is a small resort hotel in a quiet and elegant neighborhood. Most of the rooms are in individual villas.

VILLA SAN JUAN ★★★ **Carretera Siboney and Parque San Juan, tel 42478, 64 rooms.** The ex-Motel Leningrado, the Villa San Juan is located on the summit of San Juan Hill. The suites are housed in villas amid a junglelike setting.

BACANAO

BUCANERO ★★★ Parque Bacanao, tel 27126, 200 rooms. This beach resort is built at one side of a beautiful, pocket-sized cove excellent for sunbathing and swimming.

VILLA DAIQUIRÍ ★★★ Parque Bacanao, tel 24849, 157 rooms. Located on the famous Daiquirí Beach, this resort caters mainly to European package tourists, many of whom stay in the bungalows. The stark and functional decor needs to by upgraded.

VILLA LA GRAN PIEDRA ★★ Parque Bacanao, tel 51154, 44 rooms. Get away from it at all at 1,234 metres (4,113 feet) above sea level. This small hotel is built near the scenic Gran Piedra lookout, from which you have a remarkable view, weather permitting.

GUANTÁNAMO

GUANTÁNAMO ★★★ Calle 13 Norte, tel 381015, 130 rooms. The only tourist hotel in Guantánamo, this gloomy Soviet-style building needs an upgrade.

CAIMANERA

CAIMANERA ★★★ Loma Norte, tel 91414, 18 rooms. The Caimanera is a small jewel of a hotel, built around a swimming pool on a hill overlooking Guantánamo Bay. The staff is friendly and the service attentive. At night, while gazing at the bright lights of the U.S. naval base, you can contemplate the weirdness of international politics.

BARACOA

EL CASTILLO ★★★ tel 42125. This is the place to stay in Baracoa, a hotel built in an 18th-century fort on a hilltop above town. Aside from the view, it features a pool, a good restaurant, comfortable rooms and an efficient staff. Some stay for months.

LA RUSA ★ Calle Máximo Gómez 161, Baracoa, tel 43011. This spartan downtown hotel offers simple rooms that roar with the sound of waves crashing against the Malecon right out front.

Restaurants

EATING HAS SUFFERED IN SOCIALIST CUBA. Tourism authorities have only recently realized that their visitors expect better. The first problem was that the Revolution did not care about fine food. Well-prepared Cuban cuisine seems to have been associated with the reviled pre-1959 era; it was a capitalist luxury that the people could ignore while building the ideal state. In their isolation, Cuban cooks stuck to their traditional, grease- and calorie-heavy style of cooking, unaware that abroad eaters were demanding a lighter and more varied cuisine. Then the Special Period came along, cutting off the supply of fresh produce and meat. Even in the top hotels, there were—and occasionally are—shortages of certain items. Slowly, however, the tourist industry is building up links to Cuban farmers and to sources abroad.

Hotels and restaurants are also slowly learning what tourists want—Cuban food prepared with a wide variety of fresh tropical ingredients. Unfortunately, most Cubans have an extremely conservative palate, and you see their tastes reflected in menus: rice and beans, roast pork, fried chicken and ham and cheese sandwiches. They ignore this fertile island's wide variety of fresh fruits and vegetables—the kind of food tourists come here expecting.

Hotel and dollar restaurants are of widely varying quality. In most cases, your safest bet is to stick with the old stand-bys listed above (rice and beans, etc.). The most adventurous and expensive dish is usually the least successful; well-prepared seafood is tragically hard to find. In Havana, the tourist restaurant quality is usually in inverse ratio to the pretensions of its service. Of the hotels, the Cohiba offers the best and most expensive cuisine. Out in the country, the tourist restaurants are far cheaper and more reliable; Pinar del Río has a number of good choices.

In the last two years, a third eating choice has sprung up all over Cuba. Called *paladares*, small restaurants in private homes have become an excellent alternative to tourist industry food. They are priced moderately so both Cubans and tourists can afford them, and the food is almost always adequate. Occasionally (particularly in Havana) the quality reaches gourmet levels. The best main course is generally a variety of ham; they are not allowed to serve lobster or shrimp, but if you ask . . . Unfortunately, the government has imposed taxes and other restrictions on these private restaurants that make it nearly impossible for them to stay in business. Most of those that remain lie near tourist hotels in cities such as Havana and Varadero. Look for signs (occasionally neon!) or ask at the front desk for recommendations.

Cuban Food

LA BODEGUITA DEL MEDIO **Calle Empedrado 207, tel 624498.**
One of the most famous restaurants in Cuba, the 'BDM' has a
graffiti-scrawled bar—home of the mojito cocktail —on the street
level and dining rooms above. The food is typically Cuban, such
as roast pork and rice and beans, but nothing stellar.

LA CECILIA **Av 5 and Calle 110, Playa, tel 226700.** Haute Cuban
cuisine in a ritzy mansion.

LOS DOCE APOSTOLES **Fortaleza de la Cabaña, East Havana, tel
637941.** The food here is good, but the great attraction is the
setting at the base of the fort and the view of Havana.

EL RANCHON **Calles 19 and 140, Playa, tel 235838.** This restaurant out by the convention centre has the reputation for serving
the best Cuban food in Havana.

Seafood

EL FLORIDITA **Calle Monserrate 557, Old Havana, tel 631060.**
El Floridita was recently rebuilt, and Constance once again serves
his famous frozen daiquiris from behind the bar. Come here to
drink, because the food is wildly overpriced and poorly prepared.
To eat, try La Zaragozana next door.

PAPA'S **Marina Hemingway, Santa Fé, tel 331150.** A good,
Hemingway-themed seafood restaurant.

Chinese

EL PAVO REAL **Av 7 between Calles 2 and 4, Miramar, tel
332315.** This has the reputation as Havana's best Chinese restaurant.

LA TORRE DE MARFIL **Calle Mercaderes between Oficios and
Obrapía, Old Havana, tel 623466.** The food is so-so, but the setting is cheerfully tacky.

Ice Cream

COPPELIA **Calles 23 and L, Vedado.** The temple of ice cream in
Cuba. A must.

International

1830 **Malecún at Calle 20, Vedado, tel 34504.** An elegant setting in a waterfront mansion at the western edge of Vedado.

D'GIOVANNI **Calle Tacón #4 at Empedrado, Old Havana, tel 614445.** Italian food in a charming Old Havana palace.

OASIS **Prado #258, Old Havana, tel 614098.** Inexpensive Arab food.

LA PAELLA **Calles Oficios and Obrapía, Old Havana, tel 34504.** A Spanish restaurant housed in the Hostal Valencia hotel.

LA PAMPA **Av 1 and Calle 84, Miramar, tel 225551.** Argentine grilled meats.

EL PATIO **San Ignacio 54, Old Havana, tel 618511.** This restaurant is housed in an old palace on the Plaza de la Catedral. The food is passable.

LAS RUINAS **Parque Lenin, tel 324630.** Cuban and international dishes in a stunning half-ruined, half-modernistic setting.

PINAR DEL RÍO

CASTILLO DE LOS NUBES **Soroa.** A very good restaurant—try the chicken—in the hotel of the same name.

RUMAYOR **Pinar del Río.** The decor is neo-African, but the food is good country-style Cuban.

CASA DE DON TOMÁS **Viñales.** The oldest house in town has been converted into a restaurant specializing in *ajiaco criollo*.

VALLE DE PREHISTORIA **West of Viñales.** For this writer, the great attraction here is not the famous mural but the excellent roast pork.

CUEVA DEL INDIO **North of Viñales.** Good grilled chicken and ajiaco.

ISLAND OF YOUTH

EL COCHINITO **Calle 39, Nueva Gerona.** A peso restaurant with roast pork a specialty.

CAYO LARGO

All of the hotels have good restaurants; seafood, particularly lobster, is the specialty.

VARADERO

LAS AMÉRICAS **Carretera de las Américas, tel 63415.** Housed in the old Du Pont mansion, this is one of the most elegant restaurants in Cuba. The food—seafood is a specialty—does not quite reach the decor.

EL BODEGON CRIOLLO **Av Playa at Calle 40, tel 62180.** Cuban food.

LA CABAÑITA **Calle 9 and Camino del Mar, tel 62215.** Steak and seafood.

LAI-LAI **Av 1 and Calle 17, tel 63297.** Chinese.

MESON DEL QUIJOTE **Carretera Las Américas.** A Spanish restaurant housed in a castle north of downtown.

MI CASITA **Camino del Mar between Calles 10 and 11, tel 63787.** Steak and seafood.

CIENFUEGOS

PALACIO DEL VALLE **Next to the Hotel Jagua.** The food and service here are lacklustre; the setting is fantastic: a Moorish palace with ornate detailing covering every square foot.

LA VERJA **Av 54 two blocks east of Parque José Martí.** International cuisine.

SANTA CLARA

1878 RESTAURANT **One block from Parque Vidal.** So-so food, charming colonial mansion.

TRINIDAD

GUAMUHAYA **Calles Martí and Izquiereda.** Colonial atmosphere.

COLONIAL TRINIDAD **Calle Maceo #55.** International cuisine.

CAMAGÜEY

PARADOR DE LOS TRES REYES **Plaza San Juan de Dios.** Spanish food.

HOLGUÍN

MAYABE LOOKOUT **Road to Santiago.** Cuban cuisine under a thatched roof. Popular with tours.

GUARDALAVACA

EL ANCIA **On the beach.** Excellent seafood.

BAYAMO

LA CASONA **Plaza del Himno Nacional.** Cuban cuisine.

SANTIAGO DE CUBA

1900 RESTAURANT **San Basilio between Pío Rosado and Hartman.** Good international food in an elegant downtown mansion.

EL MORRO **Next to the Morro Castle south of town.** Cuban food and a stunning view from the clifftop. Horsemeat *criollo* style is the specialty.

CASA DE PEDRO EL COJO **Parque Bacanao east of town.** Famous restaurant for Cuban cuisine. You must have the roast pork.

SANTERÍA

Cubans are not a pious people (compared to, say, devoutly Catholic Mexicans). During the colonial era, the Catholic Church, one of the largest landowners, sided with the aristocracy and the repressive Spanish government—a stance that dampened many Cubans' zeal for regular church attendance. Instead, Cubans opt for whatever works: a little Catholic ritual, some spiritualism (a kind of ancestor worship wherein they communicate with the dead) and a lot of Afro-Cuban beliefs.

Of the latter, by far the most prevalent is Santería, the 'Way of the Saints', which has spread throughout the Caribbean and to the Latino neighborhoods of the United States. The Special Period has led to a reawakening of interest in religion, and none more than Santería. The inspiration of African slaves, Santería is a religion born of adversity; its rituals have special power for those who find themselves in a hopeless situation and need divine guidance to find a way out.

Santería's roots lie in Africa, specifically in the religion of the Yoruba kingdom that thrived for centuries in present-day Nigeria and Benin. Around 1800, internal splits and the toppling of the king led to invasion by the Yoruba's neighbors. The Muslim Fulani and the Dahomey captured and enslaved hundreds of thousands of Yorubans. Undoubtedly, some were *babalawos*, Yoruba priests. The slaves were marched to the Bight of Benin and there sold to European merchants who shipped them to the New World.

Over a half million slaves arrived in Cuba, the majority Yorubans. They found a kind of earthly hell in vast sugar plantations where they were sometimes worked to death. They also found a culture that was strangely conducive to the survival of their religion. The Catholic Church demanded that all slaves be baptized and taught a few basic prayers, but beyond that the Africans were largely left to their own beliefs (unlike slaves in English colonies where personal conversion was the basis for church admittance). In Catholicism, slaves found a religion alien to their own but with some striking similarities, most importantly a distant, all-powerful God who could be approached by divine intercessors in the form of saints.

When the Yoruba religion was transported to the cities, particularly Havana and Matanzas, it became Santería. It was difficult but not impossible for a slave to purchase his or her freedom, and freed slaves quickly gravitated to the urban areas, where they formed ethnic organizations called *cabildos*. The Yorubas, who called themselves the Lucumi, were the most numerous, but there were also *cabildos* for Congos, Mandingas, Araras and dozens of other African peoples.

In the *cabildos*, the Catholic Church saw an opportunity for evangelism and sent priests to instruct them in the finer points of doctrine. The Afro-Cubans—many were now of mixed blood—accepted closer involvement with the Church, because Catholic ritual gave them the opening to practice their own religion. Festivals like Carnival, Holy Week and particularly Epiphany (one of the magi was African) became a time of huge celebrations, when *cabildo* members could perform the African dances to the beat of African drums under the guise of celebrating Catholic holy days.

For the Lucumi *cabildos*, Catholic saints became manifestations of the *orishas*, the spiritual beings at the center of the Yoruba religion. The Virgen de Caridad, Cuba's patroness, became Oshun, the personification of eros; sword-carrying Santa Barbara became the overtly male Changó, the *orisha* of violence; the lame Saint Lazarus was transformed into Babaluaye, the representation of illness and suffering, and so on. Catholic ritual was also incorporated into the ceremonies of other Africa-based religions, such as ñañigo societies of the Efik people and the *palo monte* faith of the Congolese.

By the early 1900s, the basic principles of Santería had been established, and the religion began to flow out of urban slums into the larger Cuban culture. The *cabildos* had always had a few white and mixed-race members, but now white intellectuals and artists began to discover Santería as part of their wakening interest in Afro-Cuban culture. By mid-century, Santería had penetrated to the top of Cuban society: Batista actively courted the *santeros* (initiates of Santería) as a means of ensuring his government's power. Many of the Revolutionaries in the Sierra were also protected by bead necklaces that marked them as followers of the *orishas*. A sure sign that Batista had lost was when many *babalawos* switched their allegiance to Fidel in 1958.

continues

Like all religions, Santería was marginalized in the first decades of the Revolution. It became folklore, celebrated as an authentic creation of poor Afro-Cubans but relegated to museums and a few study centers. Only recently has Santería emerged from seclusion, as the government realizes that Santería tourism is economically viable and as more and more Cubans turn to it in times of trouble.

The basic tenet of Santería is that everyone has a destiny or 'way' given by the all-powerful god, called Oludamare. With the help of the *orishas*, you can find and fulfill your destiny rather than suffer from it. The *orishas* are the personifications of *ashe,* the divine force toward life, strength and righteousness along which all creation flows. Devotion to the *orishas* takes four forms: divination, sacrifice, possession by the spirit and initiation.

Believers most commonly come to *santeros* for the resolution of problems with health, money, love or the legal system. Using various methods, the *santero* will divine the will of Oludamare to find a solution for the problem. The most complex of these methods is *ifa,* which can be only practiced by a *babalawo* (a male priest).

A man had nothing to eat, so he took a pair of shoes out to the countryside to exchange for food with a peasant. On the way, he was stopped, the shoes were confiscated and he was told to appear before the tribunal to pay a large fine. Having nowhere to turn for help, he consulted a *babalawo*. To find the *ifa,* or the order in chaos, the priest cast the *ekwele,* eight discs of shell attached to a necklace. The patterns of the shell—dark or light sides up—showed one of the 256 possible combinations that represent archetypal life situations. The *babalawo* advised the man to perform certain rituals for the *orishas*. After following these instructions, the man went to the tribunal, where the prosecutor threw out the case, erased the fine and ordered the return of his shoes. All thanks to the *orishas*, believes the man.

In Santería, the successful resolution of problems means deepening your relationship with the *orishas*. The *orishas* are not immortal and, like us, must eat in order to survive. Keeping the *orishas* happy and well-fed rebounds on the believer, because his or her *ashe* and the *orishas* are inextricably linked. Each *orisha* has certain favorite foods and drinks with which you can win their favour. Yemaya, the patroness of the seas, prefers banana chips and watermelons. An even stronger bond between the *orisha* and the believer can be made with sacrifice. In the United States, Santería has become notorious for the practice of animal sacrifice. However, if done correctly, it is no less humanely killed than meat from a slaughterhouse. The animal is cleanly and quickly killed, the blood is given to the *orisha* and the rest is cooked and eaten by the believers.

Dance, drumming and song are crucial parts of Santería festivals. At important occasions—the most common is the *santero's* 'birthday' or anniversary of initiation—large quantities of food and drink are prepared for both the *orishas* and the guests, and drummers and singers are hired. The drummers begin to pound the rhythms of Eleggua, the trickster *orisha* who opens the ways, and then of the principal *orishas*. The *santeros* begin to dance, their movements reflecting their principal *orisha*. The culmination comes at the *asiento* ('mounting') of a believer's head by his or her *orisha*. The person literally becomes the *orisha*, not only dancing but speaking, delivering messages, advice and wisdom. When dancers and drummers finally tire, the *orisha* leaves the believer's head and life resumes its normal flow, forever altered by this touch of the divine.

As the person further enters Santería and cleaves to the paths of the *orishas*, one *orisha* might assert itself as the devotee's patron. At this point, the *orisha* will demand a lengthy and irrevocable initiation into its mysteries. This takes place at the home of an experienced initiate of the same *orisha* and includes a lengthy period of isolation and instruction culminating in the 'enthronement' of *orisha* in the initiate's head. For the rest of his or her life, the initiate must follow the demanding rules of the *orisha*. For example, followers of Obatalá, the patroness of purity, must wear white from head to toe and abstain from sex for the year following initiation and may never drink alcohol. (You can often see them in the Old Havana's Iglesia de la Merced, whose Virgin is Obatalá's Catholic manifestation.) For these sacrifices, the rewards are great: After years of devotion, the paths of the believer and the *orisha* may become one, and the believer can say with complete sincerity: 'I am an *orisha*'.

Language

SPANISH IS A RELATIVELY SIMPLE AND REGULAR LANGUAGE, and all visitors should come prepared with at least a few common phrases. Some Cubans speak English, particularly in the resort areas, but they always appreciate it when you attempt to communicate in their language.

The main difference between Cuban Spanish and the Spanish of Spain is that the former is spoken more slowly and without the Spaniards' lisp. Many Cuban Indian words, such as tabaco, canoa ('canoe') and 'Cuba' itself, have also entered the language.

The pronunciation of Cuban Spanish is almost totally regular. The letter 'j' is pronounced like 'h' in 'hat', and 'll' is pronounced as in the 'i' in 'machine'. Like Puerto Rican and Dominican Spanish, Cuban Spanish tends to omit the last syllable of words ending in 'as'.

PRONUNCIATION

a   as in 'father'
b   between vowels, almost like a 'v'
c   before 'a', 'o' and 'u', like a 'k'
ch as in 'church'
e   as in 'set'
g   before 'h' and 'i', like 'h' in 'hat' all other times a hard 'g' as in 'go'
h   always silent
i   as in 'machine'
j   like 'h' in hat
ñ   like 'ny' of 'canyon'
q   like 'k'
rr rolled
y   like 'i' in 'machine'
z   like 's' in 'sass'

COMMON EXPRESSIONS

yes   *sí*
no   *no*
good morning   *buenos días*
good afternoon   *buenos tardes*
good evening   *buenos noches*
good-bye   *adiós*
See you later   *Hasta luego*
thank you   *gracias*
please   *por favor*
My name is . . .   *Mi nombre es . . . /Me llamo . . .*
What is your name?   *Come se llama?*
How do you do?   *Como esta usted?*
Fine, and you?   *Bien, y usted?*
I don't understand   *No entiendo*

Do you speak English? *Habla usted inglés?*

I don't speak Spanish *No hablo español*

Pardon me *Perdóneme*

Excuse me *Con permiso*

Where is . . . ? *Dónde está . . . ?*

What is . . . ? *Que es . . . ?*

I want . . . *Quiero . . .*

How much is . . . ? *Cuanto cuesta . . . ?*

Is there . . . ? *Hay . . . ?*

Do you have . . . ? *Tiene . . . ?*

I am lost *Estoy perdido*

I do not feel well *No me siento bien*

The check, please *La cuenta, por favor*

Help! *Socorro!*

DAYS

Monday *lunes*

Tuesday *martes*

Wednesday *miercoles*

Thursday *jueves*

Friday *viernes*

Saturday *sábado*

Sunday *domingo*

TIME

What time is it? *Que hora es?*

morning *mañana*

today *hoy*

yesterday *ayer*

tomorrow *mañana*

week *semana*

month *mes*

early *temprano*

late *tarde*

later *después*

NUMBERS

one *uno/una*

two *dos*

three *tres*

four *quatro*

five *cinco*

six *seis*

seven *siete*

eight *ocho*

nine *nueve*

ten *diez*

eleven *once*

twelve *doce*

thirteen *trece*

fourteen *catorce*

fifteen *quince*

sixteen *dieciséis*

seventeen *diecisiete*

eighteen *dieciocho*

nineteen *diecinueve*

twenty *veinte*

twenty-one *veintiuno*

thirty *treinta*

thirty-one *treinta y uno*

fourty *cuarenta*

fifty *cincuenta*

sixty *sesenta*

seventy *setenta*

eighty *ochenta*

ninety   *noventa*
one hundred   *cien*
one hundred and one   *ciento uno*
five hundred   *quinientos*
one thousand   *mil*
one million   *millon*

DIRECTIONS
here   *aquí*
there   *allí/allá*
near   *cerca*
far   *lejos*
left   *izquierda*
right   *derecha*
straight   *derecho*
at the corner   *a la esquina*
behind   *atrás*
at the back   *al fondo*
city block   *cuadra*
next   *próximo/próxima*
entry   *entrada*
exit   *salida*
closed   *cerrado*
open   *abierto*
pull   *jale* or *hale*
push   *empuje*

HOTEL
room   *cuarto*
bed   *cama*
key   *llave*
front desk   *carpeta*
soap   *jabón*
towel   *toalla*

purified water   *agua purificada*
hot   *caliente*
cold   *frío*
blanket   *manta*
pillow   *almohada*
bill   *cuenta*
pool   *piscina*
credit card   *tarjeta de crédito*

RESTAURANT
table   *mesa*
waiter   *camarero*
waitress   *camarera*
breakfast   *desayuno*
lunch   *comida*
dinner   *cena*
fork   *tenedor*
knife   *cuchillo*
spoon   *cuchara*
napkin   *servilleta*
glass   *vaso*
wineglass   *copa*
cup   *taza*
plate   *plato*
bowl   *tazón*
bread   *pan*
butter   *mantequilla*
sugar   *azúcar*
milk   *leche*
cream   *crema*
ice   *hielo*
without ice   *sin hielo*
salt   *sal*
eggs   *huevos*
tea   *té*

coffee   *café*
beer   *cerveza*
soda   *refresco*
mineral water   *agua mineral*
bill   *cuenta*
change   *cambio*

LOCATIONS
money exchange
    casa de cambio
airport   *aeropuerto*
bus station   *terminal de omnibus*

bus   *guagua*
train station   *estacion de
    ferrocarriles*
ticket office   *taquilla*
post office   *correo*
ferry terminal   *embarcadero*
bathroom   *sanitario, lavabo,
    baño*
hospital   *hospital*
gas station   *gasolinera* or
    servicentro

Recommended Reading

C U L T U R E

Cabrera Infante, G., *Holy Smoke* (Faber & Faber, London, 1985)

González-Wippler, Migene, *Santería: African Magic in Latin America* (Doubleday/Anchor, Garden City, N.Y., 1973)

González-Wippler, Migene, *The Santería Experience* (Prentice-Hall, Englewood Cliffs, N.J., 1982)

Montejo, Esteban, *The Autobiography of a Runaway Slave* (Pantheon, New York, 1968)

Murphy, Joseph M., *Santería: African Spirits in America* (Beacon Press, Boston, 1988)

Núñez Jiménez, Antonio, *The Journey of the Havana Cigar* (Cubatabaco, Havana, 1988)

Ortiz, Fernando, *Cuban Counterpoint: Tobacco and Sugar* (Alfred A. Knopf, Inc., New York, 1947)

H I S T O R Y

Bethell, Leslie, editor, *Cuba: A Short History* (Cambridge University Press, Cambridge, 1993)

Brenner, Philip, and Daniel Siegal, editors, *The Cuba Reader* (Grove, New York, 1988)

Brugioni, Dino A., *Eyeball to Eyeball: The Inside Story of the Cuban Missile Crisis* (Random House, New York, 1991)

Castro, Fidel, *Face to Face with Fidel Castro: A Conversation with Tomás Borge* (Ocean Press, Melbourne, 1993)

Geyer, Georgie Anne, *Guerrilla Prince: The Untold Story of Fidel Castro* (Little, Brown and Co., New York, 1991)

Higgins, Trumbull, *The Perfect Failure: Kennedy, Eisenhower and the CIA at the Bay of Pigs* (W.W. Norton, New York, 1987)

Hinckle, Warren, *Deadly Secrets: The CIA-Mafia War Against Castro and the Assassination of J.F.K.* (Thunder's Mouth, New York, 1992)

Lockwood, Lee, *Castro's Cuba, Cuba's Fidel* (Westview Press, Boulder, Co., 1990)

Martí, José, *Our America* (Monthly Review Press, New York, 1977)

Miná, Gianni, *An Encounter With Fidel* (Ocean Press, Melbourne, 1991)

Moreno Fraginals, Manuel, *The Sugarmill: The Socioeconomic Complex of Sugar in Cuba* (Monthly Review Press, New York, 1976)

Pérez, Louis A., *Cuba: Between Reform and Revolution* (Oxford University Press, New York, 1988)

Pérez-Stable, Marifeli, *The Cuban Revolution* (Oxford University Press, New York, 1993)

Quirk, Robert E., *Fidel Castro* (W.W. Norton & Co., New York, 1993)

Suchlicki, Jaime, *Historical Dictionary of Cuba* (Scarecrow Press, Metuchen, N.J., 1988)

Thomas, Hugh, *Cuba, or The Pursuit of Freedom* (Eyre & Spottiswoode, London, 1971)

LITERATURE

Cabrera Infante, G., *Infante's Inferno* (Harper & Row, New York, 1984)

Cabrera Infante, G., *Three Trapped Tigers* (Harper & Row, New York, 1971)

Cabrera Infante, G., *View of Dawn in the Tropics* (Harper & Row, New York, 1978)

Carpentier, Alejo, *The Chase* (Farrar, Straus and Giroux, New York, 1989)

Carpentier, Alejo, *Explosion in a Cathedral* (Harper & Row, New York, 1979)

Carpentier, Alejo, *Reasons of State* (Writers and Readers, London, 1977)

Fuentes, Norberto, *Hemingway in Cuba* (Lyle Stuart, Secaucus, N.J., 1984)

Greene, Graham, *Our Man in Havana* (William Heinemann Ltd., London, 1958)

Guillén, Nicolás, *Patria o Muerte!, The Great Zoo and Other Poems* (Monthly Review Press, New York, 1972)

Hemingway, Ernest, *Islands in the Stream* (Scribner's, New York, 1970)

Hemingway, Ernest, *The Old Man and the Sea* (Scribner's, New York, 1952)

Lezama Lima, José, *Paradiso* (Farrar, Straus and Giroux, New York, 1974)

Martí, José, *Major Poems* (Holmes & Meier, New York, 1982)

T R A V E L L E R S ' A C C O U N T S

Cardenal, Ernesto, *In Cuba* (New Directions, New York, 1974)

Gébler, Carlo, *Driving through Cuba* (Simon & Schuster, New York, 1988)

Miller, Tom, *Trading With the Enemy* (Atheneum, New York, 1992)

Terry, T. Philip, *Terry's Guide to Cuba* (Houghton Mifflin, Boston, 1929)

Index